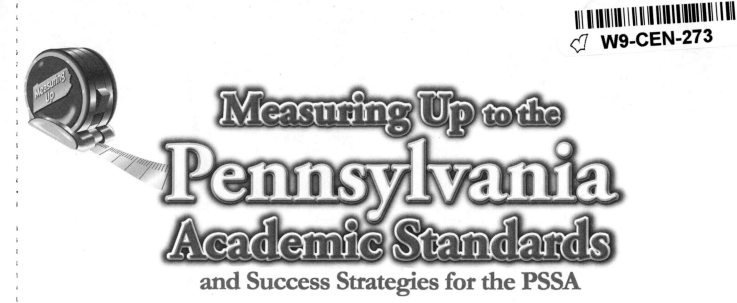

Measuring Up to the Pennsylvania Academic Standards
and Success Strategies for the PSSA

Mathematics

Level E

Developed Specifically for the PSSA

This book was designed to help you prepare to do your best on the **PSSA** in Mathematics in Grade 5. The series, *Measuring Up to the Pennsylvania Academic Standards*, includes instructional worktexts in the content areas of Reading, Writing, and Mathematics that match the **Pennsylvania Academic Standards**.

This book will help you develop the skills and confidence you need to do your very best!

The Peoples Publishing Group, Inc.

Serving the Needs of Pennsylvania Educators and Students

Visit our web site at

http://www.patesthelp.com

Editorial Development: **ELHI Publishers Services**

Pre-Press & Production Manager: **Doreen Smith**

Project Manager: **Jennifer J. Wilhelmy**

Production Editor: **Sal Esposito**

Copy Editor: **Amy Kron**

Proofreader: **Lee Laddy**

Photo Researcher/Permissions Manager: **Kristine Liebman**

Cover Design: **Armando Baéz**

Illustrations:
Brian W. Bishop
Armando Baéz
Sal Esposito
Erika L. Hillefeld
Bill Lyons
Jennifer J. Wilhelmy

Pennsylvania Reviewers:

Ronald J. Yasher–Math Consultant

R. Rene Rawhouser–Asa Packer Elementary School, Bethlehem Area School District

ISBN 1-56256-339-4

Copyright © 2001
The Peoples Publishing Group, Inc.
299 Market Street
Saddle Brook, New Jersey 07663

Printed in the United States of America.

10   9   8   7   6   5   4   3   2   1

Table of Contents

Our lessons are an exact match to the Pennsylvania Academic Standards for Mathematics and align to the PSSA.

*Our lessons are an exact match to the Pennsylvania Academic Standards
for Mathematics and align to the PSSA.*

*Our lessons are an exact match to the Pennsylvania Academic Standards
for Mathematics and align to the PSSA.*

*Our lessons are an exact match to the Pennsylvania Academic Standards
for Mathematics and align to the PSSA.*

Our lessons are an exact match to the Pennsylvania Academic Standards for Mathematics and align to the PSSA.

Correlation to the Pennsylvania Academic Standards

This workbook is 100% aligned to the Pennsylvania Academic Standards and provides complete practice for the PSSA!

As the lesson for each *Academic Standard* is completed, place a ✓ to indicate *Mastery* or an ✗ to indicate *Review Needed.*

Pennsylvania Academic Standards

Content Category 2.1.5
Numbers, Number Systems, and Number Relationships

	2.1.5A	2.1.5B	2.1.5C	2.1.5D	2.1.5E	2.1.5F	2.1.5G	2.1.50E	2.1.5PT			
A. Use expanded notation to represent whole numbers or decimals.	●							*	●			
B. Apply number theory concepts to rename a number quantity.		●						*	●			
C. Demonstrate that mathematical operations can represent a variety of problem situations.			●					*	●			
D. Use models to represent fractions and decimals.				●				*	●			
E. Explain the concepts of prime and composite numbers.					●			*	●			
F. Use simple concepts of negative numbers (e.g., on a number line, in counting, in temperature).						●		*	●			
G. Develop and apply number theory concepts (e.g., primes, factors, multiples, composites) to represent numbers in various ways.							●	*				

Pennsylvania Academic Standards

Content Category 2.2.5
Computation and Estimation

	2.2.5A	2.2.5B	2.2.5C	2.2.5D	2.2.5E	2.2.5F	2.2.5G	2.2.5H	2.2.5I	2.2.50E	2.2.5PT		
A. Create and solve word problems involving addition, subtraction, multiplication, and division of whole numbers.	●									*	●		
B. Develop and apply algorithms to solve word problems that involve addition, subtraction, and/or multiplication with decimals with and without regrouping.		●								*	●		
C. Develop and apply algorithms to solve word problems that involve addition, subtraction, and/or multiplication with fractions and mixed numbers that include like and unlike denominators.			●							*	●		
D. Demonstrate the ability to round numbers.				●						*	●		
E. Determine through estimations the reasonableness of answers to problems involving addition, subtraction, multiplication and division of whole numbers.					●					*	●		
F. Demonstrate skills for using fraction calculators to verify conjectures, confirm computations and explore complex problem-solving situations.						●				*	●		
G. Apply estimation strategies to a variety of problems including time and money.							●			*	●		
H. Explain multiplication and division algorithms.								●		*	●		
I. Select a method for computation and explain why it is appropriate.									●	*	●		

Pennsylvania Academic Standards

Content Category 2.3.5
Measurement and Estimation

	2.3.5A	2.3.5B	2.3.5C	2.3.5D	2.3.5E	2.3.50E	2.3.5PT						
A. Select and use appropriate instruments and units for measuring quantities (e.g., perimeter, volume, area, weight, time, temperature).	●					*	●						
B. Select and use standard tools to measure the size of figures with specified accuracy, including length, width, perimeter and area.		●				*	●						
C. Estimate, refine and verify specified measurements of objects.			●			*	●						
D. Convert linear measurements within the same system.				●		*	●						
E. Add and subtract measurements.					●	*	●						

* Open-Ended Questions incorporate a variety of skills from each content category.

OE: Open-Ended Questions
PT: Practice Test

This workbook is 100% aligned to the Pennsylvania Academic Standards and provides complete practice for the PSSA!

As the lesson for each *Academic Standard* is completed, place a ✓ to indicate *Mastery* or an ✗ to indicate *Review Needed*.

Pennsylvania Academic Standards

Content Category 2.4.5 — *Mathematical Reasoning and Connections*

Lessons	2.4.5A	2.4.5B	2.4.5C	2.4.5D	2.4.5E	2.4.5F	2.4.5OE	2.4.5PT
A. Compare quantities and magnitudes of numbers.	•						*	•
B. Use models, number facts, properties and relationships to check and verify predictions and explain reasoning.		•					*	•
C. Draw inductive and deductive conclusions within mathematical contexts.			•				*	•
D. Distinguish between relevant and irrelevant information in a mathematical problem.				•			*	•
E. Interpret statements made with precise language of logic (e.g., "all", "or", "every", "none", "some", "or", "many").					•		*	•
F. Use statistics to quantify issues (e.g., in social studies, in science).						•	*	•

Pennsylvania Academic Standards

Content Category 2.5.5 — *Mathematical Problem Solving and Communication*

Lessons	2.5.5A	2.5.5B	2.5.5C	2.5.5D	2.5.5E	2.5.5F	2.5.5OE	2.5.5PT
A. Develop a plan to analyze a problem, identify the information needed to solve the problem, carry out the plan, check whether an answer makes sense and explain how the problem was solved.	•						*	•
B. Use appropriate mathematical terms, vocabulary, language symbols and graphs to explain clearly and logically solutions to problems.		•					*	•
C. Show ideas in a variety of ways, including words, numbers, symbols, pictures, charts, graphs, tables, diagrams and models.			•				*	•
D. Connect, extend and generalize problem solutions to other concepts, problems and circumstances in mathematics.				•			*	•
E. Select, use and justify the methods, materials and strategies used to solve problems.					•		*	•
F. Use appropriate problem-solving strategies (e.g., solving a simpler problem, drawing a picture or diagram).						•	*	•

Pennsylvania Academic Standards

Content Category 2.6.5 — *Statistics and Data Analysis*

Lessons	2.6.5A	2.6.5B	2.6.5C	2.6.5D	2.6.5E	2.6.5OE	2.6.5PT
A. Organize and display data using pictures, tallies, tables, charts, bar graphs and circle graphs.	•					*	•
B. Describe data sets using mean, median, mode and range.		•				*	•
C. Sort data using Venn diagrams.			•			*	•
D. Predict the likely number of times a condition will occur based on analyzed data.				•		*	•
E. Construct and defend simple conclusions based on data.					•	*	•

Pennsylvania Academic Standards

Content Category 2.7.5 — *Probability and Predictions*

Lessons	2.7.5A	2.7.5B	2.7.5C	2.7.5D	2.7.5E	2.7.5F	2.7.5G	2.7.5H	2.7.5I	2.7.5J	2.7.5OE	2.7.5PT
A. Perform simulations with concrete devices (e.g., dice, spinner) to predict the chance of an event occurring.	•										*	•
B. Determine the fairness of the design of a spinner.		•									*	•

* **Open-Ended Questions incorporate a variety of skills from each content category.**

OE: Open-Ended Questions
PT: Practice Test

As the lesson for each *Academic Standard* is completed, place a ✓ to indicate *Mastery* or an ✗ to indicate *Review Needed*.

Pennsylvania Academic Standards
Content Category 2.7.5
Probability and Predictions (cont'd)

Lessons	2.7.5A	2.7.5B	2.7.5C	2.7.5D	2.7.5E	2.7.5F	2.7.5G	2.7.5H	2.7.5I	2.7.5J	2.7.5OE	2.7.5PT
C. Express probabilities as fractions and decimals.			●								*	●
D. Compare predictions based on theoretical probability and experimental results.				●							*	●
E. Calculate the probability of a simple event.					●						*	●
F. Determine patterns generated as a result of an experiment.						●					*	●
G. Determine the probability of an event involving "and", "or" or "not".							●				*	●
H. Predict and determine why some outcomes are certain, more likely, less likely, equally likely or impossible.								●			*	●
I. Find all possible combinations and arrangements involving a limited number of variables.									●		*	●
J. Develop a tree diagram and list the elements.										●	*	●

Pennsylvania Academic Standards
Content Category 2.8.5
Algebra and Functions

Lessons	2.8.5A	2.8.5B	2.8.5C	2.8.5D	2.8.5E	2.8.5F	2.8.5G	2.8.5H	2.8.5I	2.8.5OE	2.8.5PT
A. Recognize, reproduce, extend, create and describe patterns, sequences and relationships verbally, numerically, symbolically and graphically, using a variety of materials.	●									*	●
B. Connect patterns to geometric relations and basic number skills.		●								*	●
C. Form rules based on patterns (e.g., an equation that relates pairs in a sequence).			●							*	●
D. Use concrete objects and combinations of symbols and numbers to create expressions that model mathematical situations.				●						*	●
E. Explain the use of combinations of symbols and numbers in expressions, equations and inequalities.					●					*	●
F. Describe a realistic situation using information given in equations, inequalities, tables or graphs.						●				*	●
G. Select and use appropriate strategies, including concrete materials, to solve number sentences and explain the method of solution.							●			*	●
H. Locate and identify points on a coordinate system.								●		*	●
I. Generate functions from tables of data and relate data to corresponding graphs and functions.									●	*	●

Pennsylvania Academic Standards
Content Category 2.9.5
Geometry

Lessons	2.9.5A	2.9.5B	2.9.5C	2.9.5D	2.9.5E	2.9.5F	2.9.5G	2.9.5H	2.9.5I	2.9.5J	2.9.5K	2.9.5L	2.9.5OE	2.9.5PT
A. Give formal definitions of geometric figures.	●												*	●
B. Classify and compare triangles and quadrilaterals according to sides or angles.		●											*	●
C. Identify and measure circles, their diameters and their radii.			●										*	●
D. Describe in words how geometric shapes are constructed.				●									*	●
E. Construct two-and three-dimensional shapes and figures using manipulatives, geoboards and computer software.					●								*	●
F. Find familiar solids in the environment and describe them.						●							*	●

* Open-Ended Questions incorporate a variety of skills from each content category.

OE: Open-Ended Questions
PT: Practice Test

This workbook is 100% aligned to the Pennsylvania Academic Standards and provides complete practice for the PSSA!

As the lesson for each *Academic Standard* is completed, place a ✓ to indicate *Mastery* or an ✗ to indicate *Review Needed*.

Pennsylvania Academic Standards *Content Category 2.9.5* *Geometry (cont'd)*	2.9.5A	2.9.5B	2.9.5C	2.9.5D	2.9.5E	2.9.5F	2.9.5G	2.9.5H	2.9.5I	2.9.5J	2.9.5K	2.9.5L	2.9.5OE	2.9.5PT
G. Create an original tessellation.							●						*	●
H. Describe the relationship between the perimeter and area of triangles, quadrilaterals and circles.								●					*	●
I. Represent and use the concepts of line, point and plane.									●				*	●
J. Define the basic properties of squares, pyramids, parallelograms, quadrilaterals, trapezoids, polygons, rectangles, rhombi, circles, triangles, cubes, prisms, spheres and cylinders.										●			*	●
K. Analyze simple transformations of geometric figures and rotations of line segments.											●		*	●
L. Identify properties of geometric figures (e.g., parallel, perpendicular, similar, congruent, symmetrical).												●	*	●

Pennsylvania Academic Standards *Content Category 2.10.5* *Trigonometry*	2.10.5A	2.10.5B	2.10.5OE	2.10.5PT
A. Identify and compare parts of right triangles, including right angles, acute angles, hypotenuses and legs.	●		*	●
B. Create right triangles on a geoboard.		●	*	●

Pennsylvania Academic Standards *Content Category 2.11.5* *Concepts of Calculus*	2.11.5A	2.11.5B	2.11.5C	2.11.5D	2.11.5E	2.11.5F	2.11.5OE	2.11.5PT
A. Make comparisons of numbers (e.g., more, less, same, least, most, greater than, less than).	●						*	●
B. Identify least and greatest values represented in bar and circle graphs.		●					*	●
C. Identify maximum and minimum.			●				*	●
D. Describe the relationship between rates of change and time.				●			*	●
E. Estimate areas and volumes as the sums of areas of tiles and volumes of cubes.					●		*	●
F. Describe the relationship between the size of the unit of measurement and the estimate of the areas and volumes.						●	*	●

* Open-Ended Questions incorporate a variety of skills from each content category.

OE: Open-Ended Questions
PT: Practice Test

Notes

Letter to Students

Dear Student,

There are many ways you show what you have learned and what you are good at. You might play on a sports team or take part in an individual sport such as ice skating, tennis, or gymnastics. You might perform in a play or be a part of a school club. You might cook for someone or draw a picture for them. You might take a test in school. This book was written to help you do well on math tests so you can show your parents and teachers (and yourself!) what you have learned.

When you take a test, you can succeed by preparing and practicing—just as you do for a game or a musical or acting performance. The very best way to prepare for a math test is to learn the math! The lessons in this book are specially designed to help you practice and succeed on math tests.

Here are some **Tips for Taking Tests** that will help you show yourself, your family, and your teachers what you know about math.

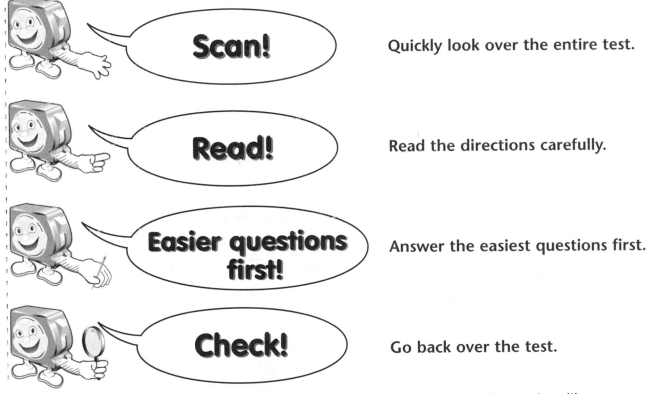

Scan! — Quickly look over the entire test.

Read! — Read the directions carefully.

Easier questions first! — Answer the easiest questions first.

Check! — Go back over the test.

This book contains multiple-choice problems and open-ended questions—just like your math tests. The next few pages have strategies and ideas for improving your "test smarts!" People with test smarts know the best way to answer multiple-choice and open-ended problems.

Throughout this book, you will see 🏠 in the lessons. This symbol is there to encourage you to take your book home and show your family members what you know about math.

Now it's time to get started! By the time you finish this book, you will be ready to do well on your math tests.

Good luck!

Measuring Up on Multiple-Choice Questions

You can do better on tests just by knowing how to take a test. On the math test, you are given four answer choices for each multiple-choice question. One of the answers is correct. After you solve the problem, you need to choose the correct answer from the choices you are given. Here are some strategies to help you with multiple-choice questions.

Read!

Read the question or problem carefully and completely.
- *Circle or underline key information in the problem.*
- *Draw a diagram or picture of the problem if possible.*
- *If the question or problem seems difficult, go to the next problem and come back to it later.*

Two sides of a triangle are equal in length. The third side is twice as long as one other side. The perimeter of the triangle is 8 cm. What is the length of the longest side of the triangle?

1. Circle the information you need to solve the problem.

Think!

Look at all the answers and eliminate any that you know are wrong.
- *Use number sense to eliminate.*

$837 + (323 \times 0 \times 2) = $ _____.

   A 323
   B 1,674
   C 837
   D 646

1. You know the answer is not A or D because you will be adding 837. In answer A, $323 < 837$. In answer D, $646 < 837$.

2. Using the Zero Property, you know that $323 \times 0 \times 2 = 0$ and that $837 + 0 = 837$. Therefore the answer is C.

- *Use estimation to eliminate.*

Which is true?

   A $898 \times 11 = 900$
   B $898 \times 11 = 898$
   C $898 \times 11 = 9,000$
   D $898 \times 11 = 9,878$

1. $900 \times 10 = 9,000$.

2. A, B, and C are not large enough. The answer must be D.

- *Look for choices that are obviously wrong and eliminate them.*

Find the area of a room 8 ft long and 4 ft wide.

A 32 ft

B 12 ft²

C 24 ft

D 32 ft²

1. Since the problem is about area, you know that the answer will be in square feet or ft².

2. Answers A and C can be eliminated because they are not in square feet.

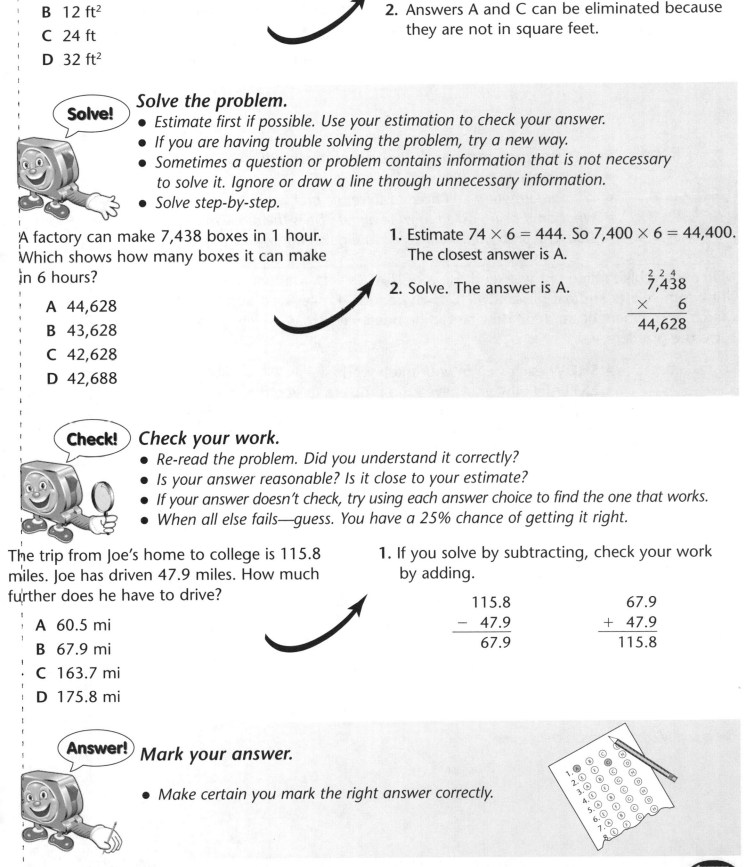

Solve! Solve the problem.

- *Estimate first if possible. Use your estimation to check your answer.*
- *If you are having trouble solving the problem, try a new way.*
- *Sometimes a question or problem contains information that is not necessary to solve it. Ignore or draw a line through unnecessary information.*
- *Solve step-by-step.*

A factory can make 7,438 boxes in 1 hour. Which shows how many boxes it can make in 6 hours?

A 44,628

B 43,628

C 42,628

D 42,688

1. Estimate 74 × 6 = 444. So 7,400 × 6 = 44,400. The closest answer is A.

2. Solve. The answer is A.

$$\begin{array}{r} \overset{2\ 2\ 4}{7{,}438} \\ \times\quad 6 \\ \hline 44{,}628 \end{array}$$

Check! Check your work.

- *Re-read the problem. Did you understand it correctly?*
- *Is your answer reasonable? Is it close to your estimate?*
- *If your answer doesn't check, try using each answer choice to find the one that works.*
- *When all else fails—guess. You have a 25% chance of getting it right.*

The trip from Joe's home to college is 115.8 miles. Joe has driven 47.9 miles. How much further does he have to drive?

A 60.5 mi

B 67.9 mi

C 163.7 mi

D 175.8 mi

1. If you solve by subtracting, check your work by adding.

$$\begin{array}{r} 115.8 \\ -\ 47.9 \\ \hline 67.9 \end{array} \qquad \begin{array}{r} 67.9 \\ +\ 47.9 \\ \hline 115.8 \end{array}$$

Answer! Mark your answer.

- *Make certain you mark the right answer correctly.*

Open-ended questions take longer to answer than multiple-choice questions, so give yourself plenty of time to read and answer these problems. It is very important that you read the question carefully and completely before you begin to solve and answer the problem. Open-ended questions ask you to explain how you solved the problem. Your explanations should be clear and easy to understand. Here are some things you can do to help you solve open-ended questions.

Read! *Read the question carefully and completely.*
- *What problem am I being asked to solve?*
- *What information do I need to solve the problem?*
- *What am I being asked to write about? Does the problem ask me to show my work? Does the problem ask me to explain how I got my answer?*

Marco went bike riding last weekend. He rode 7 miles east and then 9 miles south. He stopped to drink some water and eat his sandwich. Then he rode 4 miles west and 10 miles north. How far is Marco from where he started? How far did he ride in all? Draw a picture or diagram to help you solve the problem.

- **SHOW** each step of your math work.
- **EXPLAIN** why you solved the problem as you did.
- **WRITE** an explanation describing what you did and why you solved the problem as you did, **EVEN** if you used mental math or a calculator.

Plan! *Plan your work.*
- *What should I do to solve the problem?*
- *Is there more than one step to the problem?*
- *What strategies should I use to solve the problem?*

I need to draw a diagram showing Marco's bike ride so I can calculate how far he is from where he started and how far he rode in all.

- What is the answer to the problem?
- Be careful with your computation. Always check your math. If your first strategy doesn't work, try another strategy.
- Make sure you answer in the form requested, for example, writing a fraction in the simplest form.
- Reread the original question to make sure you answer the question correctly.

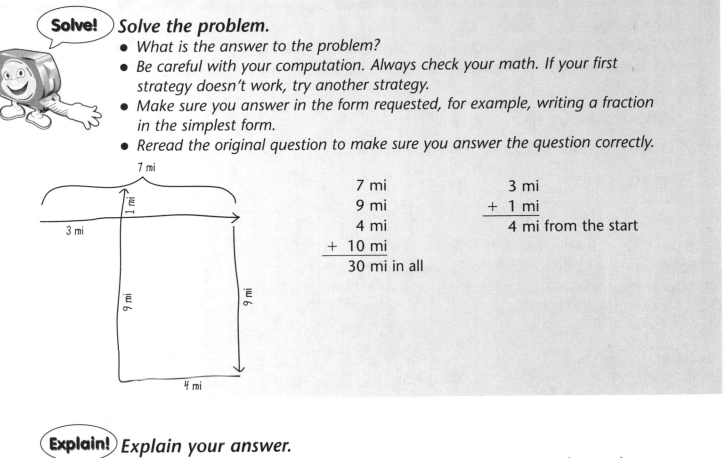

$$
\begin{aligned}
&7 \text{ mi} \\
&9 \text{ mi} \\
&4 \text{ mi} \\
+\ &10 \text{ mi} \\
\hline
&30 \text{ mi in all}
\end{aligned}
\qquad
\begin{aligned}
&3 \text{ mi} \\
+\ &1 \text{ mi} \\
\hline
&4 \text{ mi from the start}
\end{aligned}
$$

Explain! Explain your answer.

- How did you get your answer? Make sure your explanation is clear and easy to understand.
- If you can't solve the whole problem, answer any parts that you can. Partial credit is usually given even if you don't explain everything. Partial credit is better than no credit! Explain everything that you can.

My diagram shows that Marco rode 30 mi in all. 7 mi + 9 mi + 4 mi + 10 mi = 30 miles. I added each leg of his ride to find how many miles he rode in all. According to my diagram, Marco ends up 3 miles east and 1 mile north of where he started. 3 mi + 1 mi + 4 miles.

Check! Reread the question, your answer, and your explanation.

- Check that you have answered the question and solved the problem correctly and completely.
- Check your explanation. Is it easy to understand? Will someone else understand what you wrote? Have you left anything out?
- Use all the time you have left to check and recheck your work and your explanation.

Ready Reference

place value the value of a digit based on its position in a number

expanded notation writing the number in expanded form to show the value of each digit

Think About It

How do you read the number 725,341,582.21?

Here's How

Use a place value chart.

Each digit has a place value. It tells how many millions, thousands, hundreds, tens, ones, tenths, or hundredths there are. For example, the value of 3 in this number is 300,000.

MILLIONS			THOUSANDS			ONES				
hundred millions	ten millions	one millions	hundred thousands	ten thousands	one thousands	hundreds	tens	ones	tenths	hundredths
7	2	5	3	4	1	5	8	2	2	1

1. **Expanded form:**

   700,000,000 + 20,000,000 + 5,000,000 + 300,000 + 40,000 + 1,000 + 500 + 80 + 2 + .2 + .01

2. **Short word form:** 700 million + 20 million + _____5_____ million + 300 thousand + ____40____ thousand + ____1____ thousand + 5 hundred + ____80____ tens + ____2____ ones + 2 tenths + ____1____ hundredth

3. **Word form:** seven hundred twenty-five million, three hundred forty-one thousand, five hundred eighty-two and twenty-one hundredths. (Read the decimal point as *and*.)

Practice

1. The maximum distance of the planet Mercury from the sun is about 43,<u>4</u>00,000 miles. Which shows the value of the underlined digit?

   A 40

   B 4,000

   C 40,000

   D 400,000

2. The minimum distance of Earth from the sun is <u>9</u>1,400,000 miles. Which shows the value of the underlined digit?

   E 90,000,000

   F 900,000

   G .9

   H 90,000

3. Mars orbits around the sun at a speed of about 14.9<u>9</u> miles per second. Which shows the value of the underlined digit?

   A 9

   B .09

   C .9

   D 90

4. Earth orbits around the sun at a speed of about 18.<u>5</u>1 miles per second. Which shows the value of the underlined digit?

   E 50

   F 5

   G .5

   H .05

5. It takes the planet Jupiter 4,<u>3</u>31.8 days to revolve around the sun. Which shows the value of the underlined digit?

   A   3,000
   B   300
   C   30
   D   .3

6. It takes the planet Pluto <u>9</u>0,466.8 days to revolve around the sun. Which shows the value of the underlined digit?

   E   90
   F   900
   G   9,000
   H   90,000

7. It takes Earth 3<u>6</u>5.3 days to revolve around the sun. Which shows the value of the underlined digit?

   A   600
   B   60
   C   6
   D   .6

8. Earth orbits around the sun at a speed of about 1<u>8</u>.51 miles per second. Which shows the value of the underlined digit?

   E   8
   F   80
   G   800
   H   .8

9. Which shows the expanded form of the number 5,789.36?

   A   50,000 + 70,000 + 800 + 9 + .3
   B   5,000 + 700 + 80 + 9 + 36
   C   5,000 + 700 + 80 + 90 + 36
   D   5,000 + 700 + 80 + 9 + .3 + .06

10. The length of the equator is 24,901.55 miles. Which is the word name for this number?

    E   Twenty-four thousand, nine hundred and fifty-five hundredths
    F   Twenty-four million, nine hundred one thousand fifty-five
    G   Twenty-four thousand, nine hundred one and five tenths
    H   Twenty-four thousand, nine hundred one and fifty-five hundredths

11. The visible rings of the planet Saturn stretch out to a distance of one hundred thirty-six thousand, two hundred km from Saturn's center. Which shows this number in standard form?

    A   136
    B   1,360
    C   136,200
    D   13,200

12. At times, the planet Saturn is eight hundred thirty-eight million, four hundred thousand miles from Earth. Which shows this number in standard form?

    E   838,400,000
    F   838,400
    G   8,380,400
    H   838,400,400

Think About It

Tara told Michael her family has 8 rock CDs, 8 pop CDs, $\frac{16}{2}$ vocal CDs, $\frac{32}{4}$ classical CDs, $12 - 4$ swing CDs, 4×2 country CDs, and $6 + 2$ gospel CDs. Does she have the same number of each kind of CD? How do you know?

Here's How

How many ways can you rename $4\frac{1}{2}$?

1. Use mixed numbers: $4\frac{1}{2}$

2. Use words: four and _____

3. Use fractions: $\frac{9}{2}$ $\frac{}{4}$ $\frac{}{8}$

4. Use decimals: $\frac{1}{2}$ is the same as .5 so $4\frac{1}{2}$ = _____

5. Use addition facts: $4 + \frac{1}{2}$ ___ or $3 +$ ___ or $2 +$ ___

6. Use subtraction facts: $5 - \frac{1}{2}$ ___ or $6 -$ ___ or $5\frac{1}{2} -$ ___

7. Use multiplication facts: $9 \times \frac{}{2}$

Practice

1. Suppose you finish one-half of a book. Which does NOT rename how much more you have to read?

   A $\frac{1}{4} + \frac{1}{4}$

   B $\frac{1}{4} + \frac{2}{4}$

   C $1 - \frac{1}{2}$

   D .5

2. Edgetown is 299 miles from Centertown. Today you drove 155 miles. Which does NOT rename the distance left to drive? Show your work.

   E 18×7

   F $576 \div 4$

   G $173 - 29$

   H $99 + 45$

3. The fifth grade made 20 gal of punch for the school sports day. Someone spilled 2.7 gallons. Which does NOT rename the amount of punch left? Show your work.

   A 17.03

   B $17 + 0.3$

   C $18 - \frac{7}{10}$

   D $\frac{173}{10}$

4. One hundred students were asked to choose between blue and orange book covers. Twenty-three chose orange. Which does NOT rename the number of students who chose blue? Show your work.

   E $1 + 76$

   F $109 - 32$

   G $19 + 59$

   H 11×7

5. Karen has a pepperoni pizza that is divided into 10 pieces. She gives Sam 5 pieces. Which does NOT show how many pieces are left?

A $\frac{5}{10}$

B $\frac{1}{2}$

C $\frac{2}{2}$

D $\frac{2}{4}$

6. Barry saved seventeen and a half dollars by washing cars, cutting lawns, and raking leaves. Which renames the amount of money he saved?

E $10.00 + $7.00

F $17.00

G $20.00 − $2.50

H $17.05

7. Megan, Tony, and Niko collected $6\frac{2}{3}$ pounds of cans for a recycling drive at school. Which does NOT show how many pounds they collected?

A $3 + 3\frac{2}{3}$

B $10 - 3\frac{1}{3}$

C 6.23

D six and two-thirds

8. Carol-Anne had $2\frac{1}{2}$ hours of homework last week. Which does NOT rename the amount of homework?

E $1\frac{1}{2} + 1\frac{1}{2}$

F $3 - \frac{1}{2}$

G $1 \times 2\frac{1}{2}$

H $1\frac{1}{4} + 1\frac{1}{4}$

9. Sarah, Ben, and Cameron bought a present for their mother. Sarah contributed $2.95, Ben contributed $3.15, and Cameron contributed $2.90. Which does NOT show the cost of the present? Show your work.

A $5.85 + $3.15

B $81.00 ÷ $9.00

C Nine dollars and ten cents

D $3.00 × $3.00

10. Callie's mom made $9\frac{1}{2}$ gal of ice cream for a community picnic. Five and one-half gallons were chocolate. Which does NOT show the amount of strawberry ice cream she made? Show your work.

E 5.5 − 1.0

F $\frac{8}{2}$

G $\frac{1}{8} + 3\frac{7}{8}$

H 36 ÷ 9

Think About It

When you read a word problem, you have to decide which operation to use. How do you make that decision? First you read to make sure you understand the problem and then you decide which operation to use. What are some of the clues in a problem that help you decide which operation to use?

To combine groups	+ Use addition
To compare groups	− Use subtraction
To combine equal groups	× Use multiplication
To separate into equal groups	÷ Use division

Here's How

Selena compiled a table for a report that showed the weights of some African animals.

Animal	Weight in Pounds
African elephant	17,000
giraffe	18,000
hippopotamus	8,000
cheetah	120

1. How would you find the total weight of all the animals? I need to combine the weights, so I need to add all the weights.

   Write a number sentence that shows the total weight of all the animals.

   17,000 + 18,000 + _____ + _____ = _____ lb

2. How would you find how much heavier the giraffe is than the elephant? Subtract the weight of the elephant from the weight of the _____.

   Write a number sentence that shows how much heavier the giraffe is than the elephant.

   18,000 − 17,000 = _____ lb

3. How would you find the weight of 4 cheetahs?

   Multiply 4 times _____.

   Write a number sentence that shows the weight of 4 cheetahs.

   120 × _____ = _____ lb

4. If you know that 4 hippopotami weigh 32,000 lb, how would you find the weight of 1 hippopotamus? Divide the total weight by _____.

   Write a number sentence that shows the weight of 1 hippopotamus.

   32,000 ÷ _____ = _____ lb

Practice

Ali compiled information about the length of dinosaurs for this table.

Dinosaur	Length in feet
Ankylosaurus	20
Brachiosaurus	70
Deinonychus	15
Stegosaurs	25

1. How would you find the total length of the dinosaurs?

  A Multiply the lengths.

  B Add the lengths.

  C Divide the total length by 4.

  D Subtract the length of Stegosaurs from the total of all the lengths.

2. How would you find how much longer Brachiosaurus is than Deinonychus?

  E Multiply the length of Deinonychus by the length of Brachiosaurus.

  F Add the length of Deinonychus and the length of Brachiosaurus.

  G Subtract the length of Deinonychus from the length of Brachiosaurus.

  H Divide the total length by 4.

3. How would you find the length of 7 Ankylosaurus?

  A Multiply the length of Ankylosaurus by 7.

  B Divide the length of the longest dinosaur by the length of Ankylosaurus.

  C Multiply the length of Ankylosaurus by 6.

  D Divide the length of Ankylosaurus by 7.

4. Which number sentence would you use to find the length of 7 Ankylosaurus?

  E $20 \div 7 = x$

  F $70 \div 20 = x$

  G $20 \times 6 = x$

  H $20 \times 7 = x$

5. Roger made a table of population for some of the county seats in Pennsylvania.

County	County Seat	1995 Population	1990 Population
Allegheny	Pittsburgh	1,309,821	1,336,449
Bucks	Doylestown	573,901	541,174
Fayette	Uniontown	146,827	145,351
Somerset	Somerset	80,113	78,218
Greene	Waynesburg	41,114	39,550

Which number sentence shows how to find how much larger the Doylestown 1995 population is than the Somerset 1990 population?

  A $573{,}901 + 78{,}218$

  B $573{,}901 - 78{,}218$

  C $573{,}901 - 541{,}174$

  D $573{,}901 + 541{,}174$

Standard 2.1.5D ✦ Use models to show fractions and decimals

Think About It

Look at the number 1.111. Each digit has a place value. It tells how many ones, tenths, hundredths, or thousandths. How do you use grid paper and base–10 blocks to show fractions and decimals?

Here's How

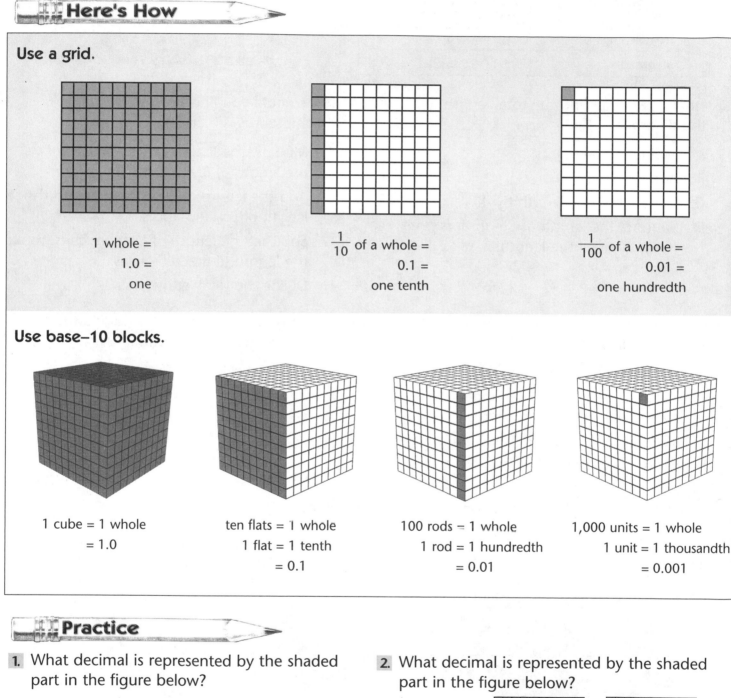

Use a grid.

1 whole =
1.0 =
one

$\frac{1}{10}$ of a whole =
0.1 =
one tenth

$\frac{1}{100}$ of a whole =
0.01 =
one hundredth

Use base–10 blocks.

1 cube = 1 whole
= 1.0

ten flats = 1 whole
1 flat = 1 tenth
= 0.1

100 rods = 1 whole
1 rod = 1 hundredth
= 0.01

1,000 units = 1 whole
1 unit = 1 thousandth
= 0.001

Practice

1. What decimal is represented by the shaded part in the figure below?

A 2.03

B 1.3

C .3

D 2.3

2. What decimal is represented by the shaded part in the figure below?

E .47

F 1.47

G 147.7

H 1.7

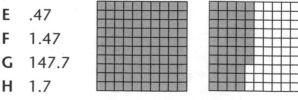

3. What fraction is represented by the shaded part in the figure below?

A $\frac{1}{5}$

B 5

C $\frac{1}{2}$

D $\frac{5}{2}$

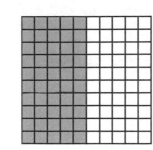

4. What decimal is represented by the shaded part in the figure below?

E 3.86

F 3.68

G 368.6

H 3.8

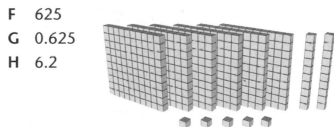

5. What decimal is represented by the shaded part in the figure below?

A 10.54

B 1.354

C 1.3

D 13.54

6. What decimal is represented by the shaded part in the figure below?

E 6.25

F 625

G 0.625

H 6.2

7. Mrs. Shea baked an apple, cherry, blueberry, and banana pie for a party. Each pie was cut into eighths. After the party, there were 3 slices of apple pie, 2 slices of cherry pie, 1 slice of blueberry pie, and 5 slices of banana pie left. Which shows the total amount of pie left?

A

B

C

D

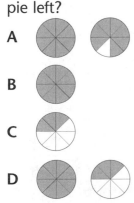

8. Mr. Carter cut a long board in half. Then he cut one of the halves in half again. He cut one of those pieces in half again and wrote a large X on one of the last two pieces. Which fraction shows the piece of wood with a large X? Make a drawing to show your work.

E $\frac{1}{2}$

F $\frac{1}{4}$

G $\frac{1}{8}$

H $\frac{1}{16}$

Ready Reference

prime number an integer greater than one whose only positive factors are 1 and itself

composite number any positive integer exactly divisible by one or more positive integers other than itslef and 1

factor the number or variable multiplied in a multiplication expression

common factor a number that is a factor of two or more numbers; *example*: 1, 2, 3, and 6 are common factors of 6 and 12

greatest common factor (GCF) the greatest number that is a factor of each of two or more numbers; *example*: the GCF of 24 and 48 is 12

Think About It

The number 1 does not have two factors, so it is not a prime number. The number 2 has only two factors (2 × 1) so it is a prime number. If a number has more than two factors, it is a composite number. How do you determine if numbers are prime by using factors?

Here's How

Mrs. Duncan is arranging the chairs for a meeting. How many different ways can 18 chairs be arranged so there is the same number of chairs in each row? She made a factor chart to help her.

Number	Rows x Chairs	Factors	Number of Factors	Prime or Composite?
1	1 x 1	1	1	Neither
2	2 x 1, 1 x 2	1, 2	2	Prime
3				
5				
9	1 x 9, 9 x 1, 3 x 3	1, 3, 9	3	Composite
12				
18				

1. Complete the rest of the chart.

2. Mrs. Duncan can arrange the chairs in 1 row of _____ , 2 rows of _____ , _____ rows of 6, 6 rows of _____ , 9 rows of _____ , _____ rows of 1.

3. Mrs. Duncan realizes she will have to add 24 stools to seat everyone. What is the least number of rows possible if stools and chairs are not combined in a row?
   Find the common factors.

   18: **1, 2, 3, 6**, 9, 18

   24: **1, 2, 3, 4, 6**, 8, 12, 24   Since 6 is the greatest common factor (GCF) of 18 and 24, the chairs and stool can be put in rows of 6.

Practice

1. How many prime numbers are between 1 and 100?

A 34

B 17

C 25

D 11

2. Which is a prime number between 48 and 58?

E 51

F 53

G 54

H 57

3. Which number is NOT a factor of 42? Show your work.

A 2

B 3

C 13

D 7

$\lceil 42$

4. Which number is NOT a factor of 87? Show your work.

E 29

F 3

G 19

H 1

$3\lceil 87$

5. Which is the greatest common factor of 10 and 12? Show your work.

A 5

B 1

C 6

D 2

$10, 5, 2$ $10, 1$

$12, 1, 12$ $6, 2$

6. Which is the greatest common factor of 24, 36, 60? Show your work.

E 6

F 12

G 8

H 13

7. The tomato plants in Kevin's vegetable garden are arranged in a 9 by 12 rectangular array. Which shows why the total number of plants is a prime or composite number? Show your work.

A 108 is a prime number because it has only 2 factors.

B 108 is a prime number because it has more than 2 factors.

C 108 is a composite number because it has only 2 factors.

D 108 is a composite number because it has more than 2 factors.

Ready Reference

negative number a whole number that is less than zero

Think About It

Is negative 3 (–3) less than 0? Is –3 less than 3? How do you order positive and negative numbers?

Here's How

Count on a number line.

How would you place these numbers on a number line? –3, 3, $\frac{1}{3}$

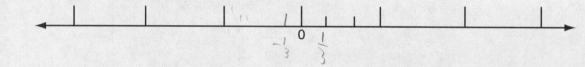

1. Count from 0 to write the numbers on the line. –3 is a negative number, so it is less than 0. Write the positive and negative numbers on the number line. Write $\frac{1}{3}$ on the number line.

2. Compare two different numbers by looking at their positions on the number line. For any two different places on the number line, the number on the right is greater than the number on the left. Every positive number is greater than any negative number. Use < or > to compare the numbers.

$$-2 \underline{\quad <\quad } 2 \qquad -2 \underline{\quad <\quad } 0 \qquad -2 \underline{\quad <\quad } -1$$

3. Is $-\frac{1}{3}$ to the left or the right of zero? _____

Use a thermometer.

1. Use the negative sign to write temperatures below zero. –8°F is read as "8 degrees below zero Fahrenheit."

2. If the temperature is 20°F and falls 30° during the night, what is the final temperature? (Use the thermometer to count.)

   _–10_

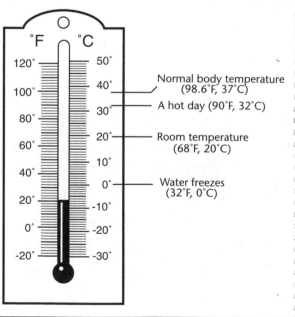

✏ Practice

1. Which shows the temperature on the thermometer?

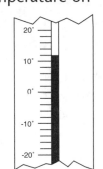

- A   −11°
- B   9°
- C   −6°
- D   11°

2. Which shows the temperature on the thermometer?

- E   16°
- F   −6°
- G   −16°
- H   6°

3. Which is shown on the number line?

- A   −1
- B $-1\frac{1}{2}$
- C $-\frac{1}{4}$
- D $-\frac{1}{2}$

4. Which is shown on the number line?

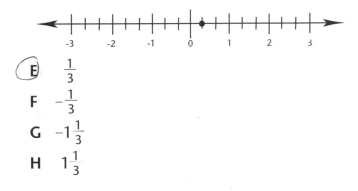

- E $\frac{1}{3}$
- F $-\frac{1}{3}$
- G $-1\frac{1}{3}$
- H $1\frac{1}{3}$

5. The temperature was 25°F, and later dropped to 13°F. How many degrees did the temperature drop? Show your work.

- A   38
- B   12
- C   10
- D   22

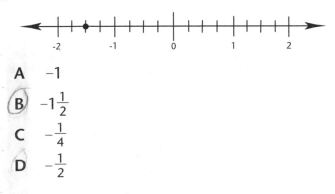

6. The morning temperature was 7°C. At night it was −7°C. How many degrees did the temperature drop? Show your work.

- E   21
- F   0
- G   7
- H   14

7. The temperature in the morning was 11°F. During the snowstorm, the temperature dropped 4° every hour. What was the temperature 3 hours later? Show your work.

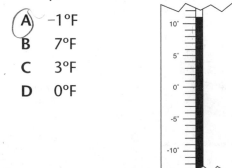

- A   −1°F
- B   7°F
- C   3°F
- D   0°F

8. Which expression is shown by the number line?

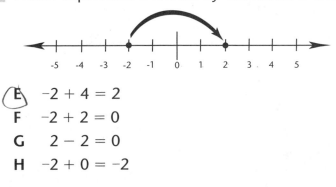

- E   −2 + 4 = 2
- F   −2 + 2 = 0
- G   2 − 2 = 0
- H   −2 + 0 = −2

Ready Reference

common multiple a multiple of 2 or more numbers; *example*: 8 is a common multiple of 2 and 4

multiple a number that is the product of a given integer and another integer; *example*: 0, 3, 6, 9... are multiples of 3

least common multiple (LCM) the least number, other than 0, that is the common multiple of two or more numbers; *example*: 6 is the least common multiple of 2 and 3

Think About It

You have learned to use common factors, greatest common factors, and prime and composite numbers to solve problems. How can understanding multiples help you solve problems?

Here's How

Carla has green beans for dinner every 4 days and mashed potatoes every 6 days. What is the first day that she will have green beans and mashed potatoes together?

Step 1 Make a list of the first several multiples of each number.

4: 4, 8, 12, 16, 20, 24 ⟶ Days Carla will have green beans:
Day 4, Day 8, Day 12, Day 16, and so on

6: 6, 12, 18, 24, 30 ⟶ Days Carla will have mashed potatoes:
Day 6, Day 12, Day 18, Day 24, and so on

Step 2 Find the common multiples.

4: 4, 8, **12**, 16, 20, **24** ⟶ Days Carla will have green beans AND
6: 6, **12**, 18, **24**, 30 ⟶ mashed potatoes: Day 12 and Day _____

Step 3 Find the least common multiple (LCM).

Since 12 is the least common multiple, Day 12 is the first time Carla will have green beans and mashed potatoes together.

Practice

1. Which is the least common multiple of 6 and 2? Show your work.

   A 4
   B 12
   C 6
   D 3

2. Which is the least common multiple of 6, 9, and 12? Show your work.

   E 36
   F 42
   G 18
   H 24

3. Which is the least common multiple of 8, 10, and 16? Show your work.

    A 64

    B 90

    C 80

    D 160

4. Which is the least common multiple of 20 and 25? Show your work.

    E 50

    F 75

    G 125

    H 100

5. Which is the least common multiple of 24, 12, and 8? Show your work.

    A 24

    B 48

    C 72

    D 120

6. Which is the least common multiple of 3, 4, and 9? Show your work.

    E 18

    F 36

    G 45

    H 27

7. Movie Time shows a comedy every 2 days, a science fiction movie every 4 days, and a drama every 5 days. What is the first day that a comedy, science fiction, and drama will be shown on the same day? Show your work.

    A Day 16

    B Day 24

    C Day 20

    D Day 40

8. Tamara has math homework every 2 days, spelling homework every 7 days, and social studies homework every 8 days. What is the first day she will have homework in all three subjects? Show your work.

    E Day 21

    F Day 56

    G Day 32

    H Day 48

1. Pam's mom traveled twenty–eight thousand, six hundred thirty-one miles last year for her job. Write the number of miles she traveled in the following ways: standard form, short word form, and expanded form. Which form should she use to describe her travels in a letter to her cousin? Explain.

- **READ** the problem and break it into parts to solve it.
- **WRITE** an explanation describing what you did and why you solved the problem as you did, **EVEN** if you used mental math or a calculator.
- **EXPLAIN** why you answered the question as you did.
- **WRITE** your answers in the spaces provided.

Explanation

Which form should she use in a letter to her cousin? Why?

Standard form _____

Short word form _____

_____

Expanded Form _____

0–5 Points

Score _____

2. Determine the numbers represented by the pictures in Part A, Part B, and Part C.
For Part A, write as a mixed number and a decimal. For Part B, write as a whole
number. For Part C, write as a whole number.

- **SHOW** each step of your math work.
- **WRITE** an explanation describing what you did and why you solved the problem as you did,
  EVEN if you used mental math or a calculator.
- **WRITE** your answers in the spaces provided.

Part A   Part B

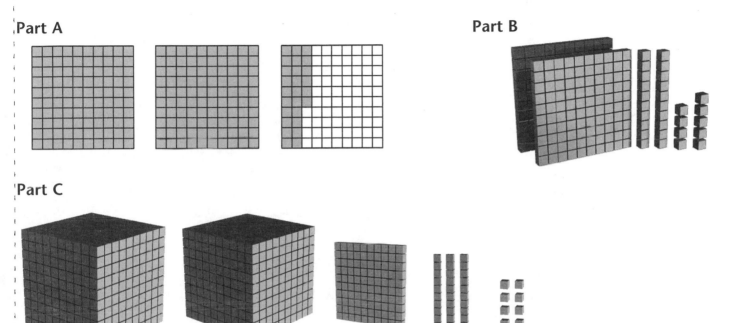

Part C

Explanation

Part A _____

Part B _____

Part C _____

0–5 Points

Score _____

3. A cake is cut into 12 equal pieces. Two brothers take three pieces each. What fraction of the cake did the brothers take? What fraction of the cake is left? Write the fractions. Simplify fractions if possible. Then check your answer by shading the cake shown in Figure 1 to show the pieces taken by the brothers.

- **SHOW** each step of your math work.
- **WRITE** an explanation describing what you did and why you solved the problem as you did, **EVEN** if you used mental math or a calculator.
- **WRITE** your answers in the spaces provided.

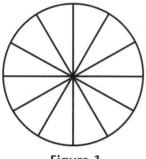

Figure 1

Explanation

Fraction of the cake taken

Fraction of the cake left

0–5 Points
Score

4. Many numbers can be expressed in more than one way. In the spaces provided, rename the number 12 using the method requested. Then explain whether 12 is a prime number or a composite number.

- **READ** the problem and break it into parts to solve it.
- **SHOW** your work, **EVEN** if you used a calculator or mental math to solve the problem.
- **EXPLAIN** why you answered the question as you did.
- **WRITE** your answers in the spaces provided.

Explanation

Use words _____

Use fractions _____

Use decimals _____

Use addition facts _____

Use subtraction facts _____

Use multiplication facts _____

Use division facts _____

Is 12 an example of a prime or composite number? _____

0–5 Points

Score _____

1. Which shows the value of the underlined digit in 2<u>7</u>,707,777?

   A 700,000

   B 7,000

   C 70,000,000

   D 7,000,000

2. Which shows the standard form of eight hundred fifty-four thousand, two hundred eleven?

   E 854,211

   F 800,054

   G 800,540

   H 805,211

3. Sonya spent $1\frac{3}{4}$ hours writing a report. Which does NOT rename the amount of time she worked?

   A $1 + \frac{3}{4}$

   B $2\frac{1}{2} - 1\frac{1}{2}$

   C $1\frac{3}{4} \times 1$

   D $2 - \frac{1}{4}$

4. Which renames 9.7?

   E 9.7×0.7

   F $10 - 9.7$

   G $9 + 0.7$

   H $9 + 1.7$

5. Sam made a table of important dates in the Middle Colonies. How would you find how much earlier New Jersey was founded than Pennsylvania?

Date	What Happened?
1664	New Netherland becomes New York
1664	New Jersey is founded
1681	Pennsylvania is founded
1704	Delaware gets its own legislature

   A Add the New Jersey date and the Pennsylvania date.

   B Subtract the New Jersey date from the Pennsylvania date.

   C Subtract the Pennsylvania date from the New Jersey date.

   D Multiply the Pennsylvania date by the New Jersey date.

6. Which number sentence would you use to find how much earlier New Jersey was founded than Pennsylvania?

   E $1{,}681 - 1{,}664 = x$

   F $1{,}681 + 1{,}664 = x$

   G $1{,}681 \times 1{,}664 = x$

   H $1{,}681 \div 1{,}664 = x$

7. Which decimal is represented by the shaded part?

   A 16

   B 1.6

   C .16

   D 1.06

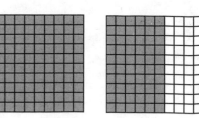

8. Which fraction is represented by the shaded part?

E $\frac{8}{10}$

F 8

G $\frac{1}{8}$

H $\frac{8}{100}$

12. Which temperature does the thermometer show?

E −12°C

F 12°C

G 2°C

H 2°C

9. Which is the GFC (greatest common factor) of 18, 24, and 36?

A 3

B 9

C 12

D 6

13. What is the LCM (least common multiple) of 6 and 10?

A 60

B 30

C 24

D 20

10. Which is a prime number?

E 20

F 21

G 22

H 23

14. Henry eats carrots every 2 days and salad every 3 days. Which is the first day he will eat them both on the same day?

E Day 2

F Day 4

G Day 6

H Day 8

11. The temperature rose from −9°F to 11°F. How many degrees did it rise?

A 9

B 19

C 20

D 10

15. What is the LCM (least common multiple) of 6 and 9?

A 18

B 9

C 12

D 6

Think About It

When you read a word problem, you have to decide which operation to use. How do you make that decision? You look for clue words. Here are some clue words that often signal an operation.

Addition	Subtraction	Multiplication	Division
altogether	fewer	times	shared equally
total	less	twice	half

Here's How

Addition

Rico has 78 stickers in one album and 134 stickers in another album. What is the total number of stickers in Rico's two albums?

1. What clue word is in the problem?
   total

2. What operation does this signal?
   addition

3. Write the number sentence.
   _78 + 134 =_

4. How many stickers are in the albums?
   _2,2_

Subtraction

Lea has read 128 pages of her book. Nan has read 39 fewer pages than Lea. How many pages has Nan read?

1. What clue word is in the problem?
   fewe

2. What operation does this signal?
   Subtraction

3. Write the number sentence.
   _128 - 39 =_

4. How many pages has Nan read? _69_

Multiplication

A fifth grade class collected 56 cans for a food drive. A fifth grade class collected four times this number. How many cans did the fifth grade class collect?

1. What clue word is in this problem?
   time

2. What operation does this signal?
   Multiplication

3. Write the number sentence.
   _56 × 4 =_

4. How many cans did the fifth grade class collect?
   _224_

Division

Ted, Jon, and Marco bought a gift for their teacher. The gift cost $21. The boys shared the cost of the gift equally. How much did each boy pay?

1. What clue word is in this problem?
   shared

2. What operation does this signal?
   division

3. Write the number sentence.
   _3 ⟌21_

4. How much did each boy pay? _7_

Practice

1. During this soccer season, the Hawks scored 46 goals. The Eagles scored half as many goals. Which shows how many goals the Eagles scored? Show your work.

   A 48
   (B) 23
   C 44
   D 26

2. This morning you counted 539 sports cards in your collection. A surprise package just arrived with 368 more cards. Which shows how many cards you have altogether? Show your work.

   E 171
   F 897
   G 452
   (H) 907

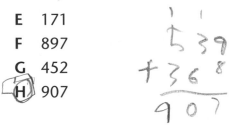

3. Kim collected 234 stamps. Tia collected twice as many stamps as Kim. Which shows how many stamps Tia has collected? Show your work.

   A 117
   (B) 468
   C 232
   D 236

4. Joe scored 3,876 points in a video game. Dee scored 452 less points than Joe. Which shows how many points Dee scored? Show your work.

   E 4,328
   F 3,476
   (G) 3,424
   H 4,012

5. Miguel and his father have 2,579 international coins in their collection. Of this total, 599 are from Asian countries. Which shows how many coins are NOT from Asian countries? Show your work.

   A 1,989
   (B) 1,980
   C 2,980
   D 1,970

6. A factory can make 7,438 boxes in 1 hour. Which shows how many boxes it can make in 6 hours? Show your work.

   (E) 44,628
   F 43,628
   G 42,628
   H 42,688

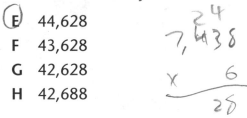

7. Mrs. Montoya bought 9 copies of a book for her book club. Each book costs $9.65. Which shows how much the books cost? Show your work.

   A $86.45
   (B) $86.85
   C $81.45
   D $81.85

8. An art show booth made $126.00 selling belts. Nine belts were sold. Which shows how much each belt cost? Show your work.

   E $14.50
   F $24.00
   (G) $14.00
   H $1,134.00

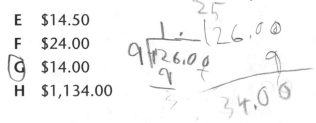

Ready Reference

decimal a number expressed using a decimal point; part of a whole

Think About It

Some word problems involve decimals. How do you add, subtract, and multiply decimals? Every time you solve a problem with money, you are using decimals.

Here's How

Addition

Mel bought a tie for 8.99. He also bought a pair of jeans for $32.50. Altogether, how much did Mel spend?

 Step 1 Line up the decimal points.

```
  32.50
+  8.99
```

Step 2 Add. Use regrouping if necessary. Start at the right and add the hundredths first, then add the tenths. Now add the ones, then the tens.

Step 3 Place the decimal point in your answer.

```
  32.50
+  8.99
    .
```

How much did Mel spend?

_____

Subtraction

Risha treated her friends to lunch. The bill was $27.85. Risha paid with two $20 bills. How much change did she receive?

 Step 1 Line up the decimal points.

```
  40.00
- 27.85
```

Step 2 Subtract. Use regrouping if necessary. Start at the right and subtract the hundredths first, then subtract the tenths. Now subtract the ones, then the tens.

Step 3 Place the decimal point in your answer.

```
  40.00
- 27.85
    .
```

How much did Risha receive?

_____

Multiplication

Dixie puts $42.75 in the bank every month. How much money has Dixie saved at the end of one year?

 Step 1 Write the problem vertically.

```
  42.75
×    12
```

Step 2 Multiply just as you do with whole numbers.

```
  42.75 →2 decimal places
×    12 →0 decimal places
   8550
  42750
$    .  →2 decimal places
```

 Step 3 Place a decimal point in the product so it has the same number of decimal places as the factors.

How much has Dixie saved?

_____

Practice

1. Maria's family is going to visit relatives. They are driving 35.8 miles to her aunt's house. Then they are driving 93.9 miles to her cousin's home. Finally, they will drive 65.2 miles back home. How many miles will Maria's family travel on this trip? Show your work.

   A 129.7
   B 159.1
   C 188.6
   D 194.9

2. Each member of a fourth-grade class contributes $3.75 for a class party. If there are 28 students in the class, how much is collected? Show your work.

   E $105.00
   F $84.00
   G $103.60
   H $98.40

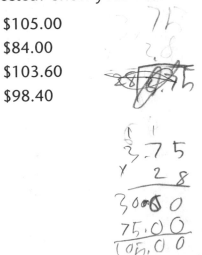

3. Greg walks to school each morning and takes the bus home. His school is 0.65 mi from his house. How far does Greg walk in 5 days? Show your work.

   A 32.5 mi
   B 325 mi
   C 3.25 mi
   D 3 mi

4. The trip from Joe's home to college is 115.8 miles. Joe has driven 47.9 miles. How much further does he have to drive? Show your work.

   E 60.5 mi
   F 67.9 mi
   G 163.7 mi
   H 175.8 mi

5. Dan has a clothing budget of $60.00. He has found a hat for $12.98, jeans for $22.45, a shirt for $19.75, and shoes for $36.50. Which three items can he buy? Show your work.

   A jeans, shirt, shoes
   B hat, jeans, shoes
   C hat, shirt, shoes
   D hat, jeans, shirt

6. David is making lemonade for a party. Each package makes 2.8 quarts. If he makes $4\frac{1}{2}$ packages, how much lemonade will he have? Show your work.

   E 12.6 qt
   F 126 qt
   G 1.26 qt
   H .126 qt

Part 1 ✦ Add, subtract, and multiply with like denominators

Think About It

How do you add and subtract fractions and mixed numbers with like denominators? What happens to the denominators? Karim walked $\frac{4}{10}$ mi from his house to the park. Then he walked $\frac{2}{10}$ mi from the park to the library. After that he walked $1\frac{3}{10}$ mi to the baseball field. How far did Karim walk? Use addition to find the answer to this problem, then check with subtraction.

$$1\frac{13}{10} + \frac{2}{10} + \frac{4}{10} \quad \frac{-9}{10}$$

Here's How

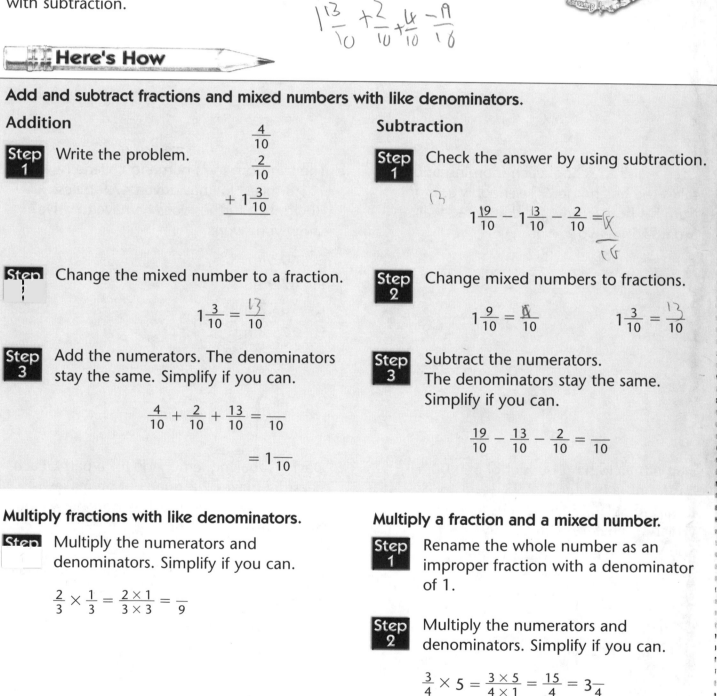

Add and subtract fractions and mixed numbers with like denominators.

Addition

Step 1 Write the problem.

$$\begin{array}{r} \frac{4}{10} \\ \frac{2}{10} \\ + 1\frac{3}{10} \\ \hline \end{array}$$

Step 2 Change the mixed number to a fraction.

$$1\frac{3}{10} = \frac{13}{10}$$

Step 3 Add the numerators. The denominators stay the same. Simplify if you can.

$$\frac{4}{10} + \frac{2}{10} + \frac{13}{10} = \frac{}{10}$$

$$= 1\frac{}{10}$$

Subtraction

Step 1 Check the answer by using subtraction.

$$1\frac{19}{10} - 1\frac{13}{10} - \frac{2}{10} = \frac{}{}$$

Step 2 Change mixed numbers to fractions.

$$1\frac{9}{10} = \frac{}{10} \qquad 1\frac{3}{10} = \frac{13}{10}$$

Step 3 Subtract the numerators. The denominators stay the same. Simplify if you can.

$$\frac{19}{10} - \frac{13}{10} - \frac{2}{10} = \frac{}{10}$$

Multiply fractions with like denominators.

Step 1 Multiply the numerators and denominators. Simplify if you can.

$$\frac{2}{3} \times \frac{1}{3} = \frac{2 \times 1}{3 \times 3} = \frac{}{9}$$

Multiply a fraction and a mixed number.

Step 1 Rename the whole number as an improper fraction with a denominator of 1.

Step 2 Multiply the numerators and denominators. Simplify if you can.

$$\frac{3}{4} \times 5 = \frac{3 \times 5}{4 \times 1} = \frac{15}{4} = 3\frac{}{4}$$

Practice

1. Carol spent $\frac{3}{7}$ of her allowance on a gift for her brother and $\frac{2}{7}$ of her allowance for a snack. How much of her allowance did she spend? Show your work.

  A $\frac{5}{14}$

  B $\frac{6}{14}$

  C $\frac{5}{7}$

  D $\frac{1}{7}$

2. Tom rode his bike for $2\frac{2}{3}$ h on Monday and $3\frac{1}{3}$ h on Wednesday. How much longer did he ride on Wednesday? Show your work.

  E $1\frac{2}{3}$ h

  F $1\frac{1}{3}$ h

  G $\frac{1}{3}$ h

  H $\frac{2}{3}$ h

3. Kim lives $\frac{5}{8}$ m from her school. Mark lives 5 times that distance from school. How far does Mark live from school? Show your work.

  A   3 m

  B $2\frac{1}{8}$ m

  C $3\frac{1}{8}$ m

  D $2\frac{7}{8}$ m

4. James bought three pieces of rope that measured $6\frac{1}{8}$ ft, $7\frac{7}{8}$ ft, and $8\frac{3}{8}$ ft. How many feet of rope did he buy in total? Show your work.

  E $22\frac{3}{8}$

  F $23\frac{3}{8}$

  G $21\frac{3}{8}$

  H $21\frac{7}{8}$

5. In Mary's garden, $\frac{4}{5}$ is planted with different kinds of peppers. Of the part planted with peppers, $\frac{2}{5}$ is planted with red peppers. What part is planted with red peppers? Show your work.

  A $\frac{10}{20}$

  B $\frac{8}{25}$

  C $\frac{1}{2}$

  D $\frac{2}{5}$

Part 2 ✦ Add, subtract, and multiply with unlike denominators

Ready Reference

least common denominator (LCD) the least common multiple of the denominators of two or more fractions; *example*: the LCD of 4 and 3 is 12

✏️ Think About It

How do you add, subtract, and multiply fractions and mixed numbers with unlike denominators? What happens to the denominators? When do the denominators change? When do they stay the same?

✏️ Here's How

Addition

1. Find the LCD of 4 and 3.
2. Write the equivalent fractions, using the LCD, 12.
3. Add. Then simplify if you can.

$$1\frac{3}{4} = 1\frac{3 \times 3}{4 \times 3} = 1\frac{9}{12}$$

$$+ 3\frac{2}{3} = 3\frac{2 \times 4}{3 \times 4} = 3\frac{8}{12}$$

$$4\frac{17}{12} = 5\frac{5}{12}$$

Subtraction

1. Find the LCD of 4 and 3.
2. Write the equivalent fractions, using the LCD, 12.
3. Subtract. Then simplify if you can.

$$4\frac{3}{4} = 4\frac{3 \times 3}{4 \times 3} = 4\frac{9}{12}$$

$$- 2\frac{2}{3} = 2\frac{2 \times 4}{3 \times 4} = 2\frac{8}{12}$$

$$2\frac{1}{12}$$

Multiply fractions.

Find $\frac{1}{3}$ of $\frac{3}{4}$.

1. Multiply the numerators and the denominators.
2. Write the product in simplest form, if possible.

$$\frac{3}{4} \times \frac{1}{3} = \frac{3 \times 1}{4 \times 3}$$

$$= \frac{3}{12} = \frac{1}{4}$$

Multiply mixed numbers.

Find $1\frac{2}{3}$ of $2\frac{1}{4}$.

1. Rename the mixed numbers as fractions.
2. Multiply the numerators and denominators.
3. Write the product in simplest form.

$$1\frac{2}{3} \times 2\frac{1}{4} = \frac{5}{3} \times \frac{9}{4}$$

$$= \frac{5 \times 9}{3 \times 4}$$

$$= \frac{45}{12}$$

$$= 3\frac{9}{12}$$

$$= 3\frac{3}{4}$$

Multiply a fraction and a mixed number.

Find $\frac{2}{3}$ of $10\frac{1}{2}$.

1. Rename the mixed numbers as fractions.
2. Multiply the numerators and denominators.
3. Write the product in simplest form.

$$\frac{2}{3} \times 10\frac{1}{2} = \frac{2}{3} \times \frac{21}{2}$$

$$= \frac{2 \times 21}{3 \times 2}$$

$$= \frac{42}{6}$$

$$= \underline{\qquad}$$

Practice

1. A bag of peaches weighs $1\frac{1}{4}$ lb. A second bag weighs $2\frac{2}{3}$ lb. How much do the bags weigh together? Show your work.

A   3 lb

B $3\frac{11}{12}$ lb

C $\frac{11}{12}$ lb

D $3\frac{3}{4}$ lb

2. Katherine has a rope that is $6\frac{1}{2}$ ft long. She wants to cut off $4\frac{1}{3}$ ft. How much rope will she have left? Show your work.

E $1\frac{1}{6}$ ft

F   2 ft

G $2\frac{1}{12}$ ft

H $2\frac{1}{6}$ ft

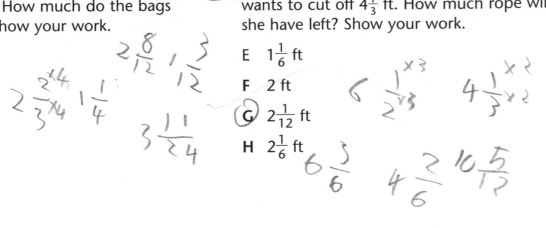

3. Mr. Green has $3\frac{3}{4}$ lb of potatoes. If he sells $\frac{2}{3}$ of them, how many pounds are left? Show your work.

A $2\frac{1}{2}$ lb

B $1\frac{1}{2}$ lb

C $3\frac{1}{2}$ lb

D $3\frac{3}{4}$ lb

4. Sam carried $2\frac{1}{2}$ lb of books. Samantha carried 4 times as many pounds. How many pounds did she carry? Show your work.

E   9 lb

F $9\frac{1}{2}$ lb

G   10 lb

H $10\frac{1}{2}$ lb

5. There were $9\frac{1}{2}$ lb of oatmeal cookies at the bake sale. Anna bought $\frac{1}{4}$ of the oatmeal cookies. How many pounds did Anna buy? Show your work.

A $2\frac{1}{8}$ lb

B $2\frac{3}{8}$ lb

C $3\frac{3}{8}$ lb

D $1\frac{3}{8}$ lb

6. Mr. Shepherd has $5\frac{3}{4}$ lb of grass seed. He needs to put $\frac{4}{5}$ of the seed in the backyard. How much seed does he need for the backyard? Show your work.

E   4 lb

F $4\frac{4}{5}$ lb

G $4\frac{2}{5}$ lb

H $4\frac{3}{5}$ lb

Ready Reference

round write a number as the nearest ten, hundred, thousand, and so on

Think About It

Every year, the fifth-grade class holds a school fair with food booths, games, and rides. Last year the fair cost $2,730. To the nearest hundred dollars, how much will this year's fair cost? You need to round $2,730 to find out.

Here's How

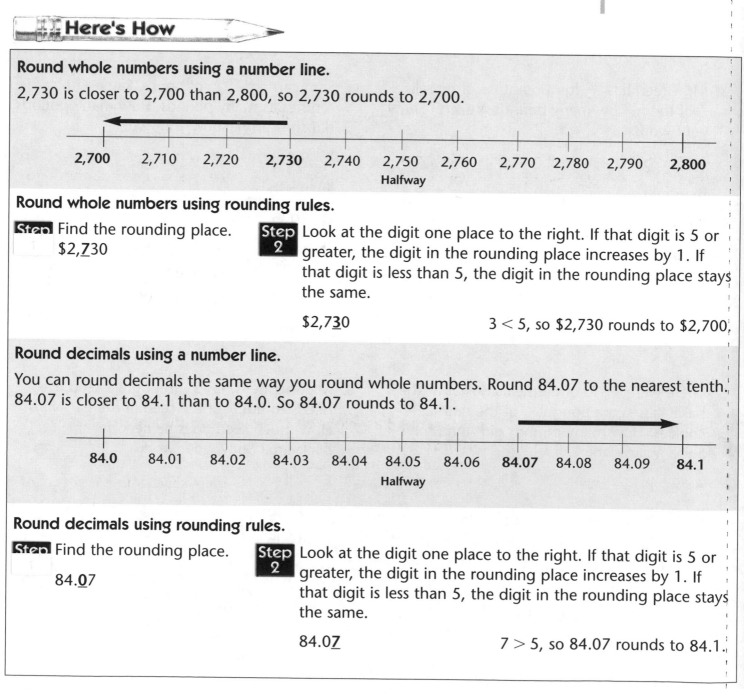

Round whole numbers using a number line.

2,730 is closer to 2,700 than 2,800, so 2,730 rounds to 2,700.

| 2,700 | 2,710 | 2,720 | 2,730 | 2,740 | 2,750 | 2,760 | 2,770 | 2,780 | 2,790 | 2,800 |

Halfway

Round whole numbers using rounding rules.

Step 1 Find the rounding place.
$2,7̲30

Step 2 Look at the digit one place to the right. If that digit is 5 or greater, the digit in the rounding place increases by 1. If that digit is less than 5, the digit in the rounding place stays the same.

$2,73̲0   3 < 5, so $2,730 rounds to $2,700.

Round decimals using a number line.

You can round decimals the same way you round whole numbers. Round 84.07 to the nearest tenth. 84.07 is closer to 84.1 than to 84.0. So 84.07 rounds to 84.1.

| 84.0 | 84.01 | 84.02 | 84.03 | 84.04 | 84.05 | 84.06 | 84.07 | 84.08 | 84.09 | 84.1 |

Halfway

Round decimals using rounding rules.

Step 1 Find the rounding place.
84.0̲7

Step 2 Look at the digit one place to the right. If that digit is 5 or greater, the digit in the rounding place increases by 1. If that digit is less than 5, the digit in the rounding place stays the same.

84.07̲   7 > 5, so 84.07 rounds to 84.1.

Practice

1. Mr. Murray sold 720 computer programs last year. How many did he sell, rounded to the nearest hundred?

A 7,000
B 700
C .7
D 7

2. On the first night of the play, 396 people attended. How many people attended the play, rounded to the nearest ten?

E 400
F 390
G 380
H 40

3. The 4th of July parade was viewed by 2,708 people. Which shows how many people watched the parade, rounded to the nearest ten?

A 27,080
B 2,710
C 2,800
D 2,709

4. Of the 15,000 people who attended the Stars baseball game, 13,438 paid full price. How many people paid full price, rounded to the nearest hundred?

E 13,500
F 14,000
G 13,400
H 14,400

5. The town collected 341,995 pounds of garbage. How many pounds were collected, rounded to the nearest thousand?

A 341,000 lb
B 341,990 lb
C 342,000 lb
D 342,900 lb

6. On Saturday, 2,967,125 people watched the awards show on television. How many people watched, rounded to the nearest million?

E 2,000,000
F 2,900,000
G 3,900,000
H 3,000,000

7. A muffin costs $0.74. How much is that rounded to the nearest tenth?

A $0.70
B $0.80
C $0.75
D $0.85

8. Milo found a weight of 0.667 g in his science experiment. How much is that rounded to the nearest hundredth?

E 1.06 g
F 0.7 g
G 1.66 g
H 0.67 g

9. Each student has exactly 44.279 g of salt for the science experiment. How much salt does each student have, rounded to the nearest tenth?

A 44.3 g
B 44.2 g
C 44.37 g
D 44.38 g

Ready Reference

estimate an approximate answer that is close to exact

Think About It

How can you tell if an answer is reasonable? You can estimate. The estimate gives you a general idea of what the answer should be. A reasonable estimate is close to the exact answer. Use rounding rules when you estimate: If the digit is less than 5, round down. If the digit is 5 or more, round up.

Here's How

Addition

Rae added 178, 504, and 893. He said the sum is 1,575. Is his answer reasonable?

1. Round each number to the nearest hundred.

   178 rounds to 200

   504 rounds to _____

   893 rounds to _____

2. Find the sum of the rounded numbers.

   200 + 500 + 900 = _____

3. Compare the estimate with Rae's answer. Since 1,600 is close to 1,575, Rae's answer is reasonable.

Subtraction

Clark had 718 trading cards. He gave 224 cards to his brother. Clark said he now has 694 cards. Is his statement reasonable?

1. Round each number to the nearest hundred.

   718 rounds to 700

   224 rounds to _____

2. Find the difference of the rounded numbers.

   700 − 200 = _____

3. Compare the estimate with Clark's answer. Since 500 is much less than 694, Clark's statement is NOT reasonable.

Multiplication

Lea multiplied 319 and 28. She said the product is 6,132. Is Lea's answer reasonable?

1. Round each number to the greatest place.

   319 rounds to 300

   28 rounds to _____

2. Find the product of the rounded numbers.

   300 × 30 = _____

3. Compare the estimate with Lea's answer. Since 9,000 is so much greater than 6,132, Lea's answer is NOT reasonable.

Division

The Cookie Company plans to bake 4,380 cookies tomorrow. The cookies will be put into boxes of 12. The manager said she needs 365 boxes to package these cookies. Is her statement reasonable?

1. Round each number to the greatest place.

   4,380 rounds to 4,000

   12 rounds to _____

2. Find the quotient of the rounded numbers.

   4,000 ÷ 10 = _____

3. Compare the estimate to the manager's answer. Since 400 is close to 365, the manager's statement is reasonable.

Practice

1. A zipper factory makes 2,195 zippers every day. The manager says that the factory will make 39,510 zippers in the next 18 days. Which answer shows why the manager's statement is reasonable? Show your work.

A $3,000 \times 20 = 60,000$

B $40,000 - 2,000 = 38,000$

C $2,000 \times 20 = 40,000$

D $2,000 + 40,000 = 42,000$

2. Enrique's family drove to the mountains for their vacation. They drove 329 miles on the first day, 498 miles on the second day, and 218 miles on the third day. Enrique said they had driven 745 miles after three days. Which answer shows why Enrique's statement is NOT reasonable? Show your work.

E $300 + 500 + 200 = 1,000$

F $300 + 400 + 100 = 800$

G $300 \times 3 = 900$

H $400 + 500 + 300 = 1,200$

3. Oakdale School collected 1,776 cans. The cans are placed in boxes of 48. Rhea said that 80 boxes are needed to package all the cans. Which answer shows why her statement is NOT reasonable? Show your work.

A $1,600 \div 20 = 80$

B $1,000 \div 50 = 20$

C $2,000 \div 50 = 40$

D $50 \times 1,000 = 50,000$

4. Jed wants to buy a car that costs $12,135. He has saved $5,809. Jed said he still needs $6,326. Which answer shows why his statement is reasonable? Show your work.

E $12,000 + 6,000 = 18,000$

F $12,000 - 6,000 = 6,000$

G $12,000 \times 2 = 24,000$

H $10,000 + 5,000 = 15,000$

5. A soccer club needs to raise $1,180 for new uniforms. There are 287 players in the club. To raise the money, the players are selling key rings. Each key ring costs $1. Al said that each player must sell 4 key rings to raise the money. Which answer shows why Al's statement is reasonable? Show your work.

A The product of 300 and $4 is $1,200.

B The difference of $1,200 and 30 is $1,170.

C The product of 300 and $1 is $300.

D The sum of $1,200 and 300 is $1,500.

Ready Reference

fraction a number that names part of a whole

✏ Think About It

A fraction is a number that names part of a whole. You can use a fraction calculator to add, subtract, multiply, or divide. You use special keys to enter fractions. The `\` key makes fractions. Use the `Unit` key to show a mixed number. Use `Simp` to simplify a fraction. If your answer is an improper fraction such as $\frac{13}{12}$, press `A b\c` to change your answer to a mixed number.

For example, to enter $1\frac{3}{4}$, press `1` `Unit` `3` `\` `4`   (1 u 3\4)

✏ Here's How

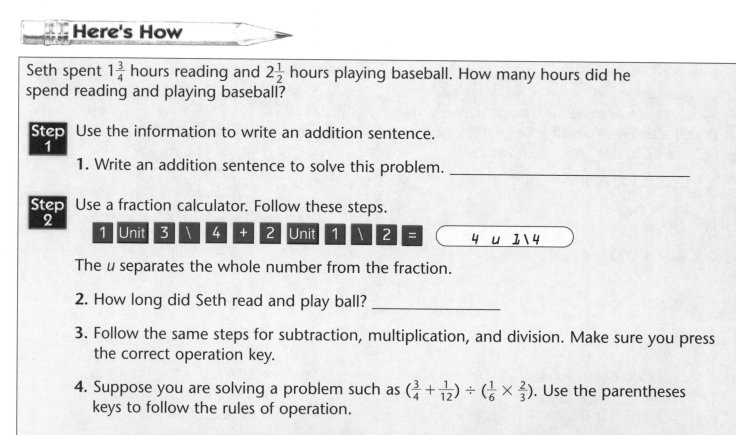

Seth spent $1\frac{3}{4}$ hours reading and $2\frac{1}{2}$ hours playing baseball. How many hours did he spend reading and playing baseball?

Step 1 Use the information to write an addition sentence.

   1. Write an addition sentence to solve this problem. _____

Step 2 Use a fraction calculator. Follow these steps.

   `1` `Unit` `3` `\` `4` `+` `2` `Unit` `1` `\` `2` `=`   (4 u 1\4)

   The *u* separates the whole number from the fraction.

   2. How long did Seth read and play ball? _____

   3. Follow the same steps for subtraction, multiplication, and division. Make sure you press the correct operation key.

   4. Suppose you are solving a problem such as $(\frac{3}{4}+\frac{1}{12}) \div (\frac{1}{6} \times \frac{2}{3})$. Use the parentheses keys to follow the rules of operation.

   Press `(` `3` `\` `4` `+` `1` `\` `12` `)` first, then continue with the rest of the problem. Remember to do all work within the parentheses first.

Practice

Use a fraction calculator to solve these problems.

1. Rico has a 21-inch piece of cloth. He cut it into $\frac{7}{8}$ inch strips. How many strips does Rico have?

   A $21\frac{7}{8}$

   B 24

   C $20\frac{1}{8}$

   D $18\frac{3}{8}$

2. The choir practiced for $1\frac{3}{4}$ hours on Monday and $2\frac{1}{3}$ hours on Friday. How long did the choir practice in all?

   E $4\frac{1}{2}$ h

   F $\frac{7}{12}$ h

   G $1\frac{1}{3}$ h

   H $4\frac{1}{12}$ h

3. Don bought 8 lb of apples. He used $5\frac{2}{3}$ lb to make pies. How many pounds of apples are left?

   A $45\frac{1}{3}$ lb

   B $1\frac{7}{17}$ lb

   C $13\frac{2}{3}$ lb

   D $2\frac{1}{3}$ lb

4. Jim has 117 sports cards. He gave $\frac{1}{3}$ of his cards to Al. How many cards did Al receive?

   E 351

   F $116\frac{2}{3}$

   G 39

   H $117\frac{1}{3}$

5. Of the 78 books in a bookcase, $\frac{1}{6}$ are biographies. How many books are NOT biographies?

   A 13

   B $78\frac{1}{6}$

   C 65

   D $93\frac{3}{5}$

6. Bill has a 6-inch piece of wire that he cut into $\frac{3}{4}$ inch strips. How many $\frac{3}{4}$ inch strips does Bill have?

   E $6\frac{3}{4}$

   F 8

   G $5\frac{1}{4}$

   H $4\frac{1}{2}$

7. Dee has $5\frac{1}{2}$ c of flour. She used $2\frac{2}{3}$ c to make muffins. How much flour is left?

   A $8\frac{1}{6}$ c

   B $14\frac{2}{3}$ c

   C $2\frac{1}{16}$ c

   D $2\frac{5}{6}$ c

8. In order to solve $\frac{1}{4} \times \frac{3}{8} + (\frac{7}{8} - \frac{1}{2}) + \frac{2}{7}$, which do you calculate first?

   E $\frac{3}{8} + \frac{7}{8}$

   F $\frac{1}{4} \times \frac{3}{8}$

   G $\frac{7}{8} - \frac{1}{2}$

   H $\frac{1}{2} + \frac{2}{7}$

Ready Reference

estimate an approximate answer that is close to exact

Think About It

Sometimes you need to estimate an answer to a time or money problem. An estimate is an answer that is close to the exact answer. The words *about, almost, more than, less than,* and *nearly* show that you should find an estimate.

Here's How

Time

Ruth practiced the piano for 25 minutes on Monday and on Wednesday. She practiced for 50 minutes on Saturday and 1 hour 10 minutes on Sunday. Altogether, about how long did Ruth practice the piano?

1. What word shows that an estimate is needed?

   _____

2. Round each time to the nearest half-hour.

   25 minutes rounds to $\frac{1}{2}$ hour

   50 minutes rounds to _____

   1 hour 10 minutes rounds to _____

3. Find the sum of the rounded times.

   $\frac{1}{2} + \frac{1}{2} + 1 + 1 =$ _____

4. Ruth practiced about 3 hours.

Subtraction

Jake spent $17.35 on groceries. He paid $12.75 for gas. Lunch at The Burger Hut cost $4.95. Was the total amount of money Jake spent more than $40 or less than $40?

1. What words show that an estimate is needed?

   _____

2. Round each amount of money to the nearest dollar.

   $17.35 rounds to $17

   $12.75 rounds to _____

   $4.95 rounds to _____

3. Find the sum of the rounded numbers.

   $17 + 13 + 5 =$ _____

4. Compare the estimate with $40.

   Did Jake spend more or less than $40? _____

Practice

1. Melanie babysat for 3 h 15 min on Saturday and 5 h 45 min on Sunday. About how long did Melanie babysit during the weekend? Which answer shows how Melanie can find the estimate? Show your work.

   A The sum of 3 h and 5 h is 8 h.

   B The sum of 3 h and 6 h is 9 h.

   C The sum of 4 h and 5 h is 9 h.

   D The sum of 4 h and 6 h is 10 h.

2. Alice wants to buy a book for $5.95, a backpack for $19.35, and a sweatshirt for $22.95. She has $50 to spend. Which answer shows how Alice can determine if the items will cost more than $50 or less than $50? Show your work.

   E $5 + $19 + $22 = $46, and $46 < $50

   F $6 + $19 + $22 = $47, and $47 < $50

   G $6 + $19 + $23 = $48, and $48 < $50

   H $6 + $20 + $30 = $56, and $56 > $50

3. Adam worked for 4 h 10 min on Monday, 6 h 50 min on Wednesday, and 5 h 45 min on Friday. Which answer shows how Adam can determine about how many hours he worked altogether? Show your work.

   A The sum of 4, 7, and 6 is 17.

   B The sum of 4, 6, and 5 is 15.

   C The sum of 5, 7, and 6 is 18.

   D The sum of 5, 7, and 7 is 19.

4. Max saved $13.85 last week. He saved $26.15 this week. Next week, Max expects to save $18.25. Which answer shows how Max can estimate if his savings are more than $55 or less than $55? Show your work.

   E $13 + $26 + $18 = $57, and $57 > $55

   F $14 + $27 + $19 = $60, and $60 > $55

   G $14 + $26 + $19 = $59, and $59 > $55

   H $14 + $26 + $18 = $58, and $58 > $55

5. Three days a week, Mike spends $3.85 on lunch. On the other two days, he spends $5.25 for lunch. Which answer shows how Mike can estimate the total amount of money he spends each week for lunch? Show your work.

   A The product of $4 and $5 is $20.

   B The product of $4 and $3 is $12. The product of $5 and $2 is $10. The sum of $12 and $10 is $22.

   C The product of $5 and $5 is $25.

   D The product of $3 and $3 is $9. The product of $5 and $2 is $10. The sum of $9 and $10 is $19.

Ready Reference

regroup use 1 ten to form 10 ones, 1 hundred to form 10 tens, and so on

Think About It

Sometimes you need to multiply to find an answer. Other times you need to divide. How do you set up a multiplication or a division expression?

Here's How

Multiplication

Don rides a bus to school 181 days a year. He spends 32 minutes on the bus each day. How many minutes does Don spend on the school bus each year?

Step 1 Multiply by the ones and write your answer. Regroup if necessary.

$$\begin{array}{r} 181 \\ \times\ 32 \\ \hline \end{array}$$

   1. Did you have to regroup? _____

Step 2 Place a 0 in the ones place. Multiply by the tens and write your answer.   _____ **0**

   2. Did you have to regroup? _____

Step 3 Add the products.

   3. What is the sum? _____

Division

The fifth–grade class is planning a talent show for the school. The show will last a total of 190 minutes. Twenty-one students will perform in the show. How much time will each student have to perform? Divide 190 minutes by 21 students.

Step 1 There are not enough hundreds to divide into 21 groups. There are not enough tens to divide into 21 groups. Regroup 1 hundred 9 tens 0 ones as 190.

Step 2 Divide the ones. Multiply and subtract.

   1. How many groups of 21 are in 190? _____

   2. How many are left over? _____
     Write the remainder (R) next to the quotient.

   3. What is the quotient? _____

$$\begin{array}{r} 9\ \text{R1} \\ 21\overline{)190} \\ -189 \rightarrow 9 \times 21 \\ \hline 1 \rightarrow \text{remainder} \end{array}$$

Step 3 Compare the remainder and the divisor.

   4. Which is larger? _____

   5. How much time will each student have to perform? _____

   6. How much time will be left over? _____

Practice

1. A total of 325 tickets have been sold to the fifth–grade talent show. The auditorium can seat 65 people. Which answer shows how to determine how many performances must be held?

   A $365 \times 5 =$

   B $365 \div 25 =$

   C $325 \times 65 =$

   D $325 \div 65 =$

2. The Sit Down Chair Factory makes 88 chairs each day. Which answer shows how to determine the number of chairs the factory will make in 225 days?

   E $225 \times 88 =$

   F $225 \div 88 =$

   G $288 \div 25 =$

   H $255 \times 80 =$

3. Every day Shanna delivers 117 newspapers. Which shows how many newspapers she delivers in 55 days? Show your work.

   A 6,405

   B 6,435

   C 6,105

   D 6,135

4. The Sweet Shop made 756 muffins. The muffins are put into boxes of 12. Which shows how many boxes are needed to package the muffins? Show your work.

   E 6

   F 63

   G 630

   H 60

5. The Break a Leg drama class decided that each member has to sell the same number of tickets. There are 536 tickets and 67 members. Which answer shows how to determine how many tickets each member must sell? Show your work.

   A $536 \times 67 =$

   B $576 \times 30 =$

   C $536 \div 67 =$

   D $67 \div 536 =$

Think About It

Many problems can be solved in more than one way. How do you decide which process to use? You use the process that makes the most sense to you.

Here's How

There are 5 fifth-grade classes in Oakville School and 29 students in each class. How many fifth-grade students are in Oakville School?

Addition

 Step 1 Find the important information.

1. How many classes are there?

   _____

2. How many are in each class?

   _____

Step 2 Write an addition sentence.

3. What addition sentence can you use to solve this problem?

   _____

4. What is the sum? _____

Multiplication

Step 1 Find the important information.

1. How many classes are there? _____

2. How many are in each class? _____

Step 2 Write a multiplication sentence.

3. What factors will you use?

   _____

4. What multiplication sentence can you use to solve this problem?

   _____

5. What is the product? _____

Four classes sold 160 tickets in all to the school play. Grades 1 and 2 sold 40 tickets each. Grade 3 sold 20 tickets. How many tickets did Grade 4 sell?

Subtraction and addition

Step 1 Find the important information.

1. How many tickets were sold in all?

   _____

2. How many tickets did Grade 1 sell?

   _____

3. How many tickets did Grade 2 sell?

   _____

4. How many tickets did Grade 3 sell?

   _____

Step 2 Write subtraction sentences.

5. What is the first subtraction sentence you will use? _____
   Solve it. _____

6. What subtraction sentence will you use next? _____
   Solve it. _____

7. What is the last subtraction sentence you will use? _____
   Solve it. _____

Step 3 Add to find the total number of tickets sold by Grades 1, 2, and 3.

1. What number sentence will you use?

   _____

2. What is the sum? _____

Step 4 Subtract this sum from the total number of tickets sold.

3. What number sentence will you use?

   _____

4. What is the difference? _____

Practice

1. A garden club is going to a flower show. The club members will ride in 14 buses. Each bus holds 38 riders. What number sentence can be used to find the total number of club members going on the trip?

   A $14 \times 38 =$

   B $38 \div 14 =$

   C $14 + 38 =$

   D $38 - 14 =$

2. Rico read 16 pages of a book each day for one week. What number sentence can be used to find the total number of pages Rico read?

   E $16 + 16 + 16 + 16 + 16 + 16 + 16 =$

   F $7 \times 16 =$

   G $16 + 7 =$

   H Both E and F

3. Annie has 2,695 pennies in a jar. She wants to surprise her little sister by giving her 958 pennies. What number sentence can be used to find how many pennies Annie will have left?

   A $2,695 \div 958 =$

   B $2,695 - 958 =$

   C $2,695 \times 958 =$

   D $2,695 + 958 =$

4. Roddy has a total of 875 football and soccer cards. Of these, 542 cards are football cards. What number sentence can be used to find the number of soccer cards Roddy has?

   E $875 \div 542 =$

   F $875 + 542 =$

   G $875 - 542 =$

   H $875 \times 542 =$

5. Carlos collects toy cars and toy trucks. He has 158 toy cars and 74 toy trucks. Jon also collects toy cars and trucks. He has twice as many cars and trucks as Carlos. What number sentence can be used to find the number of cars and trucks Jon has?

   A $158 \times 2 =$

   B $158 + 74 + 2 =$

   C $(2 \times 74) + 158 =$

   D $2 \times (158 + 74) =$

1. Yesterday morning, Crissie counted 14 sailboats and 18 ski boats that sailed into the cove. Yesterday afternoon, she counted three times as many sailboats, but only half as many ski boats. How many sailboats and ski boats did Crissie count altogether yesterday afternoon?

- **READ** the problem and break it into parts to solve it.
- **SHOW** each step of your math work.
- **EXPLAIN** why you solved the problem as you did.
- **WRITE** an explanation describing what you did and why you solved the problem as you did, **EVEN** if you used mental math or a calculator.
- **WRITE** your answer in the space provided.

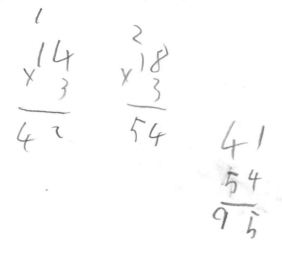

Explanation

first it said **3** times so I x 14 and 18 by 3 and it = 41 and 54 an you got to t 41 and 54 = 95

| Total number of sailboats and ski boats   95 |

| 0–5 Points |
| Score _____ |

2. At a football game, 3,429 fans showed up to cheer for the home team. An additional 2,945 fans showed up to cheer for the visitors. How many fans were in the stadium?

- **USE** front-end estimation to find a high and a low estimate. **THEN** solve the problem.
- **WRITE** your answers in the spaces provided.
- **COMPARE** your estimate to the answer and **EXPLAIN** why your estimate is reasonable.
- **SHOW** each step of your math work.
- **WRITE** an explanation describing what you did and why you solved the problem as you did, **EVEN** if you used mental math or a calculator.

$$\begin{array}{r} 3,429 \\ 2,945 \\ \hline 6,374 \end{array}$$

Explanation

I took the home and visitors and add them to gether to get 6,374

High and low estimate __6000__

Actual number of fans __6,374__

Is your estimate reasonable?
__yes__

0–5 Points

Score ____

3. Ramon's older brother has a part-time job. He earns $85.75 a week. Ramon earns $12.25 a week. If they each combine and save all their money for a year, about how much money will they have?

- **USE** estimation to solve the problem.
- **SHOW** each step of your math work.
- **WRITE** an explanation describing what you did and why you solved the problem as you did, **EVEN** if you used mental math or a calculator.
- **WRITE** your answer in the space provided.

Explanation

Answer _____

0–5 Points
Score _____

4. Ed walks $1\frac{1}{4}$ miles to school each day. Doris walks $\frac{3}{12}$ mile to school each day. What is the total distance that Ed and Doris walk to get to school each day? How far do they walk in one week?

- **READ** the problem and break it into parts to solve it. **EXPRESS** your solution in simplest terms.
- **SHOW** each step of your math work.
- **EXPLAIN** why you solved the problem as you did.
- **WRITE** an explanation describing what you did and why you solved the problem as you did, **EVEN** if you used mental math or a calculator.
- **WRITE** your answers in the spaces provided.

Explanation

| Distance per day _____ |
| Distance per week _____ |

| 0–5 Points |
| Score _____ |

1. Jon scored 1,327 points in a video game. Sue scored 455 less points than Jon. How many points did Sue score?

   A 1,782

   B 872

   C 2,654

   D 972

2. Bud has 562 sports cards. Jill has half as many cards as Bud. How many cards does Jill have?

   E 1,124

   F 564

   G 2,018

   H 281

3. Bill puts $35.75 in the bank each month. How much money has Bill saved at the end of one year?

   A $357.50

   B $71.50

   C $429.00

   D $399.00

4. The trip from Jed's home to his sister's house is 120.8 miles. Jed has driven 34.9 mi. How much farther does he have to drive?

   E 85.9 mi

   F 155.7 mi

   G 164 mi

   H 86 mi

5. Tia rode her bike for $1\frac{3}{4}$ h on Saturday and $2\frac{1}{4}$ h on Sunday. How long did Tia ride on Saturday and Sunday?

   A $\frac{1}{2}$ h

   B 4 h

   C $3\frac{1}{4}$ h

   D $3\frac{3}{4}$ h

6. Each bag holds $2\frac{1}{2}$ pounds of sugar. How much sugar is in 6 bags?

   E 12 lb

   F 3 lb

   G 10 lb

   H 15 lb

7. Which shows 17,804 rounded to the nearest thousand?

   A 20,000

   B 17,000

   C 18,000

   D 10,000

8. Which shows 982 rounded to the nearest hundred?

   E 900

   F 980

   G 990

   H 1,000

9. What is a reasonable estimate for 705 + 986?

   A 1,600

   B 300

   C 1,800

   D 1,700

10. What is a reasonable estimate for 49 × 22?

　E　1,000

　F　70

　G　800

　H　1,500

11. Rose has a 6–inch piece of cloth. She cut it into $\frac{3}{4}$–inch strips. How many strips does Rose have?

　A　18

　B　63

　C　8

　D　12

12. Carol has 65 stickers. She gave $\frac{2}{5}$ of the stickers to Amy. How many stickers did she give Amy?

　E　26

　F　13

　G　39

　H　60

13. Adam worked for $5\frac{1}{4}$ hours on Monday, $2\frac{3}{4}$ hours on Wednesday, and 3 hours on Friday. About how many hours did Adam work altogether?

　A　8

　B　10

　C　11

　D　14

14. Kim spent $6.85 for dinner, $4.15 for a cab ride, and $3.95 on a movie rental. About how much did Kim spend?

　E　$7

　F　$10

　G　$13

　H　$15

15. The Donut Shop bakes 528 donuts each day. How many donuts does the shop make in one week?

　A　3,966

　B　3,696

　C　3,669

　D　6,399

16. A total of 378 tickets have been sold for a bus trip to an amusement park. Each bus seats 45 people. Which number sentence shows how many buses are needed?

　E　378 × 45 =

　F　378 + 45 =

　G　378 ÷ 45 =

　H　378 − 45 =

17. Use a fraction calculator. Marty picked $6\frac{2}{3}$ lb of apples from the orchard. Kim picked twice as much. How many pounds did Kim pick?

　A　$8\frac{1}{3}$ lb

　B　$12\frac{1}{3}$ lb

　C　$3\frac{1}{3}$ lb

　D　$13\frac{1}{3}$ lb

18. Sue makes 17 bracelets each day. Doris makes 23 bracelets each day. How many bracelets can they make in two weeks?

　E　280

　F　391

　G　425

　H　560

Ready Reference

area the number of square units needed to cover a region; $A = l \times w$
perimeter the distance around a closed figure; $P = l + l + w + w$, or $P = 2l + 2w$
volume the amount of space inside a three-dimensional figure; $V = l \times w \times h$

Think About It

Do you measure your height the same way you measure your weight? What measurement tools and units can be used to measure perimeter, volume, weight, time, and temperature?

Here's How

Perimeter

9 ft

2 ft

1. Select a tool and unit. What tools and units can you use to measure the figure?

_____

2. Find the distance around the figure.

$$P = (2 \times 2) + (2 \times 9)$$
$$= \text{_____} + \text{_____}$$
$$= \text{_____ ft}$$

Temperature

The temperature at 6 A.M. was 31°C. Two hours later it was 8° cooler. One hour later the temperature had dropped 4 degrees more. What was the temperature?

1. Select a tool and unit. What tools and units can you use for this problem?

_____

2. Solve. $31° - 8° - 4° =$ _____

Area

1. Find the number of square units needed to cover the figure above.

2. Solve. $A = 2 \text{ ft} \times$ _____ ft
            $=$ _____ square ft

Weight

1. What measurement unit could you use to find the difference in weight between a desk and a chair? _____

2. Solve this problem. If 1 desk weighs 21 lb, how much do 13 desks weigh?

   21 lb $\times$ 13 = _____ lb

Volume

1. Select a tool and unit. What tool and unit could you use to measure the small box?

_____

2. Solve. $V = 5 \times$ _____ $\times$ _____
            $=$ _____ cubic units

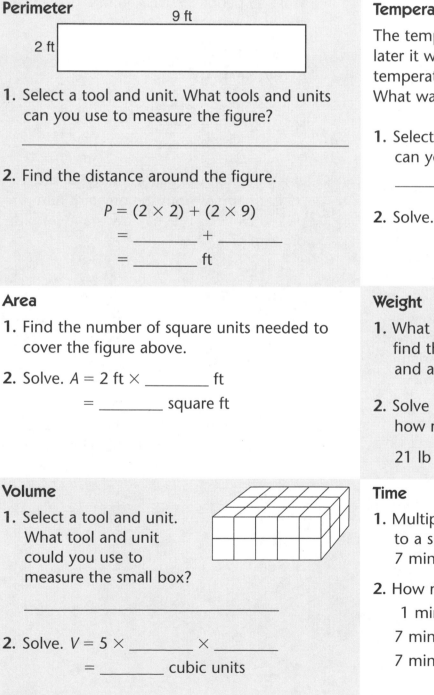

Time

1. Multiply to change from a larger unit of time to a smaller unit of time. Solve this problem.
   7 minutes = _____ seconds

2. How many seconds in a minute?
   1 minute = _____ seconds
   7 minutes = _____ $\times$ 60 seconds
   7 minutes = _____ seconds

Practice

1. Bud wants to put a fence along the outer edge of his garden. Which answer shows the best tool and unit of measure Bud should use to find the garden's perimeter?

A   Ruler, pounds, and ounces

B   Tape measure, feet, and inches

C   Scale, minutes, and seconds

D   Temperature, degrees

2. Ross has 5 oranges. Which answer shows the best tool and unit of measure Ross should use to find the weight of the oranges?

E   Scale, pounds, and ounces

F   Yardstick, yards, and feet

G   Thermometer, minutes, and seconds

H   Stopwatch, pounds, and ounces

3. Which shows the total area of a greeting card that measures 6 in. by 4 in.? Show your work.

A   10 sq in.

B   2 in.

C   24 in.

D   24 sq in.

$$\begin{array}{r} 6 \\ \times\ 4 \\ \hline 24 \end{array}$$

$$\begin{array}{r} 24 \\ 48 \\ \hline 72 \end{array}$$

4. Don wants to find the perimeter of the garden below. Which shows the perimeter? Show your work.

E   72 ft

F   288 ft

G   108 ft

H   60 ft

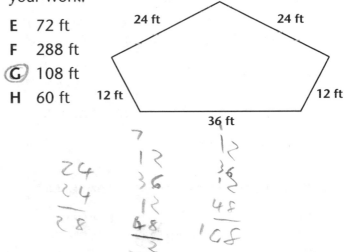

$$\begin{array}{r} 24 \\ 24 \\ \hline 28 \end{array}$$
$$\begin{array}{r} 12 \\ 36 \\ 12 \\ \hline 48 \end{array}$$
$$\begin{array}{r} 12 \\ 36 \\ 12 \\ 48 \\ \hline 108 \end{array}$$

5. There are 10 rows of unit cubes in each layer of a box. There are 10 cubes in each row. How many layers are there if there are 700 unit cubes in the box?

A   7

B   10

C   8

D   9

6. Caitlin went to the mall at 9:35 A.M. and left at 12:05 P.M. How much time did she spend at the mall? Show your work.

E $3\frac{1}{2}$ h

F $2\frac{1}{2}$ h

G   2 h 35 min

H   2 h 40 min

Ready Reference
area the number of square units needed to cover a region
perimeter the distance around a closed figure

Think About It

How do you find the perimeter and the area of this rectangle?

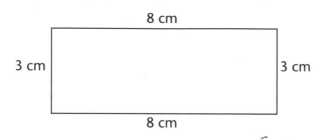

8 cm

3 cm   3 cm

8 cm

Here's How

Find the perimeter by adding.

1. The perimeter of a figure is the sum of its sides. Write an addition sentence using the measure of each side as an addend.

8 cm + 3 cm + 8 cm + 3 cm = _____

2. What is the perimeter of the rectangle?

_____ cm

Find the perimeter by using a formula.

1. Since a rectangle has two pairs of equal sides, you can multiply and then add to find the perimeter.

Use this formula: $P = (2 \times l) + (2 \times w)$

2. What are the measures of the length and the width? _____ and _____

$P = (2 \times l) + (2 \times w)$

$P = (8 \text{ cm} \times 2) + (3 \text{ cm} \times 2)$

$P =$ _____ cm + _____ cm

$P =$ _____ cm

3. What is the perimeter of the rectangle?

_____ cm

Find the area by using a formula.

1. The area of a rectangle is determined by multiplying the figure's length times its width. Area is expressed in square units. One square unit is a square that has the same length and width.

Use this formula: $A = l \times w$

2. What is the length of the rectangle?

_____ cm

What is the width of the rectangle?

_____ cm

$A = l \times w$

$A =$ _____ × _____

$A =$ _____ square cm (cm²)

3. What is the area of this rectangle?_____

Practice

1. Rod needs to find the area of the figure. Which answer shows how he can determine this measure?

6 in.

3 in. ☐ 3 in.

6 in.

A 3 in. + 6 in. =

B (3 in. × 2) + (6 in. × 2) =

C 3 in. × 6 in. = 18

D (2 × 9 in.) =

2. Tracy wants to find the perimeter of the figure. Which answer shows how she can determine this measure?

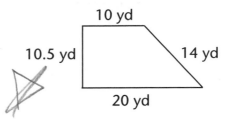

10 yd

10.5 yd   14 yd

20 yd

E 10.5 yd × 14 yd =

F 10.5 yd + 20 yd + 14 yd + 10 yd = 54.5

G 20 yd × 10 yd =

H (2 × 10 yd) + 20 yd =

3. Mica's room is 12 ft long and 9 ft wide. Which shows the perimeter of his room? Show your work.

A 42 ft

B 108 ft

C 21 ft

D 30 ft

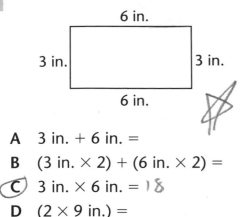

4. Rose made a square quilt with each side measuring 6 ft. Which shows the area of the quilt? Show your work.

E 24 sq ft

F 24 ft

G 12 sq ft

H 36 sq ft

5. Rod wants to put a fence around the edge of the garden shown. Which answer shows how he can determine the amount of fencing he needs? Show your work.

A (10 ft × 6) = 60

B (2 × 10 ft) + 20 ft =

C 10 ft × 10 ft =

D 10 ft + 10 ft + 10 ft + 10 ft =

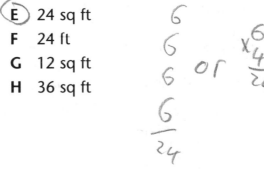

10 ft   10 ft

10 ft   10 ft

10 ft   10 ft

Think About It

When you estimate measurements, you name an amount that is close to the actual measurement. Do you know how to estimate a measurement?

Here's How

Length

1. Look at the pencil point. What numbers on the ruler is the point between?

_____

2. Which number is the point closest to?

_____

3. About how long is the pencil?

_____

4. What is the exact length? _____

Width

1. Look at the edge of the envelope.

2. What numbers on the ruler is the edge between? _____

3. Which number is the edge closest to?

_____

4. About how wide is the envelope?

_____

5. What is the exact width? _____

Temperature

1. Look at the thermometer. What numbers does the temperature lie between?

_____

2. Which temperature is the top closest to?

_____

3. Estimate the temperature. _____

Perimeter

1. Look at the bottom right edge of the square. What numbers on the ruler is the edge between? _____

2. Which number is the edge closest to?

_____

3. Estimate the perimeter of the square.

_____

Practice

1. Which answer shows an estimate of the temperature?

A 50°

B 40°

C 55°

D 60°

2. Which answer shows an estimate of the bracelet's length to the nearest inch?

E 5 in.

F $5\frac{1}{2}$ in.

G 6 in.

H $6\frac{1}{4}$ in.

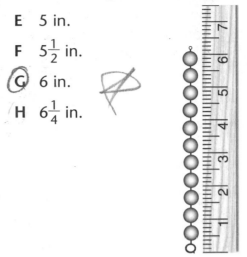

3. Which answer shows the exact width of the book?

A 4 in.

B $4\frac{1}{4}$ in.

C $4\frac{3}{4}$ in.

D 5 in.

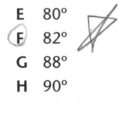

Mathematics Book

4. Which answer shows the exact temperature?

E 80°

F 82°

G 88°

H 90°

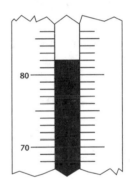

5. Which answer shows an estimate of the perimeter?

A 4 in.

B 8 in.

C 12 in.

D 16 in.

6. Which answer shows an estimate of the box's width?

E 7 in.

F $7\frac{3}{4}$ in.

G 8 in.

H $8\frac{1}{2}$ in.

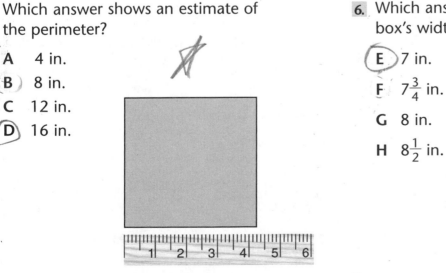

Think About It

When you convert measurements, you use a different unit to name an amount. Sometimes you want to change feet into yards or yards into feet. How do you convert a larger measurement to a smaller measurement? How do you convert a smaller measurement to a larger measurement? If you know the relationship between units of measurement, you can convert any measurement.

Here's How

To convert from a larger unit to a smaller unit, multiply.

Try this example. During a fundraiser, Ella walked 6 mi 40 ft. How many feet did she walk?

6 mi = ☐ ft   (Think 1 mi = 5,280 ft)

(6 × 5,280) + 40 = _____ + 40

6 mi 40 ft = _____ ft

How far did Ella walk? _____

To convert from a smaller unit to a larger unit, divide.

Try this example. The hardware store has 27 inches of chain. How many feet of chain is this?

27 in. = ☐ ft   (Think 12 in. = 1 ft)

27 ÷ 12 = 2 R3

27 in. = _____ ft _____in.

How many feet of chain are there? _____

Practice

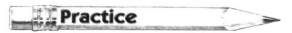

1. The distance between Town Hall and Celebration Lake is 8 mi 79 yd. Which answer shows the distance in yards? Show your work.

   A   5,280 yd
   B   14,080 yd
   C   14,159 yd
   D   632 yd

2. The Art Room is 5 yd 9 in. wide. Which answer shows this width in inches? Show your work.

   E   180 in.
   F   69 in.
   G   60 in.
   H   189 in.

3. Miguel ran 2 mi 63 ft. How many feet is that? Show your work.

A 99 ft

B 126 ft

C 3,583 ft

D 10,623 ft

4. Ryan threw a baseball 12 meters 57 cm. Which shows how many centimeters the ball traveled? Show your work.

E 12,570 cm

F 157 cm

G 1,200 cm

H 1,257 cm

5. Karen's house is 12,010 m from her grandparents' house. Which shows another way to write 12,010 m? Show your work.

A 10 km 10 m

B 12 km 10 m

C 1,000 km 10 m

D 1,000 km

6. Cam has 2 lengths of board. One board is 5 yd 2 ft long. The other is 7 yd 3 ft. How many total feet of board does he have? Show your work.

E 36 ft

F 40 ft

G 41 ft

H 17 ft

7. It is 5 mi 37 ft from Marta's house to the library. From the library to the mall, it is 2 mi 13 ft. How many feet is it from Marta's house to the library to the mall? Show your work.

A 37,010 ft

B 36,010 ft

C 36,960 ft

D 38,010 ft

8. Bill's closet is 3 ft 11 in. wide. How wide is that in inches? Show your work.

E 48 in.

F 96 in.

G 47 in.

H 36 in.

9. Richie's garden measured 9 m 4 cm. What is the length in centimeters? Show your work.

A 94 cm

B 940 cm

C 904 cm

D 9.4 cm

10. Franklin's house is 27 yd 2 ft 11 in. wide. How wide is his house in inches? Show your work.

E 972 in.

F 996 in.

G 980 in.

H 1,007 in.

Ready Reference

1 foot (ft) = 12 inches (in.)
1 yard (yd) = 36 inches
1 yard = 3 feet
1 mile (mi) = 5,280 feet or 1,760 yards

1 centimeter (cm) = 10 millimeters (mm)
1 decimeter (dm) = 10 centimeters
1 meter (m) = 100 centimeters
1 kilometer (km) = 1,000 meters

Think About It

Sometimes you need to add measurements. Other times, you need to subtract measurements. You can change units of measurements to larger or smaller units to add and subtract measurements.

Here's How

Add lengths.

The distance from the library to the music room is 15 yd 3 ft. From the music room to the art room is 12 yd 10 ft. How far did Carl walk from the library to the music room to the art room?

$$
\begin{array}{r}
15 \text{ yd } 3 \text{ ft} \\
+ \ 12 \text{ yd } 10 \text{ ft} \\
\hline
17 \text{ yd } \mathbf{13} \text{ ft} = 17 \text{ yd} + \mathbf{4} \text{ yd} + \mathbf{1} \text{ ft} = 21 \text{ yd } 1 \text{ ft}
\end{array}
$$

How far is it? _____

Subtract lengths.

Rick is 4 ft 2 in. tall. His brother is 3 ft 5 in. tall. How much taller is Rick than his brother?

$$
\begin{array}{r}
3 \text{ ft } 12 \text{ in.} \\
4 \text{ ft } 2 \text{ in.} \\
- \ 3 \text{ ft } 5 \text{ in.} \\
\hline
7 \text{ in.}
\end{array}
$$
Rename 4 ft 2 in. as 3 ft 12 in.

How much taller is Rick? _____

Add or subtract time.

$$
\begin{array}{r}
8 \text{ h } 45 \text{ min} \\
+ \ 6 \text{ h } 50 \text{ min} \\
\hline
14 \text{ h } 95 \text{ min} \\
= 14 \text{ h} + \mathbf{1} \text{ h} + 35 \text{ min} \\
= 15 \text{ h} \underline{\quad} \text{min}
\end{array}
$$

$$
\begin{array}{r}
11 \text{ h } 57 \text{ min} \\
- \ 3 \text{ h } 11 \text{ min} \\
\hline
\underline{\quad} \text{h } 46 \text{ min}
\end{array}
$$

Subtract or add weight.

$$
\begin{array}{r}
\overset{2\ 1}{2 \text{ L } 33} \text{ mL} \\
- \ 1 \text{ L } 17 \text{ mL} \\
\hline
1 \text{ L} \underline{\quad} \text{mL}
\end{array}
$$

$$
\begin{array}{r}
3 \text{ lb } 4 \text{ oz} \\
+ \ 65 \text{ oz} \\
\hline
3 \text{ lb } 69 \text{ oz} \\
= 3 \text{ lb} + \mathbf{4} \text{ lb} + 5 \text{ oz} \\
= \underline{\quad} \text{lb } 5 \text{ oz}
\end{array}
$$

Find elapsed time.

It took from 8:30 A.M. until 12:15 P.M. to drive to the hotel. How long did it take?

$$
\begin{array}{r}
11 \text{ h } \ \ 75 \text{ min} \\
\cancel{12} \text{ h } \cancel{15} \text{ min} \\
- \ 8 \text{ h } 30 \text{ min} \\
\hline
3 \text{ h } 45 \text{ min}
\end{array}
$$
Rename 12 h 15 min as 11 h 75 min.
Remember: 1 h = 60 min.

Practice

1. Tia had 4 yd 2 ft of fabric. She used 1 yd 2 ft for a craft project. Which shows how much fabric Tia has now? Show your work.

A   3 yd 2 ft

B   3 yd

C   2 yd 4 ft

D   6 yd 1 ft

2. A bus travels 8 mi 73 yd on its morning route. The bus follows the same route in the afternoon. Which answer shows the total distance the bus travels each day? Show your work.

E   16 mi 146 yd

F   64 mi 146 yd

G   16 mi

H   0 mi

3. Carol ran 5 km 12 m. Darlene ran 7 km 52 m. How much farther did Darlene run? Show your work.

A   12 km 64 m

B   2 km 30 m

C   2 km 40 m

D   12 km 40 m

4. Ty hit a golf ball 117 yd 1 ft 9 in. Jon hit a golf ball 89 yd 2 ft 6 in. Which shows the total distance hit? Show your work.

E   28 yd 3 in.

F   206 yd 3 ft 3 in.

G   207 yd 3 ft 15 in.

H   206 yd 4 ft 3 in.

5. A table is 5 ft 4 in. wide. A bookcase is 3 ft 10 in. wide. Which shows the difference in width of these items? Show your work.

A   9 ft 2 in.

B   2 ft 14 in.

C   1 ft 6 in.

D   2 ft 6 in.

6. Mia and Kerry arrived at the library at 9:15 A.M. and left at 11:03 A.M. How much time were they in the library? Show your work.

E   2 h 48 min

F   1 h 48 min

G   2 h 18 min

H   2 h 12 min

1. The clock in your classroom loses 4 minutes each day. If the clock shows 9:00 A.M. on Monday, what time will the clock show in 23 days?

- **READ** the problem and break it into parts to solve it.
- **SHOW** each step of your math work.
- **WRITE** an explanation describing what you did and why you solved the problem as you did, **EVEN** if you used mental math or a calculator.
- **WRITE** your answer in the space provided.

Explanation

Time in 23 days_____

0–5 Points

Score _____

2. Four thermometers are shown. Look carefully at each thermometer to determine the temperature. Record the temperature in the space provided. Then use your responses to identify the highest temperature, the lowest temperature, and the difference between the highest and lowest temperatures.

- **READ** the problem and break it into parts to solve it.
- **SHOW** each step of your math work.
- **WRITE** an explanation describing what you did and why you solved the problem as you did, **EVEN** if you used mental math or a calculator.
- **WRITE** your answer in the space provided.

A. 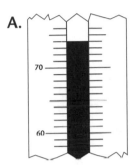   **B.** 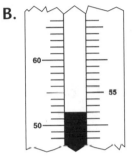   **C.** 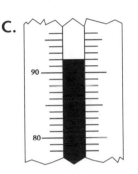   **D.**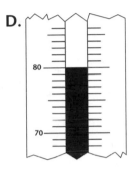

_____   _____   _____   _____

Explanation

Highest temperature _____

Lowest temperature _____

Difference between highest and lowest temperature _____

0–5 Points

Score _____

3. Several circles are shown below. Use the information given about each circle or a metric ruler to find the information asked for. Write your answers in the spaces provided. Then answer the questions.

- **READ** the problem and break it into parts to solve it.
- **SHOW** each step of your math work.
- **WRITE** an explanation describing what you did and why you solved the problem as you did, **EVEN** if you used mental math or a calculator.
- **WRITE** your answer in the space provided.

A.

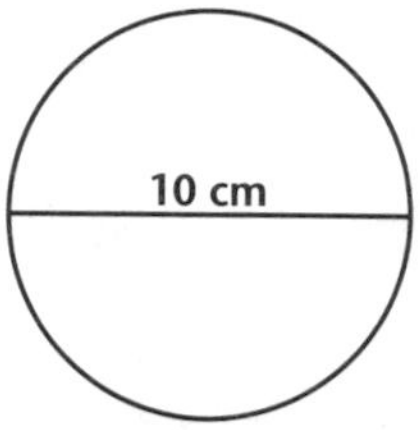

10 cm

Diameter of circle in cm _____

Diameter of circle in mm _____

Radius of circle in mm _____

B.

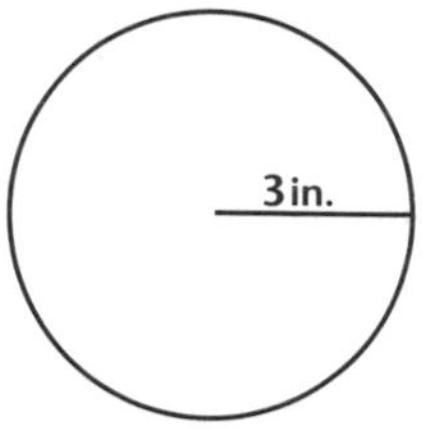

3 in.

Diameter of circle _____

Radius of circle _____

C.

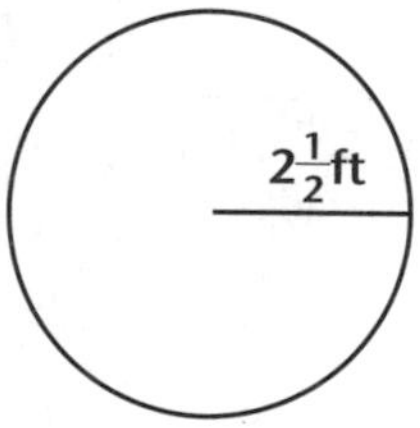

$2\frac{1}{2}$ ft

Diameter of circle _____

Radius of circle _____

D.

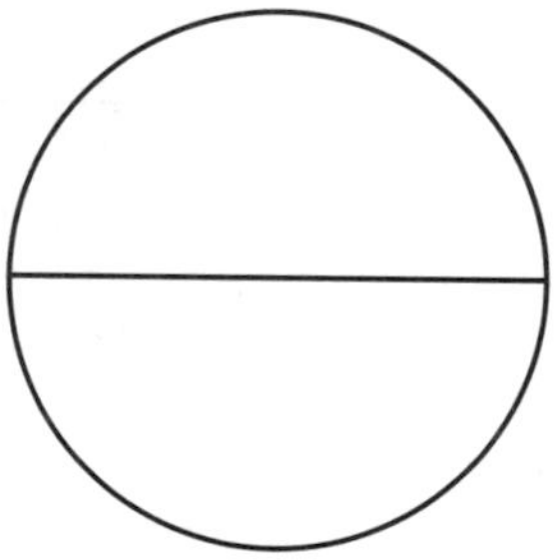

Diameter of circle in mm _____

Diameter of circle in cm _____

Radius of circle in cm _____

Radius of circle in mm _____

If you know the radius of a circle, how do you find the diameter of the circle?

If you know the diameter of a circle, how do you find the radius without measuring?

Explain how to find the circumference of circle D.

0–5 Points

Score _____

4. Each box below asks you to draw a line segment, angle, or figure. You will need a metric ruler, a compass, and a protractor. Select the appropriate tool to use for each drawing. Then complete the drawing in the space provided.

- Carefully **READ** the instructions in each box.
- **SELECT** the appropriate tool for making your drawing.
- **MAKE** your drawing in the space provided.
- **CHECK** your drawing for accuracy and **REVISE** if necessary.
- **IDENTIFY** the tool(s) you used to make your drawing.
- **WRITE** your answer in the space provided.

A. Draw a circle that has a diameter of 2 in.

B. Draw a line segment that is 15 mm in length.

Tool(s) used _____

Tool(s) used _____

C. Draw an angle that measures 45°.

D. Draw a rectangle that has a length of 3.5 cm and a width of 2 cm.

Tool(s) used _____

Tool(s) used _____

0–5 Points
Score _____

1. Mike's room is 15 ft long and 8 ft wide. Which answer shows how Mike can find the perimeter of his room?

   A $15 \times 8 =$

   B $8 + (15 \times 2) =$

   C $2 + (8 \times 15) =$

   D $(15 \times 2) + (8 \times 2) =$

2. Rose made a square quilt with each side measuring 5 ft. Which answer shows how to determine the area of the quilt?

   E $5 \times 5 =$

   F $5 + 5 + 5 + 5 =$

   G $2 \times (5 + 5) =$

   H $5 \times 2 =$

3. Which answer shows an estimate of the perimeter of the square?

   A 4 in.

   B 8 in.

   C 12 in.

   D 16 in.

4. Mara has 108 in. of cloth. How many feet of cloth does she have?

   E 3 ft

   F 6 ft

   G 9 ft

   H 10 ft

5. Annie wants to find the total area of a greeting card. Which unit of measure should she use?

   A yards

   B inches

   C feet

   D miles

6. Seth wants to find the perimeter of a window. Which unit of measure could he NOT use?

   E yards

   F inches

   G feet

   H miles

7. Which answer shows an estimate of the bracelet's length?

   A 6 in.

   B $6\frac{1}{2}$ in.

   C $6\frac{3}{4}$ in.

   D 7 in.

8. Which answer shows an estimate of the temperature?

   E 50°

   F 40°

   G 60°

   H 70°

9. Brian is 5 ft 3 in. tall. What is Brian's height in inches?

   A 53 in.

   B 60 in.

   C 63 in.

   D 65 in.

10. Last week, Suki jogged 10,560 yd. How many miles did she jog?

   E 2 mi

   F 6 mi

   G 10 mi

   H 12 mi

11. Chloe has 7 yd of wire. How many feet of wire does she have?

   A 10 ft

   B 14 ft

   C 21 ft

   D 84 ft

12. Mr. Ruiz drove 4 miles to work. How many feet did he travel?

   E 21,120 ft

   F 20,800 ft

   G 20,000 ft

   H 7,040 ft

13. Jon hit a golf ball 121 yd. Beth hit a golf ball 95 yd 2 ft. How much farther did Jon hit the ball than Beth?

   A 26 yd

   B 25 yd 1 ft

   C 216 yd

   D 216 yd 2 ft

14. A stack of books is 2 ft 3 in. tall. A stack of magazines is 10 in. tall. If the magazines are put on top of the books, how tall is the stack?

   E 3 ft 1 in.

   F 3 ft 3 in.

   G 1 ft 5 in.

   H 12 ft 3 in.

15. Deb had 5 yd of cloth. She used 3 yd 2 ft for a project. How much cloth does Deb have now?

   A 8 yd 2 ft

   B 2 yd 2 ft

   C 1 yd 2 ft

   D 1 yd 1 ft

16. The distance around a bicycle path is 2 mi. Will has ridden 1,825 yd. How much farther does Will have to go?

   E 175 yd

   F 2,095 yd

   G 1,695 yd

   H 8,735 yd

17. The distance between Marie's house and her grandmother's house is 5 mi 32 yd. Which shows the distance in yards?

   A 26,400 yd

   B 8,800 yd

   C 8,832 yd

   D 26,432 yd

18. Marisa's kitchen is 5 yd 1 ft 4 in. long. Which shows the length in inches?

   E 196 in.

   F 184 in.

   G 192 in.

   H 76 in.

19. The aisles in the hardware store are 1,258 in. long. Which shows another way to write the length?

   A 30 yd 1 ft 10 in.

   B 34 yd 2 ft

   C 34 yd 2 ft 10 in.

   D 34 ft 10 in.

Think About It

When you compare items, you describe a relationship. If the items are quantities, or amounts, you state if they are equal or unequal. If the quantities are unequal, you must name the greater amount. How do you compare quantities?

Here's How

Al needs to buy 48 hot dog rolls. A package of 12 rolls costs $2.29. A package of 8 rolls costs $1.49. Which will cost Al the least for 48 rolls?

Step 1 Determine the quantities.

1. How many packages of 12 rolls would Al need to buy? _____

2. How many packages of 8 rolls would Al need to buy? _____

Step 2 Identify the cost.

3. What number sentence can you use to find the cost of the 12 packs? _____

4. What is the cost? _____

5. What number sentence can you use to find the cost of the 8 packs? _____

6. What is the cost? _____

Step 3 Compare the costs.

7. Which digit has the greatest place value in each cost? _____

8. Compare the digits in that place. Write the ones digits using < for *less than*. _____

9. Which will cost Al the least for 48 rolls? _____

Practice

1. During a canned food drive, 28 students each collected 36 cans. Another class collected a total of 1,000 cans. Which answer shows the relationship between the 2 classes? Show your work.

   A $28 < 1,000$

   B $36 < 1,000$

   C $64 < 1,000$

   D $1,008 > 1,000$

2. Last week, Zack worked 6 hours per day on 4 different days. This week, Zack worked 8 hours per day on 3 different days. Which answer shows the relationship between Zack's total hours last week and this week? Show your work.

   E $24 > 18$

   F $10 < 11$

   G $24 = 24$

   H $24 < 32$

3. For the same amount of money, Pat can buy 12 packs of stickers with 8 stickers per pack or 6 packs of stickers with 15 stickers per pack. Which answer shows the relationship between the 8 packs and 15 packs? Show your work.

A $20 < 21$

B $96 > 90$

C $82 < 90$

D $96 < 105$

4. Lea saved $125 each month for 18 months. Ricky saved $200 each month for 1 year. Which answer shows the relationship between Lea's and Ricky's total savings? Show your work.

E $2,250 < $2,400

F $1,250 < $2,000

G $143 < $212

H $2,400 = $2,400

5. Seth practiced the piano for $2\frac{1}{2}$ h on Monday, Wednesday, and Saturday. Ann practiced the piano for 3 h 45 min on Tuesday and Thursday. Which shows the relationship between their total practice times? Show your work.

A $5 < 6\frac{1}{2}$

B $7\frac{1}{2} = 7\frac{1}{2}$

C $7\frac{1}{2} > 6$

D $7 < 7\frac{1}{2}$

6. Look at the population figures below for Pennsylvania counties in 1995. Which compares the populations from least to greatest?

Allegheny	1,309,821
Montgomery	705,178
Delaware	548,708
Philadelphia	1,498,971

E Philadelphia, Allegheny, Montgomery, Delaware

F Allegheny, Philadelphia, Montgomery, Delaware

G Delaware, Montgomery, Allegheny, Philadelphia

H Delaware, Montgomery, Philadelphia, Allegheny

7. The winners of the 100-meter freestyle at the Olympics from 1984–1996 swam their races in 49.80, 48.63, 49.02, and 48.74 seconds. Which shows these times from fastest to slowest?

A 48.63, 48.74, 49.02, 49.80

B 48.74, 48.63, 49.02, 49.80

C 49.80, 48.63, 48.74, 49.02

D 49.80, 49.02, 48.63, 48.74

8. Which number has the least value?

E 25.1

F 2.51

G .251

H .0251

Think About It

Katie, Megan, and Carl entered the 50–meter dash on field day. Each was awarded a ribbon—blue for first place, red for second place, and yellow for third place. They each wore numbers on their shirts. Katie, wearing #23, did NOT win the first place ribbon. Carl did NOT come in third. Carl, wearing #11, finished just behind the runner who wore #17. Megan did NOT come in third. Who won the ribbons for first, second, and third place? What numbers did they wear?

Here's How

Step 1 List the facts.

1. What facts are given about Katie? _____

_____

2. What facts are given about Carl? _____

_____

3. What facts are given about Megan? _____

_____

Step 2 Make a table.

Sometimes it is useful to organize information in a table. Fill in the table with the facts you already know.

Runner	1st Place	2nd Place	3rd Place	Number
Katie	No			23
Carl	No		No	11
Megan			No	

Step 3 Complete the chart.

4. If Carl wore #11 and Katie wore #23, who wore #17? _____

5. If Carl did not finish 1st or 3rd, what place did he finish in? _____

6. If Carl finished after #17 and he was second, who had to be first? _____

7. If Katie was not first or second, where did she finish? _____

8. Add your answers in Step 3 to the chart.

Step 4 Use the chart.

9. Who won the ribbons for first, second, and third place?

_____

10. What numbers did they wear?

_____

Practice

1. Don exercises on the same three days each week. Don never exercises on Sunday. He always exercises on Tuesday. Don never exercises two days in a row. Which answer shows the days he exercises? Draw a table or picture to find the answer.

A Tuesday, Wednesday, Saturday

B Monday, Wednesday, Friday

C Tuesday, Thursday, Saturday

D Wednesday, Friday, Saturday

2. Jim, Rob, Tia, and Pearl are standing in line. Tia is behind Rob. Pearl is first. Jim is in front of Rob. Which answer shows the order in which they are standing? Draw a table or picture to find the answer.

E Pearl, Jim, Rob, Tia

F Pearl, Rob, Jim, Tia

G Tia, Rob, Jim, Pearl

H Rob, Jim, Pearl, Tia

3. Pat, Conor, Amy, and Carla all collected cans for a food drive. Conor collected more cans than Amy but less than Carla. Pat collected the least number of cans. Which answer shows the students arranged from most to least cans collected? Draw a table or picture to find the answer.

A Conor, Amy, Carla, Pat

B Amy, Carla, Conor, Pat

C Pat, Amy, Carla, Conor

D Carla, Conor, Amy, Pat

4. Shawna, Kyle, Bud, and Dixie are sitting in four rows of a theater. Bud is sitting in Row 2. Dixie is sitting behind Kyle. Shawna is sitting in front of Bud. Which answer shows the order in which they are sitting? Draw a table or picture to find the answer.

E Bud, Dixie, Kyle, Shawna

F Shawna, Bud, Kyle, Dixie

G Kyle, Bud, Dixie, Shawna

H Shawna, Bud, Dixie, Kyle

5. Maylee, Sandra, Kaleen, and Joan are standing in the ticket line. Sandra is last. Joan is not first or third. Kaleen is not first. In what order are they standing? Draw a table or picture to find the answer.

A Sandra, Joan, Maylee, Kaleen

B Maylee, Joan, Kaleen, Sandra

C Joan, Kaleen, Maylee, Sandra

D Kaleen, Maylee, Joan, Sandra

Ready Reference

deductive reasoning the process of reasoning from statements accepted as true to reach a conclusion

inductive reasoning generalizations made from particular observations in a common occurrence

 Think About It

Sometimes you use deductive reasoning to solve a problem. Other solutions come through inductive reasoning. How do you decide which type of reasoning a problem calls for?

 Here's How

Deductive reasoning

The perimeter of a square quilt is 16 ft. What is the length of one side of the quilt?

Step 1 Identify true statements.

1. The problem gives the perimeter of the quilt and notes that it is a square. What is the perimeter of the quilt?

_____

2. How do you determine perimeter?

_____
_____

3. What is the definition of a square?

_____
_____

Step 2 Apply the true statements.

4. How many sides does the quilt have? _____

5. What is the sum of these sides? _____

Step 3 Solve the problem.

6. What number sentence can you use to find the length of one side?

_____

7. What is the length of one side of the quilt? _____

Inductive reasoning

What are the next two terms of this pattern?
5, 6, 8, 11, 15, _____, _____

Step 1 Determine the relationships.

1. What do you do to the first term to get the second term? _____

2. What do you do to the second term to get the third term? _____

3. What do you do to the third term to get the fourth term? _____

4. What do you do to the fourth term to get the fifth term? _____

Step 2 Identify the pattern.

5. What pattern exists in these five terms?

_____

Step 3 Use the pattern.

6. What will you do to the fifth term to get the sixth term? _____

7. What is the sixth term? _____

8. What will you do to the sixth term to get the seventh term? _____

9. What is the seventh term? _____

Practice

1. The area of a flower garden is 24 ft². The length of the garden is 6 ft. What is the width of the garden? Show your work.

   A   6 ft

   B   18 ft

   C   4 ft

   D   12 ft

2. Ruth jogged 2 miles during the first week of April. During the second week, she jogged 4 miles and in the third week she jogged 8 miles. If this pattern continues, how far did Ruth jog during the last week of April? Show your work.

   E   10 mi

   F   12 mi

   G   14 mi

   H   16 mi

3. Paula is making a necklace. She strings 2 red beads, 3 green beads, 3 white beads, and 2 blue beads. If she continues in this pattern, what color is the fifteenth bead? Show your work.

   A   red

   B   green

   C   white

   D   blue

4. Two sides of a triangle are equal in length. The third side is twice as long as one other side. The perimeter of the triangle is 8 cm. What is the length of the longest side of the triangle? Show your work.

   E   2 cm

   F   3 cm

   G   4 cm

   H   6 cm

5. Pete is putting a border along the four walls of his bedroom. The length of the room is twice its width. Pete needs 48 ft of border for the job. What is the length of the room? Draw a chart to show your answers.

   A   16 ft

   B   12 ft

   C   8 ft

   D   24 ft

Think About It

A word problem contains a lot of information. Some of the information is relevant, or needed, to find a solution. Some information may be irrelevant or unnecessary. How do you find the relevant information?

Here's How

Rico works at a hardware store. He got the job because he likes building things. Last week, Rico worked 24 hours. The owner of the hardware store, Mr. Marks, pays Rico $5.75 for each hour he works. How much money did Rico earn last week?

Step List all the information.

1. Make a list of all the information given in the problem.

_____

_____

_____

Step Identify the question.

2. What question do you need to answer?

_____

Step Find the relevant information.

3. What information from your list is needed to answer this question? _____

_____

Step 4 Use the information.

4. What operation will you use to answer the question? _____

5. What number sentence will you use? _____

Step Answer the question.

6. Solve the number sentence. _____

7. Answer the question. _____

Practice

1. Max works at an ice cream shop. He saves some of his pay each week. Max has saved $54.50. He spent $42.95 to buy a radio. How much money does Max have left? Find the relevant and irrelevant information and show your work.

   A $151.95

   B $21.50

   C $11.55

   D $10.95

2. Rosa worked 18 hours last week. She usually works 24 hours a week but had to take one day off. Rosa was paid $112.50. How much does Rosa earn an hour? Find the relevant and irrelevant information and show your work.

   E $6.25

   F $4.69

   G $11.25

   H $12.50

3. Miguel has collected baseball cards since he was five years old. He has 18 albums filled with cards. Each album holds 96 cards. How many cards are in Miguel's albums? Find the relevant and irrelevant information and show your work.

   A   114

   B   90

   C   960

   D   1,728

4. Liz sells homemade bracelets. She used 468 beads to make bracelets. Liz will sell the bracelets at a school craft fair. She puts 52 beads on each bracelet. How many bracelets did Liz make for the craft fair? Find the relevant and irrelevant information and show your work.

   E   52

   F   29

   G   9

   H   520

5. Oak School holds a craft fair each year. The money earned is used to buy new playground equipment. There were 84 booths in this year's fair. The school was paid a $15 fee for each booth. How much did the school receive in booth fees? Find the relevant and irrelevant information and show your work.

   A $99

   B $69

   C $840

   D $1,260

Think About It

Read these sentences: *All* boys in the fifth grade are in the band. *Some* boys in the fifth grade are in the band. *Many* boys in the fifth grade are in the band. One word is different in each sentence, but that word changes the meaning of the sentence. Words such as *all*, *some*, *many*, and *or* are part of the precise language of math. Using and understanding precise mathematical language helps you understand problems.

Here's How

Use the precise word "some."

Jon said that *some* numbers greater than 2 but less than 8 are odd numbers. Is this true?

1. The word *some* means part of a group, but not the entire group. How many numbers greater than 2 but less than 8 are odd numbers? _____

2. Is Jon's statement true? Why?

_____

_____

_____

Use the precise word "many."

Tiko said that *many* months of the year have 31 days. Is his statement true?

1. The word *many* means a large number. Write a ratio comparing the number of months with 31 days to the number of months in a year. _____

2. Is Tiko's statement true? Why?

_____

_____

_____

Use the precise word "all."

Rhea said that *all* even numbers greater than 11 but less than 19 are divisible by two. Is this true?

1. The word *all* means the entire group or every item in the group.

2. How many even numbers greater than 11 but less than 19 are divisible by two? _____

3. Is Rhea's statement true? Why?

_____

_____

Use the precise word "or."

Pedro said that whole numbers less than 31 that end in 0 or 5 are divisible by either 5 *or* 10. Is his statement true?

1. The word *or* means either. Which whole numbers less than 31 that end in 0 or 5 are divisible by 5? _____

2. Which numbers are divisible by 10?

_____

3. Is Pedro's statement true? Why?

_____

_____

Practice

1. Which statement is the MOST precise?

   A *All* odd numbers are divisible by 3.

   B *All* odd numbers are divisible by 3 *or* 5.

   C *Every* odd number less than 10 is divisible by 2 *or* 3.

   D *Some* odd numbers less than 10 are divisible by 3.

2. Which statement is the MOST precise?

   E One yard equals 36 inches *or* 3 feet.

   F *All* lengths measured in inches are less than 1 yard.

   G *Every* length measured in feet is greater than 1 yard.

   H One foot equals 12 inches *or* 1 yard.

3. Which statement is the MOST precise?

   A *All* even numbers are divisible by 4.

   B *Some* even numbers are divisible by 4.

   C *Every* even number is divisible by 6.

   D *None* of the even numbers are divisible by 4 *or* 6.

4. Which statement is the MOST precise?

   E *Most* fifth graders are 10 *or* 11 years old.

   F *All* fifth graders are 10 years old.

   G *None* of the fifth graders are 10 years old.

   H *All* fifth graders are 11 years old.

5. Which statement is the MOST precise?

   A *All* four–sided figures are squares.

   B *Some* four–sided figures are rectangles.

   C *Most* four–sided figures are triangles.

   D *All* four–sided figures are rectangles.

6. Which statement is the MOST precise?

   E *All* months have 30 *or* 31 days.

   F *Some* months have 30 *or* 31 days.

   G *All* months have less than 31 days.

   H *Most* months have 30 *or* 31 days.

7. Which statement is the MOST precise?

   A The product of two even numbers is an even number *or* an odd number.

   B *All* products of two even numbers are even numbers.

   C *Some* products of two even numbers are odd numbers.

   D *Most* products of two even numbers are odd numbers.

8. Which statement is the MOST precise?

   E *None* of the math problems involve addition.

   F *All* math problems involve addition.

   G *All* math problems involve addition *or* subtraction.

   H *Some* math problems involve addition.

Standard 2.4.5F ✦ Use statistics to understand issues and problems

Think About It

Graphs and tables contain information called statistics, or numerical data. When you present data, or statistics, in a graph or table, you can more easily see the relationships between these statistics and draw conclusions from the data. You often see tables or graphs of statistics in social studies and science.

Here's How

Juan asked 100 people in Hershey if they would vote in the next election. He organized his results on a bar graph. What conclusion can he draw about the number of people who will vote in the next election?

Number of People Voting

Step 1 Interpret the graph.

1. How many people said they would vote? About _____

2. How many people said they would not vote? About _____

3. How many people said they did not know if they would vote? About _____

Step 2 Look for relationships between the statistics.

4. Look at the height of the bars in the graph. Which bar is the tallest?

_____

5. Look at the height of the bar representing the people who will not vote in the next election. About how many of these bars would cover the bar representing the people who will vote? About _____

Step 3 Describe the relationship between the statistics.

6. Write a sentence that describes the relationship between the number of people who will vote and the number of people who will not vote.

_____

_____

Practice

Use the table to answer Problems 1–2.

1. Which describes the relationship between the amount of rain on the weekend and the weekdays?

A Less rain fell on the weekend than on weekdays.

B Twice as much rain fell on the weekend than on weekdays.

C Four times more rain fell on the weekend than on weekdays.

D An equal amount of rain fell on the weekend and on weekdays.

Rainfall During Vacation

Day	Rainfall(mm)
Friday	2
Saturday	4
Sunday	8
Monday	4

2. Which statement best describes the relationship between the days receiving the least and greatest amount of rain?

E The amount of rain that fell on Monday was half as much as the amount of rain that fell on Friday.

F The amount of rain that fell on Friday was twice the amount of rain that fell on Saturday.

G The amount of rain that fell on Sunday was double the amount of rain that fell on Friday.

H The amount of rain that fell on Sunday was four times the amount of rain that fell on Friday.

Use the graph to answer Problems 3–4.

3. Which describes the relationship between the number of people who think a park should be built first and those who think a recreation center should be built first?

A About an equal number of people think a park or a recreation center should be built first.

B About twice as many people think a park should be built before a recreation center.

C About half as many people think a recreation center should be built before a park.

D About four times as many people think a recreation center should be built before a park.

What Should Be Built First?

4. Which statement best describes the relationship between the answers that received the greatest and least number of votes?

E Twice as many people think a park should be built before a library.

F The number of people who want a recreation center is half the number of people who want a park.

G Four times more people want a library than a recreation center.

H The number of people who want a recreation center is half the number of people who want a library.

1. James, Kathy, Ken, and Michelle are the only students sitting in the fourth row. Neither James nor Michelle is in the first seat. Kathy sits between two boys. Sam sits beside Kathy in the fifth row. In what order are the students sitting?

- **REREAD** the problem carefully. **IDENTIFY** any information that is not needed to solve the problem.
- **CREATE** a drawing or a chart that shows where each person sits.
- **WRITE** an explanation describing what you did and why you solved the problem as you did.
- **WRITE** your answer in the space provided.

Explanation

Seating order _____

0–5 Points

Score _____

2. The state of New York uses an average of 583 gallons of water per person per day. The smallest town in the state is Dering Harbor, with a population of 28 people. How many gallons of water are used in Dering Harbor in one day? Estimate how many gallons the people of Dering Harbor use in a month with 30 days and in one year.

- **SHOW** each step of your math work.
- **EXPLAIN** why you solved the problem as you did.
- **WRITE** an explanation describing what you did and why you solved the problem as you did, **EVEN** if you used mental math or a calculator.
- **WRITE** your answer in the box below.

Explanation

Gallons of water used in one day _____	
Gallons of water used in one month _____	
Gallons of water used in one year _____	

0–5 Points

Score _____

3. Study the fraction pieces to order the sets in parts A, B, and C from greatest to least. Explain your work using < and > .

- **SHOW** each step of your math work.
- **WRITE** an explanation describing what you did and why you solved the problem as you did, **EVEN** if you used mental math or a calculator.
- **WRITE** your answer in the box below.

Part A $\frac{2}{3}, \frac{5}{6}, \frac{1}{4}$

Part B $\frac{1}{2}, \frac{5}{8}, \frac{3}{4}$

Part C $.6, \frac{7}{8}, \frac{1}{3}$

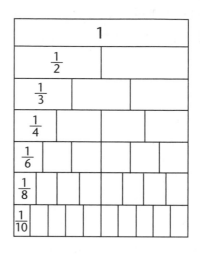

Explanation

Part A _____

Part B _____

Part C _____

0–5 Points

Score _____

4. Mr. Smith asked his students to read a book about horses. Brad has read $\frac{3}{5}$ of the book, Lynn has read $\frac{3}{4}$ of the book, and Gwen has read $\frac{3}{10}$ of the book. List the students in order from the fewest pages read to the most pages read.

- **READ** the problem and break it into parts to solve it.
- **SHOW** each step of your math work.
- **EXPLAIN** why you solved the problem as you did.
- **WRITE** an explanation describing what you did and why you solved the problem as you did, **EVEN** if you used mental math or a calculator.
- **WRITE** your answer in the space provided.

Explanation

Order of students_____

0–5 Points

Score _____

1. For the same amount of money, Glen can buy 9 packs of stickers with 6 stickers in each pack or 3 packs of stickers with 18 stickers in each pack. Which answer shows the relationship between 9 packs and 3 packs?

   A 15 < 21
   B 54 > 21
   C 15 < 54
   D 54 = 54

2. Jan saved $55 each month for 2 years. Deb saved $115 each month for 1 year. Which answer shows the relationship between their total savings?

   E $110 < $115
   F $1,320 < $1,380
   G $1,200 > $1,120
   H $1,100 = $1,100

3. For a food drive, 28 fifth graders each collected 34 cans and 42 sixth graders each collected 25 cans. Which answer shows the relationship between the total cans collected by the fifth and sixth graders?

   A 62 < 67
   B 900 < 1,200
   C 952 > 950
   D 952 < 1,050

4. Joan, Ruth, Ted, and Pam are standing in a line. Ruth is in front of Ted. Pam is first. Ted is in front of Joan. Which answer shows the order in which they are standing?

   E Pam, Ruth, Joan, Ted
   F Ruth, Joan, Pam, Ted
   G Pam, Ruth, Ted, Joan
   H Joan, Ted, Pam, Ruth

5. Max, Jake, Belle, and Dee ran a race. Max finished behind Dee. One of the girls finished first. Jake finished ahead of Dee. Which answer shows the order in which they finished the race?

   A Belle, Jake, Dee, Max
   B Dee, Max, Jake, Belle
   C Dee, Jake, Belle, Max
   D Belle, Dee, Jake, Max

6. The perimeter of a square tile is 32 inches. What is the length of one side of the tile?

   E 16 in.
   F 4 in.
   G 8 in.
   H 12 in.

7. What are the next two numbers in this pattern? 3, 6, 12, 24,_____, _____

   A 36, 48
   B 48, 96
   C 32, 44
   D 34, 46

8. What are the next two numbers in this pattern? 25, 26, 28, 31, 35, _____, _____

   E 39, 44
   F 38, 45
   G 40, 45
   H 40, 46

9. Sue works at a gift shop. Last week, she worked 15 hours. If she earns $5.85 per hour, how much did Sue earn last week?

   A $87.75
   B $75.50
   C $85.75
   D $58.50

10. Clare and Beth collect stickers. Clare has 5 albums filled with her sticker collection. Beth's collection is in 6 albums. Each album holds 144 stickers. How many stickers does Clare have?

- **E** 149
- **F** 150
- **G** 720
- **H** 864

11. Which statement is true?

- **A** *Most* numbers that end in 0 are divisible by 6.
- **B** *All* numbers that end in 5 are divisible by 3.
- **C** *Some* numbers that end in 5 are divisible by 2.
- **D** *All* numbers that end in 0 are divisible by 5.

12. A survey of 50 voters showed that 38 think the town needs a new school while 12 think the town needs a new police station. Which statement is true?

- **E** For every 1 voter who wants a new police station, there are 3 voters who want a school.
- **F** About half the voters want a new police station.
- **G** All the voters want a new school.
- **H** Twice as many voters want a new school rather than a new police station.

Use the following to answer Problems 13–15.
Tony and Sandy are making fruit punch for a party on Friday. They have $\frac{2}{3}$ lb of apples, $\frac{2}{3}$ lb of oranges, and $\frac{1}{3}$ lb of pineapple. The fruit cost $3.97.

13. What information is needed to find the total weight of the fruit?

- **A** Tony and Sandy are making fruit punch for a party.
- **B** They have $\frac{2}{3}$ lb of apples.
- **C** The fruit cost $3.97.
- **D** The party is on Friday.

14. What information is NOT needed to find the total weight of the fruit?

- **E** They have $\frac{2}{3}$ lb of apples.
- **F** They have $\frac{2}{3}$ lb of oranges.
- **G** The fruit cost $3.97.
- **H** They have $\frac{1}{3}$ lb of pineapple.

15. Which tells how to find the total weight of the fruit?

- **A** Multiply the weight of the apples by 3.
- **B** Divide the total cost of the fruit by 3.
- **C** Add the weights of the apples, oranges, and pineapple.
- **D** Multiply the weights of the apples, oranges, and pineapple.

Think About It

Did anyone ever give you step–by–step instructions about how to do something? Many math problems can be broken into parts, or steps, which makes the problem easier to solve.

Here's How

Mrs. Smith's class is planning a field trip to the museum. There are 28 children in the class and 4 children can ride in each car. How many cars will they need?

Step 1 Develop a plan.

I need to put the children into groups; therefore I need to divide.

Step 2 Identify the information needed to solve the problem.

28 children in the class

4 children can ride in each car

Step 3 Carry out the plan.

_____ ÷ 4 = _____

Step 4 Check whether the answer makes sense.

Yes, because there are 4 children in each car and there are seven cars.

4 × 7 = _____

Step 5 Explain how you solved the problem.

I know that when you have a total number and you need to break it into parts you have to divide. I know the division answer is correct because you can use multiplication to check division.

Practice

1. Alexis invited 9 girls to her birthday party. Her mom baked 36 cookies. How many cookies can each guest have if they each receive an equal amount? Show your work.

   A 4
   B 6
   C 3
   D 8

2. Scott is training for a track event. He ran 2 miles every day for three weeks. How many total miles did he run? Show your work.

   E 36
   F 28
   G 42
   H 18

3. The first through sixth grades at Grove Elementary School sold 200 tickets to their fall carnival. Grades 1, 2, and 3 each sold 22 tickets. Grade 4 sold 52 tickets. Grade 5 sold 5 more than grade 4. How many tickets did grade 6 sell? Show your work

A 35

B 20

C 40

D 25

4. Daybreak Donuts sells 36 varieties of doughnuts. If you tried 3 new doughnuts every day, how many days would it take you to try every doughnut? Show your work.

E 6 days

F 8 days

G 12 days

H 24 days

5. Peter mows lawns during the summer. He charges $15 for every yard he mows. He mowed 20 lawns in June. How much money did he make? Show your work.

A $300

B $200

C $150

D $30

6. The school nurse saw 14 children on Monday, 12 children on Tuesday, 18 children on Wednesday, 9 children on Thursday, and 15 children on Friday. How many children did she see this week? Show your work.

E 57

F 68

G 63

H 48

7. Mr. Chung has 128 endangered animal stickers to give to his class. He gives 4 stickers to each student. How many students are there in his class? Show your work.

A 28

B 30

C 32

D 34

8. The store sells stamp booklets that each hold 20 stamps. How many stamp booklets are needed for 13,660 stamps? Show your work.

E 1,366

F 683

G 83

H 68

9. Alma wants to make 75 necklaces to sell at the school fair. Each necklace uses 72 in. of wire. How many feet of wire does she need? Show your work.

A 5,400

B 450

C 147

D 5,250

10. If Alma sells her 75 necklaces for $3.97 each, how much will she make? Show your work.

E $297.75

F $5.29

G $2,977.50

H $300

Ready Reference

mean the sum of the set of numbers divided by *n*, the number of numbers in the set

✏️ Think About It

The weatherman gave the following seven-day forecast: Sunday–57 degrees, Monday–52 degrees, Tuesday–59 degrees, Wednesday–63 degrees, Thursday–61 degrees, Friday–54 degrees, and Saturday–60 degrees. How do you use mathematical vocabulary, symbols, and graphs to answer the following questions?

1. On what day was the temperature the highest?
2. On what day was the temperature the lowest?
3. What was the mean temperature for the week?
4. Use the *greater than* and *less than* signs to compare Sunday's temperature and Monday's temperature.
5. How much cooler was it on Monday than on Wednesday?

✏️ Here's How

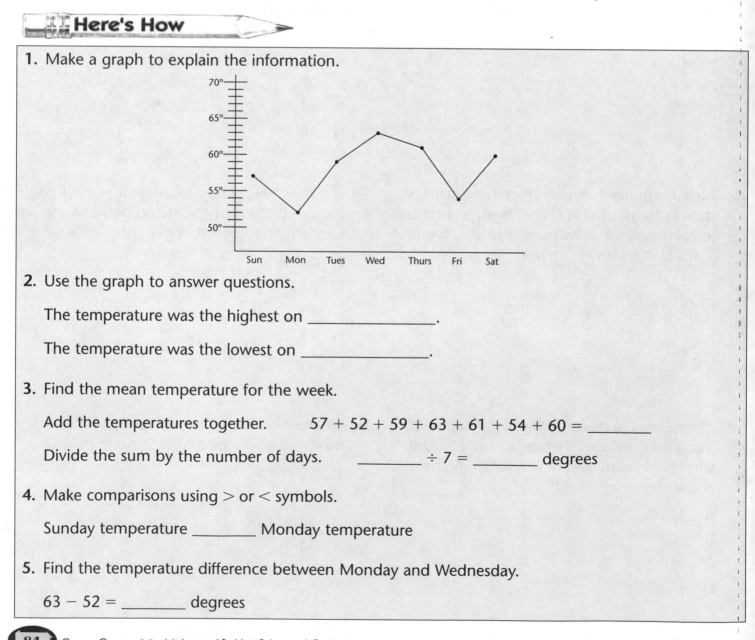

1. Make a graph to explain the information.

2. Use the graph to answer questions.

The temperature was the highest on _____.

The temperature was the lowest on _____.

3. Find the mean temperature for the week.

Add the temperatures together.   57 + 52 + 59 + 63 + 61 + 54 + 60 = _____

Divide the sum by the number of days.   _____ ÷ 7 = _____ degrees

4. Make comparisons using > or < symbols.

Sunday temperature _____ Monday temperature

5. Find the temperature difference between Monday and Wednesday.

63 − 52 = _____ degrees

Practice

Use the graph to answer Problems 1–4.

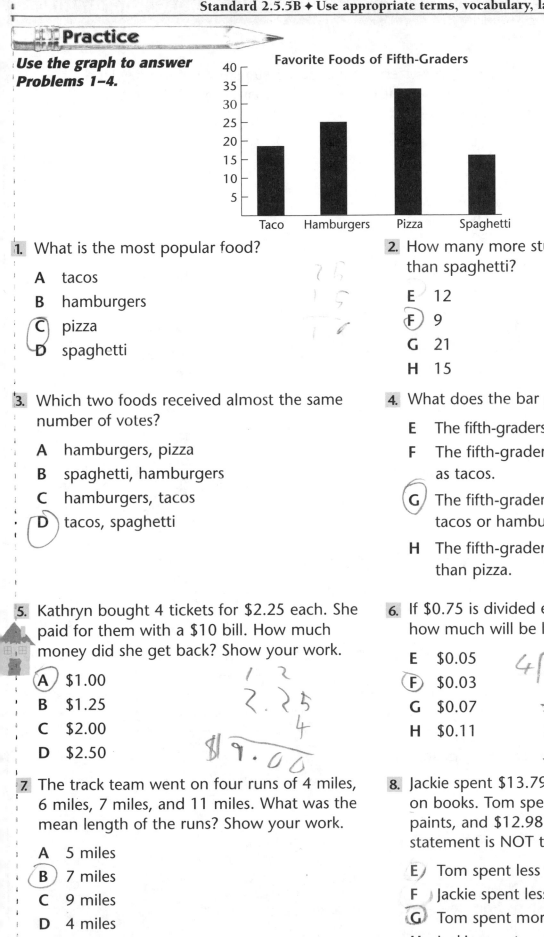

Favorite Foods of Fifth-Graders

1. What is the most popular food?

   A   tacos

   B   hamburgers

   C   pizza

   D   spaghetti

2. How many more students like hamburgers than spaghetti?

   E   12

   F   9

   G   21

   H   15

3. Which two foods received almost the same number of votes?

   A   hamburgers, pizza

   B   spaghetti, hamburgers

   C   hamburgers, tacos

   D   tacos, spaghetti

4. What does the bar graph show?

   E   The fifth-graders like tacos better than pizza.

   F   The fifth-graders like hamburgers as much as tacos.

   G   The fifth-graders like pizza better than tacos or hamburgers.

   H   The fifth-graders like tacos better than pizza.

5. Kathryn bought 4 tickets for $2.25 each. She paid for them with a $10 bill. How much money did she get back? Show your work.

   A $1.00

   B $1.25

   C $2.00

   D $2.50

6. If $0.75 is divided equally among 4 people, how much will be left? Show your work.

   E $0.05

   F $0.03

   G $0.07

   H $0.11

   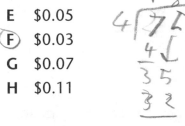

7. The track team went on four runs of 4 miles, 6 miles, 7 miles, and 11 miles. What was the mean length of the runs? Show your work.

   A   5 miles

   B   7 miles

   C   9 miles

   D   4 miles

8. Jackie spent $13.79 on a backpack and $9.98 on books. Tom spent $2.67 on pens, $6.36 on paints, and $12.98 on books. Which statement is NOT true?

   E   Tom spent less than Jackie.

   F   Jackie spent less on books.

   G   Tom spent more in all.

   H   Jackie spent more in all.

✏ Think About It

When Jodie was learning to walk she took 1 step the first day, 3 steps the second day, and 5 steps the third day. If she keeps progressing at this pace, how many steps will she take on the seventh day? You can use a variety of ways to solve this problem.

✏ Here's How

Draw a picture and look for a pattern.

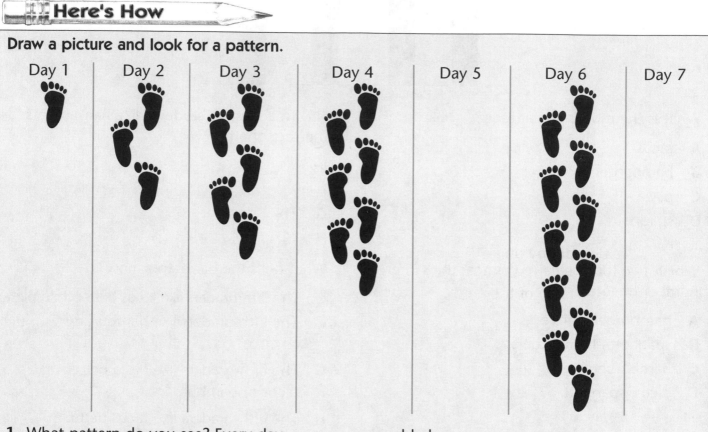

| Day 1 | Day 2 | Day 3 | Day 4 | Day 5 | Day 6 | Day 7 |

1. What pattern do you see? Every day, _____ are added.

2. How many steps did Jodie take on Day 7? _____

Make a table.

Look for a pattern. Then make a table to show the pattern. Complete the table for Day 5 and Day 7.

Day	1	2	3	4	5	6	7
Number of steps	1	3	5	7		11	

Use words and numbers to solve the problem.

1. Jodie took 2 new steps each day. You know she took 5 steps on the third day.

   How many days until Day 7? _____

2. You can write an expression to solve the problem using numbers.

   2 steps per day for 4 days = 2 + 2 + 2 + 2 = _____

   8 steps added to the 5 steps from the first 3 days equals _____ steps.

   8 + _____ = 13

Practice

1. Addison and Bailey built a card house. The first floor was made of 23 cards, the second floor was made of 20 cards, and the third floor was made of 17 cards. How many cards were used on the sixth floor? Show your work.

A 11
B 13
C 8
D 5

2. How many boxes will be used in the sixth figure? Show your work.

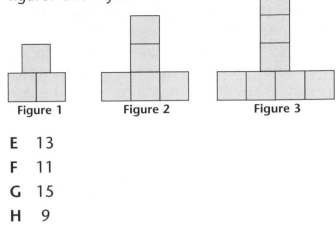

Figure 1   Figure 2   Figure 3

E 13
F 11
G 15
H 9

3. Allen bought his puppy on a Thursday, the tenth day of the month. What day of the week was the first day of the month? Show your work.

A Thursday
B Tuesday
C Friday
D Wednesday

4. A package of paper plates is $3.00 and a package of napkins is $2.00. You need the same amount of plates and napkins for a party. If you spend $24.00 for plates, how much would you spend for napkins? Show your work.

E $24.00
F $12.00
G $16.00
H $21.00

5. Callie, Grace, Emily, and Rosie sat on the same side of the table in the cafeteria. Callie sat between Emily and Grace. Emily sat between Rosie and Callie. Which two girls sat on the ends? Show your work.

A Grace, Rosie
B Emily, Callie
C Emily, Rosie
D Grace, Callie

6. Mubeen participated in a triathlon. He swam 2 miles. He ran twice as far as he swam. He rode a bicycle 6 more miles than he ran. How many miles was the triathlon? Show your work.

E 14
F 10
G 26
H 16

Think About It

What does math have to do with social studies, science, literature, or going to the grocery store? Have you ever thought about how math is related to other subjects? In *The Incredible Journey*, by Sheila Burnford, 3 runaway pets—a young Labrador retriever, a wise bull terrier, and a Siamese cat—help one another through hardships and danger as they travel 200 miles through the Canadian wilderness to make their way home. How long would it take the animals to travel 200 miles if they traveled 5 miles a day?

Here's How

Step 1 Identify the information given.

I know that the animals traveled a total of _____ miles.

They could travel _____ miles in 1 day.

Step 2 Plan how to solve the problem. Decide if you need to add, subtract, multiply or divide.

What should you do to find the number of days the journey took?

A Subtract the number of miles traveled each day from the total miles.
B Multiply the number of miles traveled each day by the total miles.
C Add the number of miles traveled each day to the number of total traveled miles.
D Divide the total number of miles by the number of miles traveled each day.

Step 3 Write and solve the problem.

$200 \div 5 =$ _____ days

Step 4 Check to see if your answer is reasonable.

If the animals traveled 5 miles each day for 40 days, then they would travel _____ total miles.

Practice

1. A 12–pack of soda at the market costs $2.76. How much do the individual cans cost? Show your work.

   A $0.23
   B $0.34
   C $0.26
   D $0.18

2. Mark's family went out to dinner. His dad's meal cost $7.75, his mom's meal cost $6.56, and his meal cost $4.69. They had to add 10% tax to their total bill. Mark's dad paid with a $20 bill and a $5 bill. How much change will he get back? Show your work.

   E $6.00
   F $5.10
   G $5.60
   H $4.10

3. Regan's school starts at 8:10 A.M. It takes 15 minutes to drive to school. Regan allows 10 minutes to stop on the way for breakfast. What time does Regan need to leave for school? Show your work.

A   7:35 A.M.

B   7:45 A.M.

C   7:50 A.M.

D   8:00 A.M.

4. Heather's teacher assigned the book *Walk Two Moons,* by Sharon Creech, to be read in two weeks. Heather wants to read the same number of pages each night. The book has 280 pages. How many pages will she need to read each night? Show your work.

E   14

F   10   .

G   20

H   18

5. It takes $\frac{3}{4}$ c flour to make 1 dozen cookies. Cori needs to make 12 dozen cookies for the school carnival. How many cups of flour will she need? Show your work.

A $4\frac{1}{4}$

B   12

C $7\frac{3}{4}$

D   9

6. Wyoming is the least populous state with 481,400 people. California is the most populous state with 31,878,234 people. How many more people live in California than in Wyoming? Show your work.

E   31,396,834

F   30,486,513

G   32,395,674

H   31,286,736

7. A liter bottle of soda holds 3 servings. Each serving has 125 milliliters of sodium. How many milliliters of sodium are in a 1–liter bottle? Show your work.

A   125

B   150

C   250

D   375

8. It is 49 miles from Allentown to Wilkes-Barre. The delivery truck drives from Allentown to Wilkes-Barre and back again to Allentown every day. How many total miles will the truck travel if it makes the trip Monday through Friday? Show your work.

E   490

F   245

G   98

H   49

Ready Reference

make a diagram drawing a diagram helps you organize information visually

guess and check guess a solution, test whether it is correct, then refine your guess

make a table put information in rows and columns to see patterns

solve a simpler problem use easier numbers to make a problem less complicated

work backwards start with the answer and use inverse operations to undo the steps

write an equation use the numbers you know to find an unknown number

make a graph put your data in a graph to understand the problem

Think About It

Many different strategies can be used to understand and solve problems. Some of these are to work backwards, solve a simpler problem, draw a diagram, make a table, write an equation, make a graph, guess and check, and use manipulatives.

Eduardo owns a sporting goods store that sells footballs, baseballs, basketballs, and soccer balls. Last month Eduardo sold 86 soccer balls and 5 times as many basketballs. How many basketballs did he sell? Which strategy would you use to solve this problem?

Here's How

Step Identify the information given.

Eduardo sold 86 soccer balls and 5 times as many basketballs.

Step 2 Plan.

The phrase *5 times as many* means you should multiply. Therefore, the best strategy to use to solve this problem is to write an equation.

Step 3 Solve.

86 × _____ = _____

Step Check to see if the answer is reasonable. If it is not reasonable, try using another strategy.

86 × 10 = 860 *Since half of ten is 5 you can find half of 860 to check your answer.*

860 ÷ 2 = _____

There are lots of ways to solve a problem. You can use more than one strategy to solve a problem. You can use whatever strategy works for you.

Practice

1. Ben and Jack have a total of 22 coins. Ben has 1 more coin than twice the number of coins Jack has. Which strategy would you use to find out how many coins each boy has?

   A draw a diagram

   B guess and check

   C work backwards

   D make a table

2. The breakfast diner sold 12,850 eggs, 7,586 pancakes, 14,325 pieces of bacon, and 23,758 cups of coffee. Estimate how many items were sold. Which strategy would you use to solve this problem?

   E solve a simpler problem

   F work backwards

   G use manipulatives

   H guess and check

3. Mrs. Baker's class took a class survey on pets. Eight children had dogs, 6 children had cats, 3 children had fish, and 2 children had no pets. Which strategy would you use to show which was the most popular pet and the least popular pet?

   A write an equation

   B make a graph

   C work backwards

   D use manipulatives

4. Ms. Smith kept all of her jewelry in a box. The earrings were to the left of the necklaces, the necklaces were in between the watches and the earrings. The rings were to the right of the watches. What order was the jewelry in from left to right? Which strategy would you use to solve this problem?

   E solve a simpler problem

   F write an equation

   G draw a diagram

   H make a table

5. Celie gave 10 pieces of bubble gum to Sara. Then she gave 6 pieces to Mary and 4 pieces to Beth. Celie had 5 pieces left. How many pieces of bubble gum did Celie have at the beginning? Choose a strategy and solve. Show your work.

   A 25

   B 20

   C 15

   D 18

6. The cleaning solution called for 3 liters of water for every one liter of solution. How many liters of water will you need for 6 liters of solution? Choose a strategy and solve. Show your work.

   E 15

   F 21

   G 12

   H 18

7. Macy was making a scrapbook. She needed an album that would hold 144 pictures. If she wanted 8 pictures on each page, how many pages would need to be in the album? Choose a strategy and solve. Show your work.

   A 18

   B 20

   C 14

   D 12

8. Danny paid $42 for a sweater and a pair of gloves. The sweater cost $18 more than the gloves. How much did the sweater cost? Choose a strategy and solve. Show your work.

   E $12

   F $24

   G $30

   H $34

Part 1 ✦ Solve a simpler problem/Draw a diagram

Think About It

Sometimes the numbers in a problem make the problem look large and difficult. Making the numbers in a problem smaller or easier can help you solve a problem. Drawing a diagram can help you visualize a problem and make it easier to understand.

Here's How

Solve a simpler problem.

The bookstore sold 685 books in November. They sold 1,023 books in December. How many more books did they sell in December?

Step 1 Use smaller numbers.

Replace 685 with 70.
Replace 1,023 with 100.

Step 2 Choose the operation.

$100 - 70 = $ _____   What operation will you use? _____

Step 3 Solve the original problem.

$1,023 - 685 = $ _____

Step 4 Check your computation.

$685 + $ _____ $= 1,023$

Draw a diagram.

Andrew, Chris, Jacob, and Eli are standing in line. Jacob is first and Chris is last. Andrew is in front of Chris. Eli is between Andrew and Jacob. In what order are they standing in line?

Step 1 Draw a diagram.

Back ←————+————+————+————+————→ Front

Step 2 Use the information in the problem to place the people into the appropriate places on the diagram.

Back ←——Chris——+————+————Jacob——→ Front

Step 3 Solve the problem.

1st in line—Jacob
2nd in line—_____
3rd in line—_____
4th in line—Chris

Practice

1. The concession stand sold 2,708 sodas, 1,895 hotdogs, and 987 candy bars. How many total items did they sell? Show your work.

   A 5,579
   B 5,590
   C 5,570
   D 5,600

2. Lori, Paige, Gabrielle, and Jennifer were the first four girls to finish the race. Lori finished after Gabrielle. Jennifer finished before Gabrielle but after Paige. In what order did they finish? Show your work.

   E Jennifer, Paige, Gabrielle, Lori
   F Paige, Gabrielle, Jennifer, Lori
   G Paige, Jennifer, Gabrielle, Lori
   H Lori, Gabrielle, Jennifer, Paige

3. On the bookshelf, the math books are to the left of the spelling books, and the spelling books are between the dictionaries and the math books. The dictionaries are between the spelling books and the reading books. What books are on the farthest left of the shelf? Show your work.

   A math books
   B spelling books
   C reading books
   D dictionaries

4. The high school football stadium can seat 8,500 people. Tickets cost $5.50. If the game sells out, how much money would the school make on ticket sales? Show you work.

   E $47,750
   F $45,000
   G $40,000
   H $46,750

5. Sam is taller then Jeff. Todd is shorter than Jeff. Aaron's height is between Todd's and Jeff's. What is the order of the boys by height from the shortest to the tallest? Show your work.

   A Todd, Aaron, Jeff, Sam
   B Aaron, Todd, Jeff, Sam
   C Todd, Aaron, Sam, Jeff
   D Sam, Jeff, Aaron, Todd

6. The school has 875 students. If they are grouped equally into 35 classrooms, how many students are in each classroom? Show your work.

   E 23 students
   F 35 students
   G 25 students
   H 30 students

Part 2 ✦ Guess and check/Working backwards

Think About It

Sometimes when you are solving a problem, you must first come up with a strategy. You can work backwards to solve some math problems. If you know the end and you know the steps in the middle, you can find the beginning by working backwards. When you use the guess and check strategy, you make a thoughtful guess, then check your guess to see if it is correct. If it's not correct, guess again!

Here's How

Work backwards.

Mrs. Zimmerman's class had a bake sale with cookies donated by a local bakery. They sold 68 cookies at lunch. They divided the rest of the cookies equally among the 14 students in the class. Each student received 3 cookies. How many cookies did the bakery donate?

Step Since each of the 14 students got 3 cookies, multiply to find out how many cookies the class received.

3 cookies × 14 children = _____ cookies given to the class

Step Since the class received 42 cookies, you will need to add that to the number of cookies sold. This will be the number of cookies the bakery donated.

42 cookies given to the class + 68 cookies sold = _____ cookies donated by the bakery

Use guess and check.

A small fruit bar costs $0.25 and a large fruit bar costs $0.60. Lauren spent $2.30 on fruit bars. How many of each fruit bar did she buy?

Step Make a guess. If it's not right, make a better guess.

Guess: 2 small fruit bars, 2 large fruit bars

Step Check your guess.

2 small = $0.50, 2 large = $1.20

$0.50 + $1.20 = _____ This guess is too low.

Step 3 Guess and check until you are correct.

2 small = $0.50, 3 large = _____

$0.50 + $1.80 = _____ This guess is correct.

Practice

1. Nick had $17 in his pockets. In one pocket, he had three more dollars than he had in the other pocket. How much money did he have in each pocket? Show your work.

A $14, $3

B $10, $7

C $12, $5

D $13, $4

2. Mrs. Smith was having a garage sale. She sold 9 pairs of shoes. She gave away 2 pairs to her sister, 3 pairs to her mother, and 1 pair to her neighbor. How many pairs of shoes did she start with? Show your work.

E 14

F 9

G 15

H 11

3. At the football game, Ashley spent $2.00 on a hotdog, $1.50 on a soda, and $2.50 on popcorn. She gave her father back $1.00 in change. How much money did she take to the concession stand? Show your work.

A $5.50

B $7.00

C $6.00

D $7.50

4. There are 54 fifth graders in the school. There are twice as many girls as boys. How many boys are in fifth grade? Show your work.

E 36

F 12

G 18

H 24

5. Big Mario's Pizza Palace sold 60 pizzas. They sold 12 more sausage pizzas than cheese pizzas. How many sausage pizzas did they sell? Show your work.

A 12

B 36

C 48

D 30

6. Ms. Curtis played a game with her class. She thought of two numbers and asked her class to guess the numbers. She told them the difference of the two numbers was 6 and the product of the two numbers was 40. What numbers was Miss Curtis thinking of? Show your work.

E 8, 5

F 12, 6

G 9, 3

H 10, 4

1. Jason has 3 quarters, 4 dimes, and 2 nickels. He wants to donate $1.00 to a school fund. Which coins could he use for the donation?

- **SHOW** each step of your math work.
- **EXPLAIN** why you solved the problem as you did.
- **WRITE** an explanation describing what you did and why you solved the problem as you did, **EVEN** if you used mental math or a calculator.
- **WRITE** your answer in the chart below.

School Fund

Number of coins	Type	Value
3	quarters	75¢
2	dimes	20¢
1	nickels	5¢

Explanation

Well I know 3 quarters is 75¢
and 2 dimes is 20¢ + 5¢ = 25
and 75¢ + 75¢ = $1.00.

0–5 Points

Score _____

2. You are in your school's library. You observe that each bookcase in the library has five shelves. The five shelves hold six books each. Determine how many books are held by one bookcase. Use an array, an addition sentence, and a multiplication sentence to describe how books are arranged in one bookcase.

- **SHOW** each step of your math work.
- **WRITE** an explanation describing what you did and why you solved the problem as you did, **EVEN** if you used mental math or a calculator.
- **WRITE** your answer in the space provided.

Array

Addition sentence _____

Multiplication sentence _____

Explanation

0–5 Points
Score _____

3. Each day, Charlotte, Kate, and Amanda practice playing their flutes. The table below shows how much time each girl spends playing her flute each day. Complete the table to show how many minutes each girl practices. Circle the name of the girl who practices the most.

- **READ** the problem and break it into parts to solve it.
- **SHOW** each step of your math work.
- **WRITE** your answer in the correct spaces in the table.
- **EXPLAIN** why you solved the problem as you did.
- **WRITE** an explanation describing what you did and why you solved the problem as you did, **EVEN** if you used mental math or a calculator.

Student	Min per day	Min in 7 days	Min in 30 days	Min in a year
Charlotte	33	231	6930	83760
Kate	38	266	7800	93600
Amanda	40	280	8400	100800

40
× 7
─────
780

38
× 7
─────
266

33
× 7
─────
231

280
× 30
─────
000
8400
─────
8400

260
38
─────
000
7500

amanda

231
30
─────
000
6930

8400
× 22
─────
16800
84000
─────
100800

Explanation

I Just × the min
it gave me × 7 and
the answer × by 30 and the answer
× by 12.

0–5 Points

Score _____

4. There are three jobs at the hot dog stand. One job is cooking (C), one is serving hot dogs (M), and one is running the cash register (R). Your co–workers are Suki and Keith. Each person can do one job at a time. Make a diagram to show all the possible combinations for filling the jobs. How many combinations are there?

- **REREAD** the problem carefully.
- **CREATE** a diagram to show the possible combinations.
- **WRITE** an explanation describing what you did and why you solved the problem as you did.
- **WRITE** your answer in the space provided.

Explanation

| Number of combinations_____ |

| 0–5 Points |
| Score _____ |

1. You purchased a pair of socks, giving the store clerk a $10 bill. The clerk gave you $5.86 back in change. How much did the socks cost?

   A $4.24

   B $4.14

   C $5.36

   D $5.14

2. Miss Brunk's class went on a photo tour of the zoo. Each group of four students had three rolls of 24–exposure film. If they each took the same number of pictures, how many pictures could each student take?

   E 24

   F 19

   G 16

   H 18

3. Susan's cat had kittens. She gave half of the kittens to Mina. Mina gave away 2 kittens and kept 2 for herself. How many kittens did Susan have at the start?

   A 8

   B 4

   C 12

   D 6

4. The product of two numbers is 56. The sum of the two numbers is 15. What are the two numbers?

   E 9, 6

   F 10, 5

   G 4, 11

   H 8, 7

5. Jane, Adam, Maria, and James are standing in line at the water fountain. Maria is standing between James and Adam. Jane is last in line. Adam is standing next to Maria, and Jane is standing next to James. Who will be the first to get a drink?

   A Jane

   B Adam

   C Maria

   D James

6. You have a baby-sitting job during the summer. You make $3.00 an hour and you babysit for 4 hours a day, Monday through Friday. If you work 8 weeks this summer, how much money will you make?

   E $360.00

   F $540.00

   G $480.00

   H $240.00

7. To make lemonade, you have to add 6 cups of water for every 2 scoops of lemonade mix. How many cups of water will you use for 10 scoops of lemonade?

   A 30

   B 24

   C 36

   D 12

8. Jared ate 640 calories for breakfast, 890 calories for lunch, and 1,272 calories for dinner. How many calories did he average for each meal?

   E 844

   F 934

   G 946

   H 856

9. Sharon planted spring flowers next to her house. The red flowers are to the right of the house. The yellow flowers are to the right of the red flowers and to the left of the white flowers. There are purple flowers to the right of the white flowers. Which flowers are the farthest from the house?

   A yellow flowers

   B red flowers

   C white flowers

   D purple flowers

10. Shelley bought 3 bags of chips. The low-fat chips cost $0.75 more than the regular potato chips. The potato chips cost $0.25 more than the corn chips. The corn chips cost $2.50. How much did the low-fat chips cost?

    E $2.75

    F $3.50

    G $3.25

    H $3.75

11. Lynn is on the school track team. She can run $\frac{1}{2}$ mile in 5 minutes. If she continues at this pace, how far could she run in 1 hour?

    A 6 miles

    B 12 miles

    C 8 miles

    D 5 miles

12. Louisa opened a checking account and a savings account. The total amount of money in both accounts is $168.00. She has twice as much money in her savings account as in her checking account. How much money does she have in her checking account?

    E $84.00

    F $73.00

    G $56.00

    H $48.00

13. Morgan spent $4\frac{3}{6}$ hours working on her science fair project on Thursday and $3\frac{2}{3}$ hours on Sunday. How much longer did she spend working on Thursday than on Sunday?

    A 1 hour

    B 1 hour 10 minutes

    C 50 minutes

    D 40 minutes

14. The florist delivered 216 roses to be placed on the tables for the reception. There are 9 tables. If the roses are divided equally among the tables, how many roses will be on each table?

    E 12

    F 24

    G 21

    H 18

15. Trent spent 4 hours drawing. If he spent $\frac{1}{2}$ hour on each drawing, how many drawings did he complete?

    A 8

    B 2

    C 4

    D 6

16. There are 36 students participating in the school play. Each costume takes 2 yards of material. The material cost $3.90 per yard. How much money should the school budget for the cost of the material?

    E $260.30

    F $282.90

    G $276.80

    H $280.80

Part 1 ✦ Organize and display data using pictures and tallies

 **Think About It**

Many times, it is easier to solve a problem by organizing the data. You can draw a picture or use tallies to organize and display data.

Here's How

Use pictures.

Micah has a bag of marbles. It contains 4 striped marbles, 2 black marbles, and 2 white marbles. What is the probability that Janet will choose a white marble when she reaches into the bag without looking?

1. Draw a picture. Show the striped marbles together, the black marbles together, and the white marbles together.

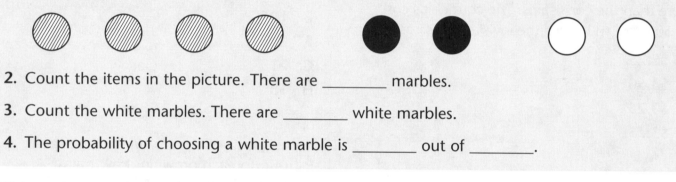

2. Count the items in the picture. There are _____ marbles.

3. Count the white marbles. There are _____ white marbles.

4. The probability of choosing a white marble is _____ out of _____.

Use a tally table.

A tally table allows you to record responses or data as it is collected. In a tally table, responses are recorded as vertical lines beside the choice they represent. However, each fifth response in a given category is recorded as a slash across the first four vertical lines. If another similar response is given, another vertical slash is made, and so on, until another group of five is reached. Since tallies are shown in groups of five, they are easy to count.

Diane asked each of the students in her class to identify their favorite snack. She recorded her results in the tally table below.

Snacks	Tally
Pretzels	ℍℍ ‖
Potato chips	ℍℍ ℍℍ
Cheese curls	‖‖
Ice cream	ℍℍ ℍℍ ‖‖‖‖
Cookies	ℍℍ ‖

1. How many people said their favorite snack was ice cream? _____

2. How many people said cheese curls were their favorite snack? _____

Practice

1. Amy has a box of shapes—4 squares, 3 circles, 2 triangles, and 3 rectangles. What is the probability she will pick a square if she reaches into the box without looking? Draw a picture to find the answer.

A 1 out of 4

B 3 out of 12

C 4 out of 12

D 4 out of 8

2. Skip took a survey at his school to find out what kind of music most people preferred. Twenty people preferred hip-hop, 12 preferred country, 5 preferred jazz, and 27 preferred rock. If Skip recorded his results in a tally table, which of the following shows how many people preferred country music?

E ͵Ht͵

F ||||||||||||

G ͵Ht͵ ͵Ht͵

H ͵Ht͵ ͵Ht͵ ||

3. Dale conducted a survey to find out the favorite lunch of students in his school. He recorded the data in a tally table. According to the table, how many more people preferred cheeseburgers than pizza?

Pizza	͵Ht͵ ͵Ht͵ ͵Ht͵	
Tuna	||||
Meatloaf	||
Cheeseburger	͵Ht͵ ͵Ht͵ ͵Ht͵ ||

A 1

B 2

C 15

D 12

4. Raul has a box of different shapes—5 squares, 2 circles, 4 triangles, and 6 rectangles. How many four-sided objects are in the box? Draw a picture to help find the answer.

E 5

F 6

G 9

H 11

5. Stefanie wants to use a tally table to record the number of people who said they liked different ice cream flavors. If 7 people said they liked vanilla and 9 said they liked chocolate, which shows how Stefanie should record these responses in a tally table?

A vanilla 7; chocolate 9

B vanilla ͵Ht͵ ||; chocolate ͵Ht͵ ||||

C vanilla |||||||; chocolate |||||||||

D vanilla ͵Ht͵ ||||; chocolate ͵Ht͵ ||

6. Greg drew 3 triangles, 4 squares, and 2 rectangles on a piece of paper. What is the total number of sides of the objects he drew? Make a drawing to help find the answer.

E 9

F 24

G 33

H 36

Part 2 ♦ Organize and display data using tables and graphs

Think About It

Mr. Fontaine's fifth-grade class gathered data on basketball. They surveyed 4 students in the class to find out how many games of basketball each student played during the past month. How can the class organize this data?

Mario	ЖЖ ЖЖ ЖЖ
Nora	ЖЖ ЖЖ ЖЖ ЖЖ
Phillip	ЖЖ
Samantha	ЖЖ ЖЖ

Here's How

Make a table.

Step 1 Write a title for the table telling what the table is about.

_____

Step 2 Determine how many cells, or boxes of information are needed for the table and draw the table in the space below.

Step 3 Label each cell telling what information will be in the column.

Step 4 Fill in the table with the tallied data.

Make a circle or a bar graph.

Fill in the missing information in the circle graph.   Shade in the number of games in the bar graph.

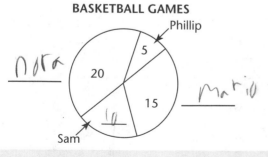

BASKETBALL GAMES

nora   Phillip 5   20   Mario   15   Sam   10

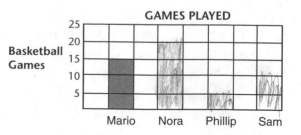

GAMES PLAYED

Basketball Games — 25, 20, 15, 10, 5 — Mario Nora Phillip Sam

Make a pictograph.

A pictograph uses pictures to represent data. Look at the pictograph on the right showing how many games of basketball each student in Mr. Fontaine's class played.

NUMBER OF GAMES PLAYED			
Mario	🏀	🏀	🏀
Nora	🏀	🏀	🏀 🏀
Phillip	🏀		
Sam	🏀	🏀	
Each 🏀 stands for 5 games.			

Practice

Use the table below to answer Problems 1–2.

Money Earned at Home Each Week by the Students Of Mr. Poe's Class

Amount Earned	Number of Students
$2.00	4
$5.00	10
$8.00	5
$10.00	3

1. According to the table above, how many students earned $10.00 per week?

   A 3
   B 4
   C 5
   D 10

2. What was the amount earned by the greatest number of students?

   E $2.00
   F $5.00
   G $8.00
   H $10.00

3. In a class poll about ice cream, 6 students liked vanilla, 8 said chocolate, 7 said strawberry, and 3 said pistachio. Which of the following tallies correctly shows how many students preferred vanilla?

   A III
   B ℍℍ III
   C IIIIII
   D ℍℍ I

4. Jeremy made this pictograph to show how many books the students in his class read over a four-year period. If the students read a total of 60 books in 1997, how many books does each symbol in Jeremy's graph equal?

   E 5
   F 7
   G 10
   H 12

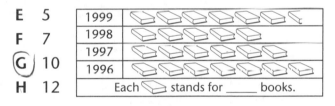

5. Which of the following bar graphs correctly shows that the boys collected 250 cans and the girls collected 300?

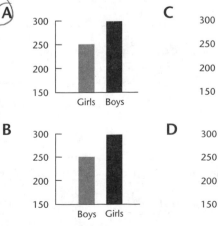

6. Chip made this line graph to show how many pizzas his class sold over a four-year period. During which year did students sell the fewest number of pizzas?

   E 1996
   F 1997
   G 1998
   H 1999

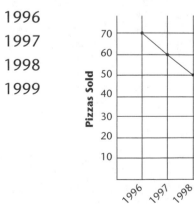

Ready Reference

mean the sum of the set of numbers divided by *n*, the number of numbers in the set

median the number that lies in the middle when a set of numbers is arranged in order. If there are two middle values, the median is the mean of these values

mode the number(s) that occurs most often in a set of numbers; *example:* in the set 1, 2, 3, 3, 5, 8; the mode is 3. There may be one mode, more than one mode, or no mode

range the difference between the greatest number and the least number in a set of data

Think About It

Students in Tim's class got the following scores on their tests: 79, 82, 78, 84, 89, and 91. Tim wants to calculate the mean score for the test. He also wants to calculate the range, median, and mode of the scores. How can Tim determine this information?

Here's How

Find the mean.

1. Add the numbers of the test scores. $79 + 82 + 78 + 85 + 89 + 91 =$ _____

2. Divide the sum by the number of addends (number of test scores). _____ $\div 6 =$ _____

   What is the mean test score? _____

Find the range.

1. What is the greatest, or highest, test score? 91

2. What is the smallest, or lowest, test score? 78

3. Find the difference between the highest test score and the lowest test score. The difference is the range.

$$\begin{array}{r} 91 \\ -78 \end{array}$$ ← highest score ← lowest score ← range

Find the mode.

1. Look at the test scores of Tim's classmates: 79, 82, 78, 84, 89, and 91. Is there a mode? Explain.

   no mode

2. What is the mode for this group of scores? Explain.   79, 83, 83, 85, 89, 92

Find the median.

1. What is the median test score from these test scores?   79, 82, 78, 84, 89, 91

   There are two numbers in the middle of this group of numbers. 82 and _____

2. The median is the mean of these two numbers. The mean is $(82 + 84) \div 2 =$ _____

Practice

Use this graph to answer Problems 1–2.

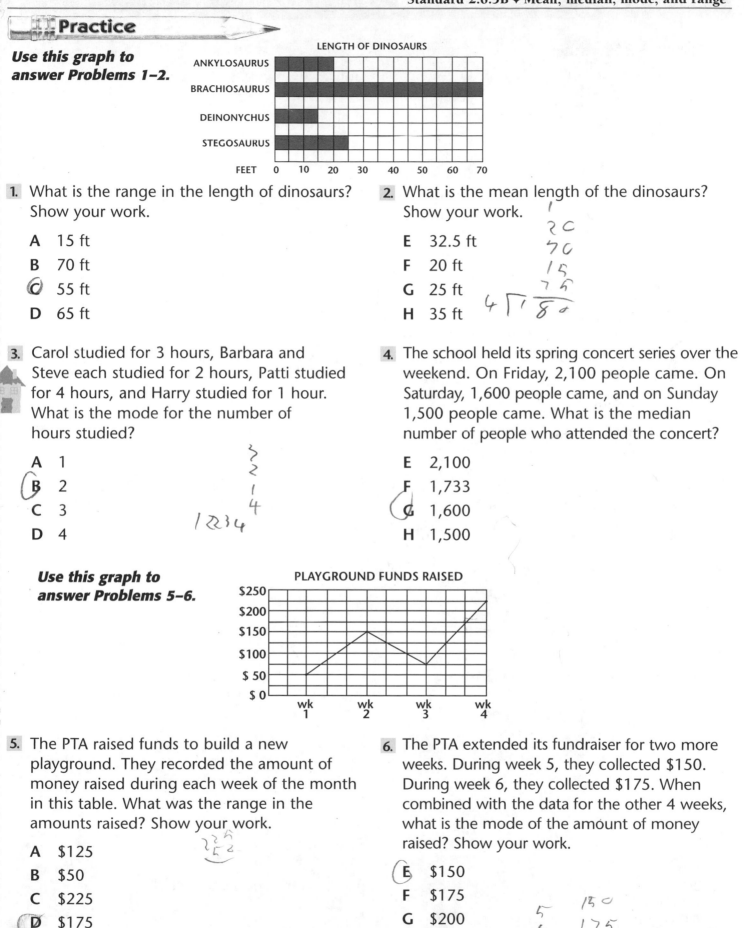

LENGTH OF DINOSAURS

ANKYLOSAURUS
BRACHIOSAURUS
DEINONYCHUS
STEGOSAURUS

FEET 0 10 20 30 40 50 60 70

1. What is the range in the length of dinosaurs? Show your work.

   A   15 ft
   B   70 ft
   C   55 ft
   D   65 ft

2. What is the mean length of the dinosaurs? Show your work.

   E   32.5 ft
   F   20 ft
   G   25 ft
   H   35 ft

3. Carol studied for 3 hours, Barbara and Steve each studied for 2 hours, Patti studied for 4 hours, and Harry studied for 1 hour. What is the mode for the number of hours studied?

   A   1
   B   2
   C   3
   D   4

4. The school held its spring concert series over the weekend. On Friday, 2,100 people came. On Saturday, 1,600 people came, and on Sunday 1,500 people came. What is the median number of people who attended the concert?

   E   2,100
   F   1,733
   G   1,600
   H   1,500

Use this graph to answer Problems 5–6.

PLAYGROUND FUNDS RAISED

$250
$200
$150
$100
$ 50
$ 0
       wk   wk   wk   wk
       1   2   3   4

5. The PTA raised funds to build a new playground. They recorded the amount of money raised during each week of the month in this table. What was the range in the amounts raised? Show your work.

   A $125
   B $50
   C $225
   D $175

6. The PTA extended its fundraiser for two more weeks. During week 5, they collected $150. During week 6, they collected $175. When combined with the data for the other 4 weeks, what is the mode of the amount of money raised? Show your work.

   E $150
   F $175
   G $200
   H $50

Ready Reference

Venn diagram a display that pictures unions and intersections of sets

Think About It

Jim has a pet cat and a pet bird. He wanted to find out how many of his friends from school also had pet cats or birds so he took a survey. Jim discovered that like him, his friend Jan also had both a cat and a bird. His friends Paul, Ben, and Pamela had only birds as pets. Sue, Tim, Kareem, and Julio all had cats. Tim's teacher suggested that he use a Venn diagram to show the results of his survey.

Here's How

1. A Venn diagram is a drawing that allows you to show relationships among sets of data. Before you can make a Venn diagram, you need to decide how many sets of data you have and how the data are related.

2. Tim has three sets of data: Bird Owners, Cat Owners, and _____. This data can be shown using two overlapping circles like the ones shown below.

3. Notice that the names of the people who own birds are written in the circle on the left. The names of the people who own cats are listed in the circle on the right. Look at the space created where the circles overlap. This space includes the names of the people who own BOTH birds and cats.

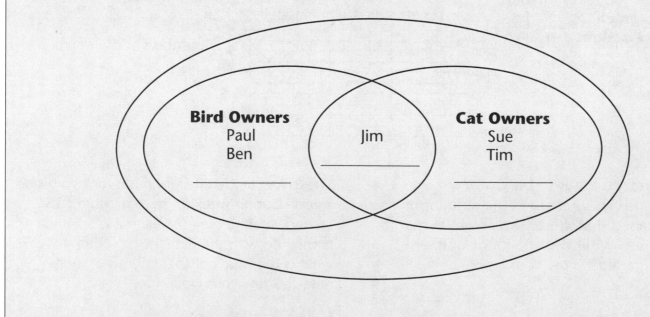

Bird Owners
Paul
Ben
_____

Jim
_____

Cat Owners
Sue
Tim
_____
_____

4. Complete the diagram by filling in the missing names in the spaces provided.

5. Write a title for the overlapping circle. _____

Practice

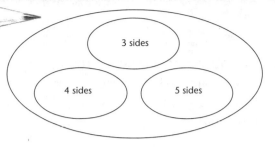

1. The Venn diagram above shows the relationship among different types of polygons. Where in the diagram would you place a right triangle?

   A   only in the large outer oval

   B   in the oval labeled 3 sides

   C   in the oval labeled 4 sides

   D   in the oval labeled 5 sides

2. If you were completing the Venn diagram above, where would you include a rectangle?

   E   only in the large outer oval

   F   in the oval labeled 3 sides

   G   in the oval labeled 4 sides

   H   in the oval labeled 5 sides

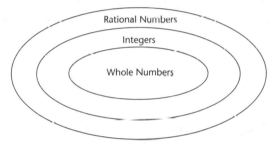

3. In which sets shown in the Venn diagram above does the number 13 belong?

   A   only in the set of rational numbers

   B   only in the set of integers

   C   in the integers and whole numbers sets

   D   in the whole numbers, integers, and rational numbers sets

4. In which sets in the Venn diagram above would you place the number 1.25?

   E   only in the set of rational numbers

   F   only in the set of integers

   G   in the integers and whole numbers sets

   H   in the rational numbers and whole numbers sets

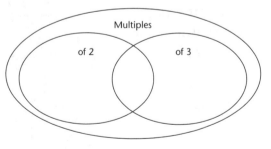

5. Where in the Venn diagram above would the number 30 appear?

   A   only in the Multiples oval

   B   in the oval labeled "of 2"

   C   in the oval labeled "of 3"

   D   in the place where the smaller ovals overlap

6. Where in the diagram above would you write the number 14?

   E   only in the Multiples oval

   F   in the oval labeled "of 2"

   G   in the oval labeled "of 3"

   H   in the place where the smaller ovals overlap

Think About It

Predictions are statements about what might happen. Predictions can be made from known information called data. Data can be collected from newspapers, magazines, and surveys known as polls. Mrs. Wright asked Julie to predict what game the class will choose to play during recess. What data does Julie need to collect? How can she gather this information?

Here's How

Decide what data is needed.

1. To make a reasonable prediction, Julie needs to find the favorite _____ of the class.

Decide how to collect the data.

2. Julie decides to take a poll of the class. In her poll, she asks each student to name his or her favorite game. Julie makes a chart similar to the one below to list the games each student names.

Baseball	Soccer	Basketball
⊬⊬⊬/	⊬⊬⊬ ⊬⊬⊬	///

3. According to the chart, which game do most of the students like best? _____

4. Julie predicts that the class will choose to play _____ during recess.

Practice

1. Roberto's local newspaper published the data shown about the current baseball season. Which team do you predict will win first place?

   A   Diamond Backs

   B   Aces

   C   Clubs

   D   Diamond Backs and Aces will tie

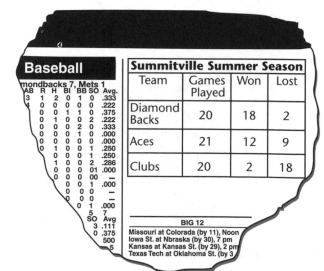

2. A magazine article reports that the sales of tennis shoes have increased every year for the past ten years. During the same period, sales of boots decreased each year. Based on this data, what do you predict will happen to the sales of tennis shoes this year?

E More boots will be sold than tennis shoes.

F Sales of tennis shows will be lower than last year.

G Sales of tennis shoes will be higher than last year.

H Sales of tennis shoes will be less than sales of boots.

3. Maya's newspaper reports that 3 out of 5 babies born in her town are boys. Her new brother or sister will be born next month. Based on this report, which of the following predictions is MOST reasonable?

A She will have a new brother.

B She will have a new sister.

C Her mother will have twins.

D She has a one in five chance of having a baby sister.

4. A newspaper published information about last year's community events. The results are shown in the table to the right. Based on this data, which month do you predict will be busiest this year?

E March

F April

G June or July

H December

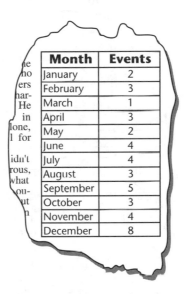

Month	Events
January	2
February	3
March	1
April	3
May	2
June	4
July	4
August	3
September	5
October	3
November	4
December	8

5. Bo asked each family in his apartment building to name their favorite desert. He put the data into the chart shown below.

Pie	Cake	Cookies	Pudding
ℍℍℍ ///	ℍℍℍ ℍℍℍ ℍℍℍ ℍℍℍ	ℍℍℍ /	ℍℍℍ

A new family moved into Bo's building. Bo predicts that their favorite desert is

A pie

B cake

C cookies

D pudding

6. Sarina is trying to solve a puzzle in a magazine. The magazine shows the following pattern.

Sarina must identify what the next pattern in the sequence will be. Which of the following should she choose?

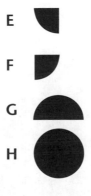

E

F

G

H

Think About It

Graphs and charts can help you make predictions and draw conclusions. Thinking about the information in graphs can help you understand the data and draw conclusions about other things that might happen.

Here's How

1. Look at the information in the graph. According to the information, who won the greatest number of races? _____

2. Who won the least number of races? _____

3. Who do you predict will win the next race? Why?

_____

_____

_____

4. Who do you predict will come in second in the next race? Why? _____

_____

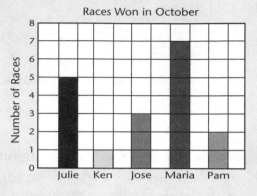

Practice

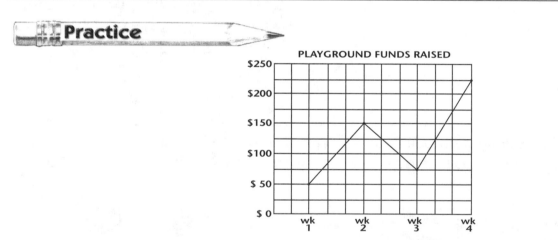

1. Look at the line graph above. Use the graph to determine the total amount of money that was raised by the end of Week 4.

    A $75

    B $150

    C $300

    D $500

2. Based on the trend shown in the graph above, how many more weeks will the school need to continue to raise money if they wish to buy a piece of equipment that costs $550.00?

    E   1 week

    F   2 weeks

    G   3 weeks

    H   4 weeks

Rainfall During Vacation

Day	Rainfall in Millimeters
Monday	8
Tuesday	6
Wednesday	0
Thursday	4
Friday	10

3. According to the chart above, during which three days of vacation did the least amount of rain fall?

A Monday, Tuesday, Wednesday

B Tuesday, Wednesday, Thursday

C Wednesday, Thursday, Friday

D Monday, Thursday, Friday

4. According to the chart, what was the total amount of rainfall between Wednesday and Friday?

E 6 mm

F 10 mm

G 14 mm

H 20 mm

Science Fair Attendance

Thurs	🚶 🚶 🚶
Fri	🚶 🚶 🚶 🚶
Sat	🚶 🚶 🚶 🚶 🚶 🚶
Each 🚶 stands for 20 people.	

5. According to the pictograph above, how many people attended the science fair on Thursday?

A 3

B 30

C 20

D 60

6. The science fair attendance has been the same for the past two years. What day next year do you think the most people will attend the fair?

E Thursday

F Friday

G Saturday

H Sunday

HOW SCOTT SPENDS HIS ALLOWANCE

7. Scott made the pie graph above to show how he spends his allowance. According to Scott's graph, what does he spend most of his money on?

A movies

B books

C sports

D clothes

8. If the graph shows all of Scott's earnings for a one-month period, what percentage of his earnings does Scott spend on movies?

E 10.5%

F 15.7%

G 26.3%

H 2%

1. Yesterday it rained heavily in several cities throughout Pennsylvania. It rained 8 inches in Philadelphia, 3 inches in Harrisburg, 15 inches in Pittsburgh, and $2\frac{1}{2}$ inches in Erie. Organize the data in a chart, and in a bar graph. Draw the chart in the space below. Then answer the questions.

- **REREAD** the problem carefully.
- **ORGANIZE** the data in a chart and use the grid provided to make a bar graph.
- Be sure to **LABEL** your chart and graph appropriately.
- Then, **ANSWER** the questions. Explain your answers.
- **WRITE** your answers in the spaces provided.

A. What is the total amount of rainfall that fell in these four cities? _____

Was this information easier to determine from the graph or the chart? Why? _____

_____

_____

B. Which city had the most rainfall? _____ The least? _____

Is this information easier to determine from the chart or the graph? Explain.

_____

_____

_____

C. Which is more helpful to you—the chart or the bar graph? Why? _____

_____

_____

_____

0–5 Points
Score _____

2. Terri conducted a survey at her school to find out what kinds of sandwiches students liked best for their lunch. She surveyed a total of 100 people. Seventeen people said they liked peanut butter and jelly best. Forty-four people liked turkey, but thirty-two preferred ham and cheese. Two students said liverwurst was their favorite sandwich. Five students said their favorite was a cheese sandwich. Determine what percentage of students preferred each kind of sandwich. Then, show your results in a circle graph.

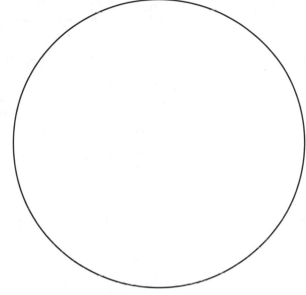

- **REREAD** the problem carefully.
- **SHOW** each step of your math work.
- **ORGANIZE** the data as a circle graph.
- Be sure to **LABEL** your graph appropriately.
- **WRITE** your answers in the spaces provided.
- **WRITE** an explanation describing what you did.

Explanation

0–5 Points
Score _____

3. The table below shows the high temperatures in Valley Forge during one week in April. Study the data in the table. Then find the range and mean for the data provided. Express the mean to the nearest hundredth.

Day	Sunday	Monday	Tuesday	Wednesday	Thursday	Friday	Saturday
Temperature	55°	62°	73°	85°	65°	91°	78°

- **REREAD** the problem carefully. **IDENTIFY** any information that is needed to solve the problem.
- **SHOW** each step of your math work.
- **WRITE** an explanation describing what you did and why you solved the problem as you did, **EVEN** if you used mental math or a calculator.
- **WRITE** your answers in the spaces provided.

mean = 74 r1

range 17

Explanation

I get the mend by adding the tempeatures to gether and I got 519 the ÷ by 7. to get the rang 7 — the lesso a forgoitems a subtract

Range __36__   Mean __7̶8̶v̶5̶__

0–5 Points

Score _____

4. Review the information you know about polygons. Then develop a Venn diagram that arranges 3-sided, 4-sided, and 5-sided polygons (triangles, squares, rectangles, and pentagons) according to the number of sides. Label each section of your Venn diagram.

- **REREAD** the problem carefully. **IDENTIFY** any information that is needed to solve the problem.
- **DRAW** a Venn diagram to show how the polygons are related and how they are different.
- **LABEL** your drawing clearly.
- **WRITE** an explanation describing what you did and why you solved the problem as you did, **EVEN** if you used mental math or a calculator.

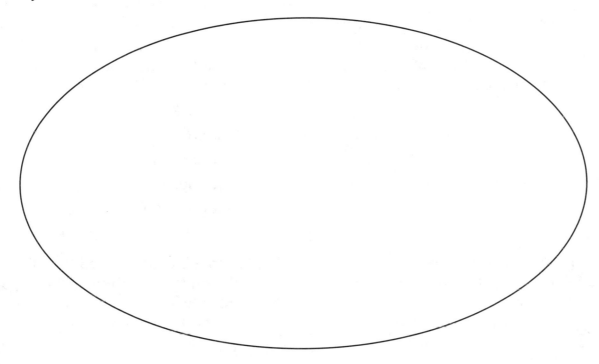

Explanation

0–5 Points
Score _____

1. According to the graph below, in which year did the fifth grade class have the most race winners?

   A 1994

   B 1995

   C 1997

   D 2000

   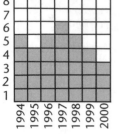

2. Sam's class recorded the temperature each day from Monday through Friday. The temperatures were 28°, 36°, 35°, 26°, and 30°. What was the mean temperature for the week?

   E 10°

   F 31°

   G 30°

   H 32°

3. Krista received test scores of 56, 99, 98, 84, 86, and 87 on her Spanish quizzes. What is her median test score?

   A 86.5

   B 42

   C 76.6

   D 56

4. There are 4 red marbles, 2 purple marbles, and 3 blue marbles in a bag. What is the probability that you will pick a red marble from the bag without looking?

   E 4 out of 4

   F 1 out of 9

   G 4 out of 9

   H 9 out of 10

5. A poll shows that 8 students prefer brownies, 3 prefer pie, 4 prefer cake, and 15 prefer ice cream. What do you predict a student will order for dessert?

   A pie

   B cake

   C brownies

   D ice cream

6. In a survey, 7 people said they liked hot dogs best. If Jamal records this data in a tally table, how should he show these results?

   E hot dogs 7

   F hot dogs IIIIIII

   G hot dogs seven

   H hot dogs ℍℍ II

7. Mr. Tahoe's class received the following grades on their math tests: 89, 89, 90, 45, 72, 89, 78, 78, and 97. What is the mode for these math scores?

   A 89

   B 52

   C 80.7

   D 78

8. The graph below shows how fast different animals can run. According to the graph, what is the total range in the speeds of the animals?

   E 30

   F 40

   G 42.5

   H 170

   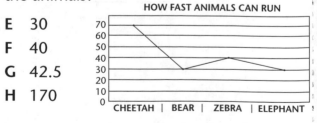

   HOW FAST ANIMALS CAN RUN

9. Review the graph in Problem 8. What is the total combined speed of all the animals shown?

- **A** 30
- **B** 40
- **C** 42.5
- **D** 170

10. What is the mean speed of the animals shown in the graph in Problem 8?

- **E** 10
- **F** 40
- **G** 42.5
- **H** 190

11. The table below shows Jim's test scores in spelling for the week. What is Jim's median score?

- **A** 10
- **B** 80
- **C** 85
- **D** 90

Day	Test Score
Monday	85
Wednesday	80
Friday	90

12. The number of hours of television watched by the students in Mrs. Rizzo's class is shown in the tally table below. What is the mean number of hours spent watching TV during one week by Mrs. Rizzo's students?

- **E** 2
- **F** 16
- **G** 19
- **H** 24

Hours	Number of Students
7							
10					
19											
20									
24			

13. Sabrina drew a Venn diagram to show how the sets of rational numbers, integers, and whole numbers are related. In which group or groups in the diagram would Sabrina include −3?

- **A** only rational numbers
- **B** only whole numbers
- **C** only integers
- **D** in both integers and rational numbers

14. The pictograph below shows how many apples were picked by three friends in a single outing. Which shows the range of apples picked?

- **E** 20 apples
- **F** 40 apples
- **G** 2 apples
- **H** 9 apples

Apples picked on Saturday	
Angela	🍎🍎🍎
Barry	🍎🍎🍎🍎
Juan	🍎🍎
Each 🍎 stands for 20 apples	

15. In the pictograph above, what is the mean for the apples picked on Saturday?

- **A** 60 apples
- **B** 50 apples
- **C** 40 apples
- **D** 35 apples

16. Twenty-five students collected cans for the local recycling center. They received $0.05 for each can. If they received $17.50, what is the mean number of cans collected by each student?

- **E** 12
- **F** 13
- **G** 14
- **H** 15

Think About It

Julie's mother prepared a basket of fruit to take on a picnic. The basket contains 1 pear, 2 apples, 1 orange, 1 banana, 1 grapefruit, and 1 tangerine. If Julie picks a fruit without looking, is it more probable that she will pick an apple or a tangerine? What are the possible outcomes when Julie reaches into the basket of fruit?

$\frac{2}{7}$ $\frac{1}{7}$

Here's How

1. If you toss a fair coin, what are the two possible outcomes of how it will land? _____ H or F _____

2. If you toss the coin five times and it lands with "heads" up all five times, what will likely be the outcome on the next toss? _____ 50/50 H or T _____

3. The outcome will still have an equal chance of landing either "heads" up or "tails" up.

Practice

Use the picture of the cube to answer Problems 1–4. The sides of the cube are labeled A, B, C, D, E, and F.

1. How many outcomes are possible if the cube is rolled one time?

   A 5

   B 1

   C 6

   D 12

2. Which of the following would NOT be a possible outcome using this cube?

   E E

   F D

   G J

   H B

3. If you rolled the cube 6 times and it landed with side A up every time, which side would land up on the next turn?

   A A

   B E

   C D

   D Each of the six sides has an equal chance of landing up.

4. If two sides of the cube were labeled with the same letter, how would that change the probable outcome?

   E The letter on the two sides would never come up.

   F The letter on two sides would come up more often.

   G The other letters would come up more often.

   H There would be no change.

     Measuring Up to the PA Academic Standards • Mathematics

Use the following information to answer Problems 5–6.

A box contains a slip of paper for each month of the year. Six students are drawing a slip from the box and then replacing it.

5. How many different outcomes are possible?

   A 6

   Ⓑ 12

   C 24

   D 3

6. Which month of the year is the first student most likely to choose?

   E January

   F December

   Ⓖ Each month has an equal chance of being chosen.

   H July

Use the following information and chart to answer Problems 7–10.

Matt and Ross are playing a board game. They made a chart showing all the possible outcomes for each roll of the dice.

Die #1	Die #2	Outcomes				
1	1	2	3	4	5	6
2	1	2	3	4	5	6
3	1	2	3	4	5	6
4	1	2	3	4	5	6
5	1	2	3	4	5	6
6	1	2	3	4	5	6

7. How many combinations are possible each time they roll the dice?

   Ⓐ 36

   B 42

   C 6

   D 72

8. What are Matt's chances of rolling double 6s as compared with rolling double 1s?

   E There is no chance of rolling doubles.

   F There is a greater chance of rolling double sixes.

   Ⓖ There is an equal chance of rolling either one.

   H There is a greater chance of rolling double ones.

9. If Ross rolled a 1–1 on his first roll, what would he most likely roll on his second turn?

   A 2–2

   B Any combination on the chart

   C 5–6

   D 1–1

10. Which of the following is NOT a possible combination on a roll of the dice?

   E 1–3

   F 6–4

   G 2–1

   Ⓗ 6–10

Think About It

Haley and Justin are playing a game in which they use a spinner to determine how many spaces they can move. Will the game be fair or unfair if they both use Spinner A? Will the game be fair if Haley uses Spinner A and Justin uses Spinner B? Does fair mean that each player will get equal results?

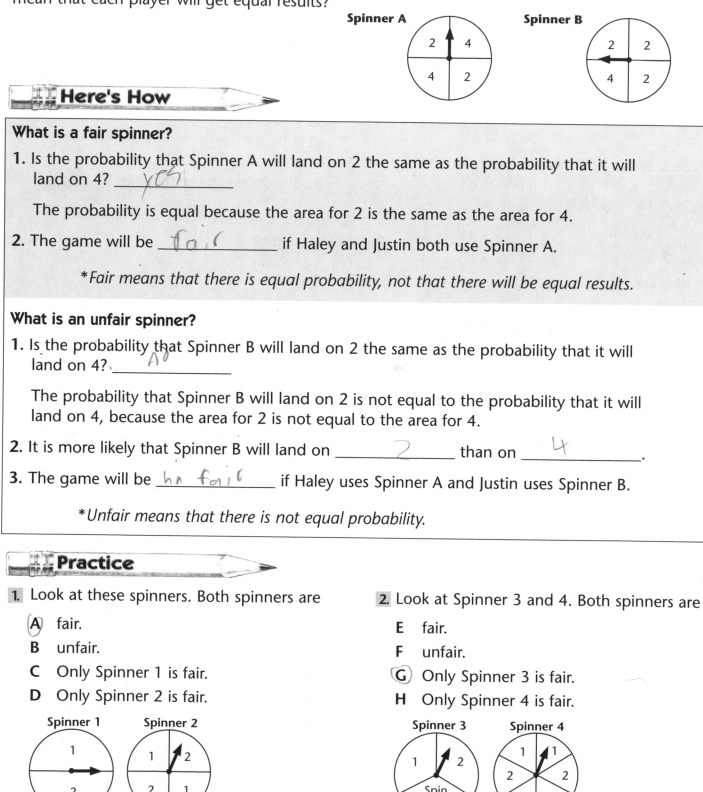

Spinner A

Spinner B

Here's How

What is a fair spinner?

1. Is the probability that Spinner A will land on 2 the same as the probability that it will land on 4? _____yes_____

   The probability is equal because the area for 2 is the same as the area for 4.

2. The game will be _____fair_____ if Haley and Justin both use Spinner A.

   Fair means that there is equal probability, not that there will be equal results.

What is an unfair spinner?

1. Is the probability that Spinner B will land on 2 the same as the probability that it will land on 4? _____No_____

   The probability that Spinner B will land on 2 is not equal to the probability that it will land on 4, because the area for 2 is not equal to the area for 4.

2. It is more likely that Spinner B will land on _____2_____ than on _____4_____.

3. The game will be ___be fair___ if Haley uses Spinner A and Justin uses Spinner B.

   Unfair means that there is not equal probability.

Practice

1. Look at these spinners. Both spinners are

   (A) fair.

   B unfair.

   C Only Spinner 1 is fair.

   D Only Spinner 2 is fair.

   Spinner 1   **Spinner 2**

2. Look at Spinner 3 and 4. Both spinners are

   E fair.

   F unfair.

   (G) Only Spinner 3 is fair.

   H Only Spinner 4 is fair.

   Spinner 3   **Spinner 4**

3. Look at Spinner 5 and 6. Both spinners are

   A   fair.

   B   unfair.

   C   Only Spinner 5 is fair.

   D   Only Spinner 6 is fair.

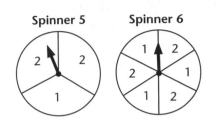

4. Look at Spinner 7 and 8. Both spinners are

   E   fair

   F   unfair.

   G   Only Spinner 7 is fair.

   H   Only Spinner 8 is fair.

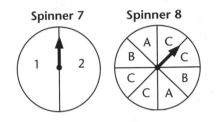

Use this spinner to answer Problems 5–8.

5. What animal should go in the empty space for the spinner to be fair?

   A   horse

   B   rhinoceros

   C   cat

   D   dog

6. If a dog is placed in the blank space, how many outcomes are possible if you spin the spinner one time?

   E   3

   F   6

   G   8

   H   5

7. If the empty section pictured a cat, then a spin would land most often on which animal?

   A   dog

   B   cat

   C   horse

   D   rhinoceros

8. If the empty section is left blank, then a spin would land the least number of times on which section?

   E   dog

   F   cat

   G   horse

   H   empty section

Ready Reference

probability a number from 0 to 1 that indicates how likely something is to happen

0 = Impossible. The result cannot occur.   1 = Certain. The result must occur.

Think About It

At a school picnic, 5 kinds of lunches are being served. They are hot dogs, baked turkey, cold cuts, tuna salad, and chicken salad. You have an equal chance of getting any of the lunches. Your favorite food is chicken salad. What is the probability that you will get chicken salad for lunch? How do you express a probability as a fraction and a decimal?

Here's How

Step 1 Count the number of possible outcomes.

   1. How many kinds of lunches are being served? _____5_____

Step 2 Find out how many chances you have of getting the outcome you want.

   2. How many of the lunches are chicken salad? _____1_____

   3. How many of the lunches contain something other than chicken salad? _____4_____

Step 3 Write the probability as a fraction. Use *P* to stand for probability.

   4. $P = \dfrac{\text{the number of lunches with chicken salad}}{\text{the number of different lunches being served}}$

   5. The probability of getting chicken salad for lunch is 1 in _____5_____ chances, or $\frac{1}{5}$ or 20%.

   $P = \frac{1}{5} = 20\%$

   Remember that $P = \dfrac{\text{number of favorable outcomes}}{\text{number of possible outcomes}}$

   6. What is the probability of getting a hamburger? $P = \frac{0}{5} = 0$ It is impossible.

Practice

1. You must choose one of these circles from a box without looking.

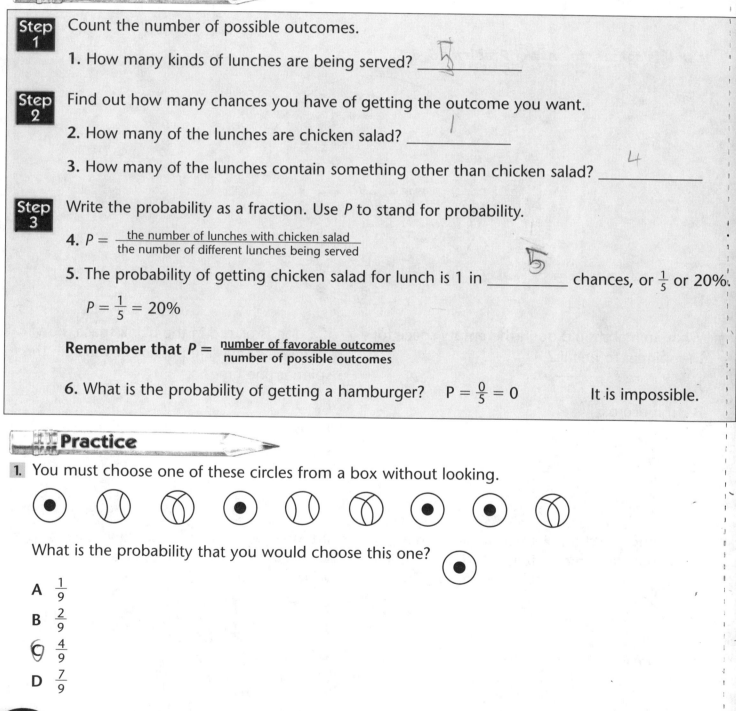

What is the probability that you would choose this one?

A $\frac{1}{9}$

B $\frac{2}{9}$

C $\frac{4}{9}$

D $\frac{7}{9}$

2. A box of 15 pencils contains 4 red pencils, 3 blue pencils, 5 green pencils, and 3 purple pencils. You can have 1 pencil. What is the probability that you will choose a blue pencil? Show your work.

E $\frac{1}{3}$

F $\frac{4}{15}$

G $\frac{1}{5}$

H $\frac{3}{5}$

3. There were 30 tickets purchased for a drawing at school. Of these, Marta bought 3 and Brent bought 7. What is the probability that either Marta or Brent will win the prize? Show your work.

A $\frac{3}{30}$

B $\frac{10}{30}$

C $\frac{3}{7}$

D $\frac{7}{30}$

4. A bag contains 2 red marbles, 3 green marbles, and 4 blue marbles. What is the probability you will pick red?

E $\frac{2}{3}$

F $\frac{5}{9}$

G $\frac{2}{9}$

H $\frac{2}{4}$

5. A bag contains 2 red marbles, 3 green marbles, and 4 blue marbles. What is the probability you will pick blue?

A $\frac{4}{9}$

B $\frac{6}{9}$

C $\frac{4}{5}$

D $\frac{4}{4}$

Use the spinner to answer Problems 6–9.

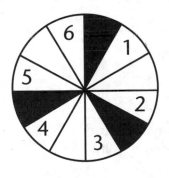

6. What is the probability of getting a number?

E $\frac{1}{6}$

F $\frac{6}{12}$

G $\frac{2}{3}$

H $\frac{1}{12}$

7. What is the probability of getting a black space?

A $\frac{6}{12}$

B $\frac{3}{6}$

C $\frac{3}{12}$

D $\frac{1}{3}$

8. What is the probability of getting the number 4?

E $\frac{1}{6}$

F $\frac{2}{6}$

G $\frac{1}{12}$

H $\frac{2}{12}$

9. The first time you spin the spinner you land on 2. What is the probability that you will land on 2 on your next spin?

A $\frac{0}{12}$

B $\frac{1}{12}$

C $\frac{2}{12}$

D $\frac{1}{6}$

Think About It

You do not know what the outcome will be when you spin a spinner, roll a number cube, or pick something out of a group of items without looking. You can predict the probability of getting a particular outcome and the result. If you spin the spinner, can you predict where it will land?

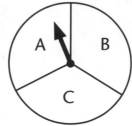

Here's How

Suppose Chris decided to spin the spinner shown above 60 times. Then she recorded her results on this chart:

Outcome	A	B	C
Total	19	24	17

1. Since the three outcomes (A, B, and C) have the same chance of occurring, the theoretical probability of spinning an A is $\frac{1}{3}$ or $P(A) = \frac{1}{3}$.

2. Based on the experiment, the experimental probability of spinning A is $\frac{19}{60}$ or $P(A) = \frac{19}{60}$

3. In this experiment, Chris found that although the theoretical probability is $\frac{1}{3}$, the spinner was more likely to land on _____.

Practice

Use the following information to answer Problems 1–2.

Alisha's favorite board game uses a color cube. Players toss the cube. The player whose color shows on top gets the next turn. One side is red, one is blue, one is yellow, two are orange, and one is purple.

1. The theoretical probability of the cube showing blue is

   A $\frac{6}{1}$

   B $\frac{1}{6}$

   C $\frac{3}{6}$

   D $\frac{1}{3}$

2. The theoretical probability of the cube showing orange is

   E $\frac{4}{6}$

   F $\frac{1}{6}$

   G $\frac{2}{3}$

   H $\frac{2}{6}$

Use the following information to answer Problems 3–6.

Alisha used the same cube to do an experiment and kept track of which colors appeared on top. The results are shown in this chart.

Red	Blue	Yellow	Orange	Purple
16	12	18	27	17

3. According to the chart, the experimental probability of the cube landing on yellow is

A $\frac{1}{6}$

B $\frac{18}{90}$

C $\frac{20}{100}$ or .20

D $\frac{3}{6}$

4. The experimental probability of the cube landing on orange is

E $\frac{2}{6}$

F $\frac{30}{100}$ or .30

G $\frac{17}{90}$

H $\frac{27}{90}$

5. According to the theoretical probability, how many times should it have landed on yellow?

A 25

B 18

C 15

D 12

6. According to the theoretical probability, how many times should it have landed on orange?

E 27

F 30

G 15

H 50

Use the following information to answer Problems 7–10.

Malik prepared a bag with 15 slips of paper numbered 1–15. Each slip had a different number.

7. If you take a slip of paper out of the bag without looking, what is the probability of choosing a number that matches your age?

A $\frac{1}{9}$

B $\frac{1}{10}$

C $\frac{1}{15}$

D $\frac{1}{2}$

8. If you take a slip of paper out of the bag without looking, what is the probability of choosing an odd number?

E $\frac{8}{15}$

F $\frac{7}{15}$

G $\frac{3}{15}$

H $\frac{1}{15}$

9. If you take a slip of paper out of the bag without looking, what is the probability of choosing a number that is less than 8?

A $\frac{8}{15}$

B $\frac{7}{15}$

C $\frac{6}{15}$

D $\frac{1}{8}$

10. If you take a slip of paper out of the bag without looking, what is the probability of choosing a number larger than 9?

E $\frac{1}{9}$

F $\frac{8}{15}$

G $\frac{7}{15}$

H $\frac{6}{15}$

Ready Reference

simple event an event whose probability can be obtained from consideration of a single occurrence; *example*: the tossing of a coin is a simple event

Think About It

In order to determine the probability of a simple event, it is necessary to know the number of ways that the event can occur. If you have a bag of cookies containing 1 chocolate chip cookie, 1 oatmeal cookie, and 1 sugar cookie, what is the probability that you will reach into the bag without looking and select the oatmeal cookie?

Here's How

Step 1 How many cookies are in the bag? _____

Step 2 How many oatmeal cookies are in the bag? There is _____ oatmeal cookie in the bag, so there is 1 chance of getting an oatmeal cookie.

Step 3 What is the probability that you will select the oatmeal cookie when you reach into the bag? The probability is _____ out of 3.

Step 4 If you do not pick the oatmeal cookie the first time, there will be 2 cookies left in the bag. If you reach into the bag again, the probability of picking the oatmeal cookie is 1 out of _____.

To find the probability of a simple event, you must determine the number of ways the event can occur and the number of different outcomes that are possible.

$$\text{Probability } (P) = \frac{\text{Number of favorable outcomes}}{\text{Total number of possible outcomes}}$$

Practice

1. How many ways can you pick a grape ice pop from a box that contains 3 cherry, 3 grape, 3 orange, and 3 strawberry ice pops?

   A 12

   B 6

   C 4

   D 3

2. What is the probability that you will choose a grape ice pop from a box that contains 3 cherry, 3 grape, 3 orange, and 3 strawberry ice pops?

   E $\frac{1}{3}$

   F $\frac{3}{12}$

   G $\frac{6}{12}$

   H $\frac{3}{9}$

3. A letter cube has one A, two Bs, one C and two Ds. How many ways can the cube land on D?

A 6

B 4

C 2

D 1

4. A letter cube has one A, two Bs, one C and two Ds. What is the probability that the cube will land on D?

E $\frac{1}{3}$

F $\frac{4}{6}$

G $\frac{1}{2}$

H $\frac{5}{12}$

5. There are 12 marbles in a bag. Six are black, 3 are blue, and 3 are purple. How many ways can you pick a purple marble?

A 12

B 6

C 5

D 3

6. There are 12 marbles in a bag. Six are black, 3 are blue, and 3 are purple. What is the probability that you will pick a purple marble?

E $\frac{3}{6}$

F $\frac{9}{12}$

G $\frac{1}{4}$

H $\frac{6}{12}$

7. Joseph's family wants to go to the movies. The theater has 8 screens. Two cartoon features, 1 animal adventure, 2 mysteries, 1 sports story, 1 foreign film, and 1 love story are showing. How may ways can his family see a mystery?

A 6

B 2

C 1

D 16

8. Two cartoon features, 1 animal adventure, 2 mysteries, 1 sports story, 1 foreign film, and 1 love story are showing. What is the probability that Joseph's family will see a mystery?

E .20

F $\frac{4}{16}$

G $\frac{1}{4}$

H $\frac{7}{8}$

9. Seth wrote the names of each of the 20 students in his class on a slip of paper. No one in his class has the same name. There are 12 girls and 8 boys. What is the probability that he will choose his name?

A $\frac{19}{20}$

B $\frac{1}{20}$

C $\frac{1}{8}$

D $\frac{8}{20}$

10. Using the same bag of 20 names from Problem 9, Seth drew three girls' names in a row. What is the probability that he will choose a girl's name next?

E 0

F $\frac{12}{20}$

G $\frac{4}{12}$

H $\frac{1}{20}$

Think About It

You can use probability to help predict what the outcome of an experiment might be. In a paper bag containing blocks of different shapes, there is a cube, a rectangular prism, a sphere, and a triangular prism. Reach into the bag, take out a block, and then return it to the bag. What shape will you pull out each time? What are the possible outcomes? How many different outcomes are there?

Here's How

1. How many blocks are in the bag? _____

2. Are all the blocks the same shape? _____

3. List the different shapes.

_____

4. Every time you reach into the bag and take out a block, there is an outcome. Name the possible outcomes each time you reach into the bag.

_____

5. Is it possible to have a cylinder–shaped block as an outcome? _____

6. How many different outcomes do you think are possible? _____

You would have to reach into the bag at least 4 times to get each shape at least once, but it might take more than 4 times. It is equally probable that you will pick the cube, the rectangular prism, the sphere, or the triangular prism. If you reach into the bag 100 different times, you may notice a pattern that a certain shape is chosen more than $\frac{1}{4}$ of the time.

Practice

Use the chart to answer Problems 1–4.

Roll a 1	Roll a 2	Roll a 3	Roll a 4	Roll a 5	Roll a 6
15	10	17	17	18	21

1. Evan rolled a die 100 times and recorded the outcomes on a chart. What is the theoretical probability that Evan would roll a 2?

   A $\frac{1}{2}$

   B $\frac{2}{10}$

   C $\frac{1}{6}$

   D $\frac{6}{100}$

2. What is the experimental probability that Evan would roll a 2?

   E .15

   F .10

   G .20

   H .75

3. According to the experiment, which number on the die is most likely to come up?

A 6

B 3

C 2

D 1

4. According to the experiment, which number on the die is least likely to come up?

E 6

F 3

G 2

H 1

5. A deck of cards has 52 cards. Twelve of the cards are face cards. Sarah did an experiment and pulled a card out of the deck 100 times. She pulled out a face card 25 times. What is the theoretical probability that Sarah would select a face card?

A $\frac{1}{4}$

B $\frac{25}{52}$

C $\frac{12}{52}$

D $\frac{25}{100}$

6. Using the information in Problem 5, what is the experimental probability that Sarah would select a face card?

E $\frac{1}{52}$

F $\frac{25}{52}$

G $\frac{12}{52}$

H $\frac{25}{100}$

Use the spinner to answer Problems 7–10.

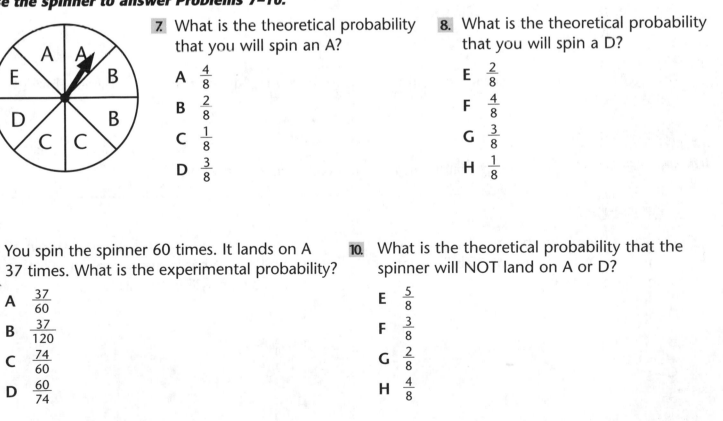

7. What is the theoretical probability that you will spin an A?

A $\frac{4}{8}$

B $\frac{2}{8}$

C $\frac{1}{8}$

D $\frac{3}{8}$

8. What is the theoretical probability that you will spin a D?

E $\frac{2}{8}$

F $\frac{4}{8}$

G $\frac{3}{8}$

H $\frac{1}{8}$

9. You spin the spinner 60 times. It lands on A 37 times. What is the experimental probability?

A $\frac{37}{60}$

B $\frac{37}{120}$

C $\frac{74}{60}$

D $\frac{60}{74}$

10. What is the theoretical probability that the spinner will NOT land on A or D?

E $\frac{5}{8}$

F $\frac{3}{8}$

G $\frac{2}{8}$

H $\frac{4}{8}$

Think About It

A weather forecaster predicts that there is a 40% chance of rain in Harrisburg. What is the chance that it will not rain? If the forecaster also predicts that there is a 40% chance of rain in Pittsburgh, what is the probability that it will rain in both places? What is the probability that it will not rain in either city?

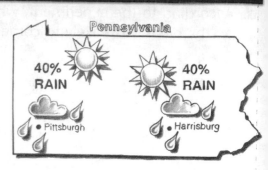

Here's How

1. When you consider the probability of an event like rain, you know it will either rain or it won't rain. If there is a 40% ($\frac{40}{100}$) probability of rain, then there is a 60% ($\frac{60}{100}$) probability that it will not rain.

   If the probability of a certain outcome is x, the probability that it will not occur is $1 - x$.

   $1.00 - .40 = $ _____ or _____ %

2. When the probabilities of two events are independent of each other, such as rain falling in Harrisburg and rain falling in Pittsburgh, you find the probability of it raining in both places by multiplying the probabilities.

   $.40 \times .40 = .16$

   There is a _____ % probability that it will rain in Harrisburg AND Pittsburgh.

3. This also means that there is an 84% probability that it will NOT rain in both cities, but it could rain in either Harrisburg OR Pittsburgh.

   $1.00 - .16 = $ _____

4. The probability that it will rain in neither city is found by multiplying the probabilities that it won't rain.

   $.60 \times .60 = .36$

   There is a _____ % probability that it will NOT rain in either city.

Practice

1. Fred and Wilma are both tossing a coin at the same time. What is the probability that Fred's coin will be heads?

   A $\frac{1}{2}$

   B $\frac{2}{1}$

   C $\frac{1}{4}$

   D $\frac{3}{4}$

2. Fred and Wilma are both tossing a coin at the same time. What is the probability that Wilma's coin will be heads?

   E $\frac{1}{2}$

   F $\frac{2}{1}$

   G $\frac{1}{4}$

   H $\frac{3}{4}$

3. Fred and Wilma are both tossing a coin at the same time. What is the probability that both coins will be heads on the same toss?

A $\frac{1}{2}$

B $\frac{2}{1}$

C $\frac{1}{4}$

D $\frac{3}{4}$

4. Fred and Wilma are both tossing a coin at the same time. What is the probability that both coins will NOT be heads on the same toss?

E $\frac{1}{2}$

F $\frac{2}{1}$

G $\frac{1}{4}$

H $\frac{3}{4}$

5. You are playing a game and must roll a die to see how many spaces to advance. What is the probability that you will roll a 2 two times in a row?

A $\frac{1}{12}$

B $\frac{2}{6}$

C $\frac{1}{36}$

D $\frac{10}{20}$

6. You are playing a game and must roll a die to see how many spaces to advance. What is the probability that you will NOT roll a 2 two times in a row?

E $\frac{11}{12}$

F $\frac{6}{8}$

G 99%

H $\frac{35}{36}$

Use this information to answer Problems 7–10.
Lynn keeps socks in two drawers in her dresser. In one drawer, there is a white sock, a blue sock, and a red sock. In another drawer are the three matching socks.

7. If Lynn reaches in one drawer and takes out a sock without looking, what is the probability that she will pull out the red sock?

A $\frac{1}{6}$

B $\frac{1}{3}$

C $\frac{4}{16}$

D $\frac{1}{9}$

8. What is the probability that she will NOT pull out the red sock?

E $\frac{2}{3}$

F $\frac{2}{6}$

G $\frac{9}{12}$

H $\frac{1}{8}$

9. If Lynn reaches in both drawers and takes out one sock without looking, what is the probability that she will pull out a matching pair?

A $\frac{1}{6}$

B $\frac{1}{3}$

C $\frac{4}{16}$

D $\frac{1}{9}$

10. If Lynn reaches in both drawers without looking, what is the probability that she will NOT pull the red sock out of either drawer?

E $\frac{2}{3}$

F $\frac{1}{6}$

G $\frac{4}{9}$

H $\frac{4}{6}$

Think About It

Some events have no chance of occurring. We use the word *impossible* to describe these events. Some events must happen. We use the word *certain* to describe these events.

What is the probability that an egg will break if it is dropped from a height of 3 feet onto a cement floor—certain or impossible?

Other events may be described as *more likely*, *less likely*, or *equally likely* to happen. What is the probability that it will rain tomorrow?

Here's How

Some events are certain.

Think: How likely is it that an egg will break when dropped from a height of 3 feet onto a cement floor?

1. What do you know about eggs? Are they easy to break? ___Yes___

2. What do you know about cement? Is it a hard or soft surface? ___Yes___

3. When something as fragile as an egg is dropped onto a hard surface, it is
___Epica___ to break.

   It is *certain* that an egg will break if it is dropped 3 feet onto a cement floor.

Some events are more likely, less likely, or equally likely.

1. If the weather forecaster predicts that there is a 30% chance of rain tomorrow, the probability that it will rain is $\frac{30}{100}$. It is not *impossible*, neither is it *certain*.

2. Since there is a 70% chance that it will NOT rain, we say that it is *less* likely to rain tomorrow.

3. Remember that probability is a number between 0 and 1. If a probability is $\frac{1}{2}$, the event is *equally likely* to happen. If a probability is less than $\frac{1}{2}$, it is *less likely* to happen. If a probability is greater than $\frac{1}{2}$, but less than 1, it is *more likely* to happen.

0	$\frac{1}{2}$	1
Impossible	*Maybe/Maybe not*	*Certain*

Practice

1. The probability of flipping a coin and it landing on tails is $\frac{1}{2}$. When Kyle flips a coin, what are his chances of the coin landing on tails rather than heads?

A equally likely

B more likely

C impossible

D certain

2. The probability of rolling double threes on a pair of dice is $\frac{1}{36}$. When Jordan rolls the dice, what are the chances that she will roll double threes rather than another combination?

E more likely

F certain

G impossible

H less likely

Use this information to answer Problems 3–6.

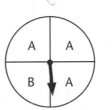

3. Antonio and Annie are using this spinner to play a game. What is the probability that Antonio will spin a B?

A $\frac{3}{4}$

B $\frac{1}{4}$

C $\frac{2}{3}$

D $\frac{1}{3}$

4. Antonio and Annie are using this spinner to play a game. What are the chances that Antonio will spin a B rather than an A?

E certain

F equally likely

G less likely

H more likely

5. What is the probability that Annie will not spin a B?

A $\frac{1}{2}$

B $\frac{1}{4}$

C $\frac{2}{3}$

D $\frac{3}{4}$

6. What are the chances that Annie will spin an A rather than a B?

E impossible

F more likely

G less likely

H equally likely

7. A bag contains 20 marbles: 6 blue, 8 green, and 6 yellow. What are the chances that you will reach into the bag without looking and take out a blue marble rather than a yellow marble?

A more likely

B equally likely

C certain

D less likely

8. A bag contains 20 marbles: 6 blue, 8 green, and 6 yellow. What are the chances that you will reach into the bag without looking and take out a green marble rather than a yellow marble?

E more likely

F equally likely

G certain

H less likely

Standard 2.7.5I ✦ Combinations and arrangements

✏ Think About It

Jenny wants to order lunch. She is offered a turkey sandwich, a ham sandwich, or a vegetable sandwich, and her choice of either white or wheat bread. How many combinations of sandwiches is Jenny being offered?

✏ Here's How

1. How many bread choices does Jenny have? _____

2. How many sandwich filling choices does Jenny have? _____

3. Jenny could have a turkey, ham, or vegetable sandwich on white bread or she could have a turkey, ham, or vegetable sandwich on wheat bread. That would be _____ different choices of sandwiches.

4. Jenny could also multiply: 2 bread choices × 3 sandwich fillings = 6 sandwich choices

   If there are x ways one event can occur and y ways a second event can occur, then for the two events to occur is $x \times y$.

✏ Practice

Use this information to answer Problems 1–4.

Sam and Sue are playing a game. They must spin both spinners on each turn to determine how to move their game pieces.

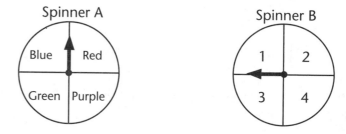

Spinner A

Spinner B

1. How many choices are shown on Spinner A?

   A 2

   B 3

   C 4

   D 5

2. How many choices are shown on Spinner B?

   E 8

   F 6

   G 5

   H 4

3. Which formula could you use to determine the total number of combinations possible on each turn?

   A $\frac{1}{4} \times \frac{1}{4}$

   B 4×4

   C 2×4

   D $4 + 4$

4. How many total combinations are possible?

   E 16

   F $\frac{1}{16}$

   G $\frac{15}{16}$

   H 8

5. An ice cream shop has five flavors of ice cream and three different toppings. What formula could a customer use to determine how many combinations of ice cream and toppings are available?

A $3 + 5$

B $\frac{3}{5} \times \frac{3}{5}$

C 3×5

D $\frac{1}{3} \times \frac{1}{5}$

6. An ice cream shop has five flavors of ice cream. They have three different toppings. How many combinations of ice cream and toppings are possible?

E 8

F $\frac{9}{25}$

G 15

H $\frac{1}{15}$

7. A store is offering 4 lamp styles and 6 lampshades that are sold separately. What formula could a customer use to determine how many kinds of lamps are for sale?

A $\frac{4}{6} \times \frac{4}{6}$

B $\frac{1}{6} \times \frac{1}{4}$

C $4 + 6$

D 4×6

8. A store is offering 4 lamp styles and 6 lampshades that are sold separately. How many different combinations of lamp styles and lampshades are possible?

E $\frac{16}{36}$

F $\frac{1}{24}$

G 10

H 24

Use the following information for Problems 9–12.

There are two cabinets with sports equipment in the gym. In one cabinet is a baseball, a tennis ball, and a ping pong ball. In the second cabinet is a baseball bat, a tennis racquet, and a ping pong paddle. Jake goes to the gym and takes equipment from one cabinet and equipment from the other cabinet without looking.

9. What formula could Jake use to find out how many different combinations he could take out?

A $3 + 3$

B 3×3

C 9×9

D $\frac{1}{3} \times \frac{1}{3}$

10. How many combinations of sports equipment are there?

E 6

F 9

G 81

H $\frac{1}{9}$

11. Which of these combinations would NOT be possible for Jake to take out?

A baseball bat–tennis ball

B ping pong paddle–basketball

C tennis racquet–tennis ball

D ping pong ball–baseball bat

12. What is the probability that Jake will take out a matched pair of equipment?

E $\frac{3}{9}$

F 30%

G $\frac{1}{9}$

H $\frac{3}{6}$

Standard 2.7.5J ✦ Develop a tree diagram and list the elements

Ready Reference
tree diagram a diagram used to show the total number of possible outcomes in a probability experiment

Think About It

Organizing data helps determine the probability of a simple event. Making a list in the form of a tree diagram helps organize the data. Tree diagrams can help you find all the possible outcomes.

Here's How

Make a list from a tree diagram.

Joseph's team is ordering uniforms. Their choices are navy or purple. The letters can be white, red, or green. What is the probability they will pick a navy uniform with white letters?

1. Draw a tree diagram.

navy uniform < white —— navy and white
              red ——— navy and red
              green ——— navy and green

purple uniform < white —— purple and white
                red ——— purple and red
                green ——— purple and green

2. Make a list of the possible choices: navy–white, navy–red, navy–green, purple–white, purple–red, purple–green.

3. How many possible choices are there? _____

4. The probability of choosing a navy uniform with white letters
   is _____ out of _____.

Practice

Use the diagram to answer Problems 1–2.
An art assignment requires the use of a black or a blue pen and one red, purple, or green marker. Michael made a tree diagram showing the possibilities.

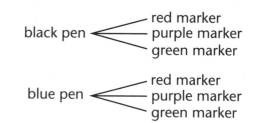

black pen < red marker
            purple marker
            green marker

blue pen < red marker
           purple marker
           green marker

1. How many possible combinations of pen and marker colors are there?

A 2

B 12

C 6

D 3

2. What is the probability that Michael will choose to use a blue pen and a purple marker?

E $\frac{1}{3}$

F $\frac{3}{6}$

G $\frac{1}{12}$

H $\frac{1}{6}$

Use the tree diagram below to help answer Problems 3–6.

Angela has a choice of vanilla or chocolate ice cream. She can choose one topping. The available toppings are strawberry, hot fudge, caramel, or marshmallow.

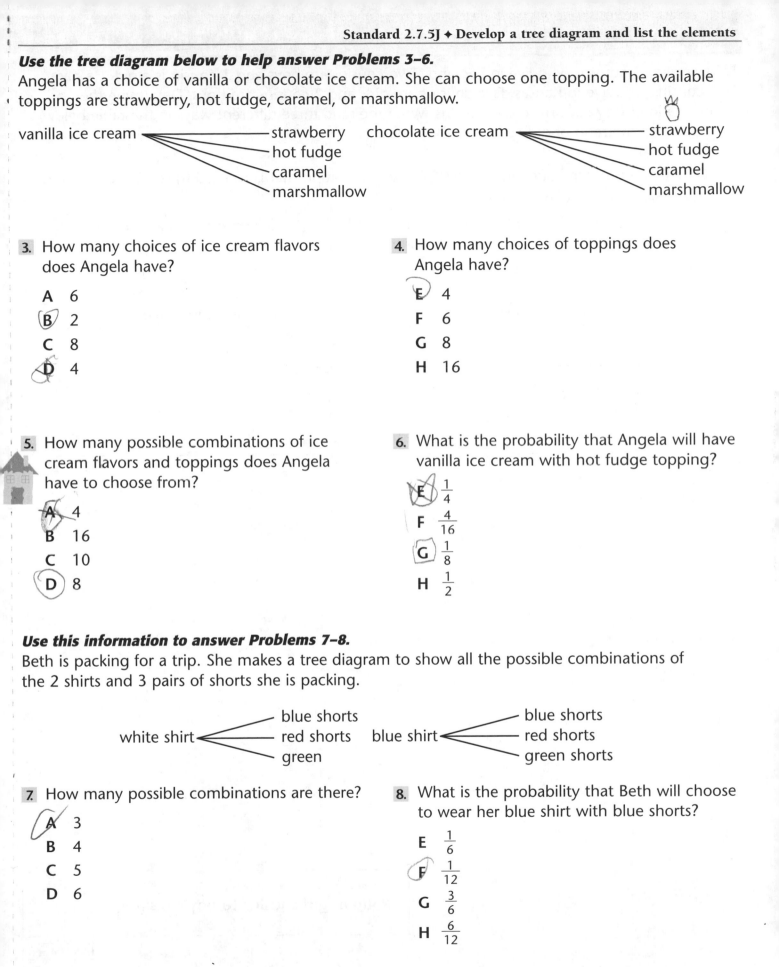

vanilla ice cream ——— strawberry
——— hot fudge
——— caramel
——— marshmallow

chocolate ice cream ——— strawberry
——— hot fudge
——— caramel
——— marshmallow

3. How many choices of ice cream flavors does Angela have?

   A 6
   B 2
   C 8
   D 4

4. How many choices of toppings does Angela have?

   E 4
   F 6
   G 8
   H 16

5. How many possible combinations of ice cream flavors and toppings does Angela have to choose from?

   A 4
   B 16
   C 10
   D 8

6. What is the probability that Angela will have vanilla ice cream with hot fudge topping?

   E $\frac{1}{4}$
   F $\frac{4}{16}$
   G $\frac{1}{8}$
   H $\frac{1}{2}$

Use this information to answer Problems 7–8.

Beth is packing for a trip. She makes a tree diagram to show all the possible combinations of the 2 shirts and 3 pairs of shorts she is packing.

white shirt ——— blue shorts
——— red shorts
——— green

blue shirt ——— blue shorts
——— red shorts
——— green shorts

7. How many possible combinations are there?

   A 3
   B 4
   C 5
   D 6

8. What is the probability that Beth will choose to wear her blue shirt with blue shorts?

   E $\frac{1}{6}$
   F $\frac{1}{12}$
   G $\frac{3}{6}$
   H $\frac{6}{12}$

1. Taylor has 3 cousins who live in England. Two cousins are boys and 1 cousin is a girl. He has 7 cousins who live in Kansas. Five cousins are girls and 2 cousins are boys. Determine the total ratio of boy cousins to girl cousins. Write the ratio three different ways in the table below. Then write the ratio of girl cousins to boy cousins.

- **REREAD** the problem carefully. **IDENTIFY** any information that is needed to solve the problem.
- **SHOW** each step of your math work.
- **WRITE** an explanation describing what you did and why you solved the problem as you did, **EVEN** if you used mental math or a calculator.
- **WRITE** your answers in the spaces provided.

Boy cousins to girl cousins	Girl cousins to boy cousins

Explanation

Ratio of girl cousins to boy cousins _____

0–5 Points

Score _____

2. A bag contains 9 blocks of the same size, but different colors. Four blocks are red, 3 blocks are green, 1 block is yellow, and 1 block is purple. If you reach into the bag without looking, what is the probability that you will choose a green block? What color block are you most likely to select? Why?

- **REREAD** the problem carefully. **IDENTIFY** any information that is needed to solve the problem.
- **SHOW** each step of your math work.
- **WRITE** an explanation describing what you did and why you solved the problem as you did, **EVEN** if you used mental math or a calculator.
- **WRITE** your answer in the spaces provided.

Explanation

Probability of picking green _____

Color you predict is most likely to be picked _____

0–5 Points
Score _____

3. The spinner shown at the right is used in a game. In the game, you may spin the spinner only once. Calculate the probability of getting each of the following on a single spin, then explain your answers: an A, a B, a C, a D, a blank space. Write each probability as a ratio on the line.

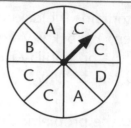

- **REREAD** the problem carefully. **IDENTIFY** information needed to solve the problem.
- **SHOW** each step of your math work.
- **WRITE** an explanation describing what you did and why you solved the problem as you did, **EVEN** if you used mental math or a calculator.
- **WRITE** your answers in the spaces provided. **EXPRESS** your probabilities as fractions.

Probability of getting A _____ $\frac{2}{8}$
Explain.

I took how many spaces and put it in a fraction.
Put it in a
Put it in t 8
and A's there-rafe

Probability of getting B _____ $\frac{1}{8}$
Explain.

I took how many spaces there are and how many Bs there are and putt it in a fraction.

Probability of getting C _____ $\frac{4}{8}$
Explain.

I took how many C's and spaces there are and put it in fraction

Probability of getting D _____ $\frac{1}{8}$
Explain. take

Probability of getting a blank space _____ 0
Explain.

0–5 Points
Score _____

4. Jill is choosing an outfit to wear to visit her grandmother. She has 4 T-shirts—purple, blue, red, and green. She can wear a T-shirt with either a skirt or pants. What is the probability she will choose a purple T-shirt with a skirt? How many different combinations can Jill choose from?

- **REREAD** the problem carefully. **IDENTIFY** information needed to solve the problem.
- **DRAW** a picture or a tree diagram. Then make a list of the combinations.
- **SHOW** each step of your work.
- **WRITE** an explanation describing what you did and why you solved the problem as you did, **EVEN** if you used mental math or a calculator.
- **WRITE** your answers in the spaces provided.

Explanation

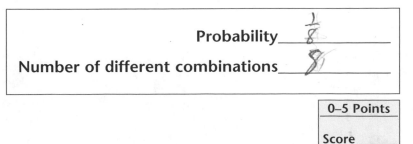

I take purple and cont how many combinations there are, then take the purple section and a skirt and pants wich is 2 and 2 is your d and take how many skirt ther ale and thats is 1 So 1/2

Probability ___1/8___

Number of different combinations ___8___

0–5 Points
Score _____

1. Pat has a bag of marbles. There are 5 red, 3 blue, and 2 white marbles. If she reaches into the bag without looking, which color of marble is she most likely to choose?

   A red
   B blue
   C white
   D There is an equal chance of choosing any of the three colors.

2. What is the probability that Pat will choose a white marble?

   E 3 out of 10
   F 1 out of 2
   G 2 out of 10
   H 2 out of 8

3. What vehicle should go in the empty space for the spinner to have an equal chance of landing on each one?

   A boat
   B car
   C truck
   D airplane

4. If the empty space on the spinner above was left blank, what is the probability that the spinner would land on the airplane?

   E $\frac{1}{2}$
   F $\frac{1}{8}$
   G $\frac{2}{10}$
   H $\frac{1}{7}$

5. You have a box of markers including 1 black, 1 red, 1 blue, 1 green, and 1 yellow. If you reach in the box without looking, what is the probability that you will choose the green marker?

   A $\frac{1}{5}$
   B $\frac{1}{2}$
   C $\frac{5}{1}$
   D $\frac{10}{1}$

6. What is the probability that you will NOT choose the green marker?

   E $\frac{5}{1}$
   F $\frac{1}{5}$
   G $\frac{4}{5}$
   H $\frac{5}{10}$

7. Taylor tossed a coin 50 times and found that heads came up 30 times and tails 20 times. What is the theoretical probability of having heads come up?

   A $\frac{1}{3}$
   B $\frac{2}{10}$
   C $\frac{1}{2}$
   D $\frac{3}{5}$

8. In Taylor's experiment, what was the experimental probability of having heads come up?

   E $\frac{1}{2}$
   F $\frac{30}{50}$
   G $\frac{20}{50}$
   H $\frac{25}{50}$

9. If you write the names of the months of the year on separate slips of paper and put them in a box, what is the probability that you will reach in without looking and take out the slip with "March" written on it?

   A $\frac{11}{12}$
   B 30%
   C $\frac{2}{6}$
   D $\frac{1}{12}$

0. In Maggie's dresser drawer there are 4 pairs of white socks, 3 pairs of black socks, and 2 pairs of red socks. If she reaches into the drawer without looking, what is the probability that she will choose a pair of black socks?

E $\frac{1}{9}$

F $\frac{3}{7}$

G $\frac{3}{9}$

H $\frac{7}{10}$

1. What is the probability that Maggie will choose a pair of white socks?

A $\frac{1}{9}$

B $\frac{4}{5}$

C $\frac{5}{10}$

D $\frac{4}{9}$

2. A weather forecaster predicts a 50% chance of rain for Philadelphia. What is the probability that it will NOT rain?

E 75%

F 100%

G 50%

H 25%

3. If the weather forecaster also predicts there is a 50% chance of rain in New York City on that day, what is the probability that it will rain in both cities?

A 75%

B 100%

C 50%

D 25%

4. If you roll a die, what is the probability that a 3 will come up on top?

E $\frac{3}{6}$

F $\frac{1}{6}$

G $\frac{1}{2}$

H $\frac{5}{6}$

15. What is the probability that you will roll a 3 two times in a row?

A $\frac{1}{6}$

B $\frac{5}{6}$

C $\frac{3}{36}$

D $\frac{1}{36}$

16. If you spin this spinner one time, what is the probability that the spinner will point to A?

E $\frac{2}{8}$

F $\frac{2}{10}$

G $\frac{1}{8}$

H $\frac{1}{6}$

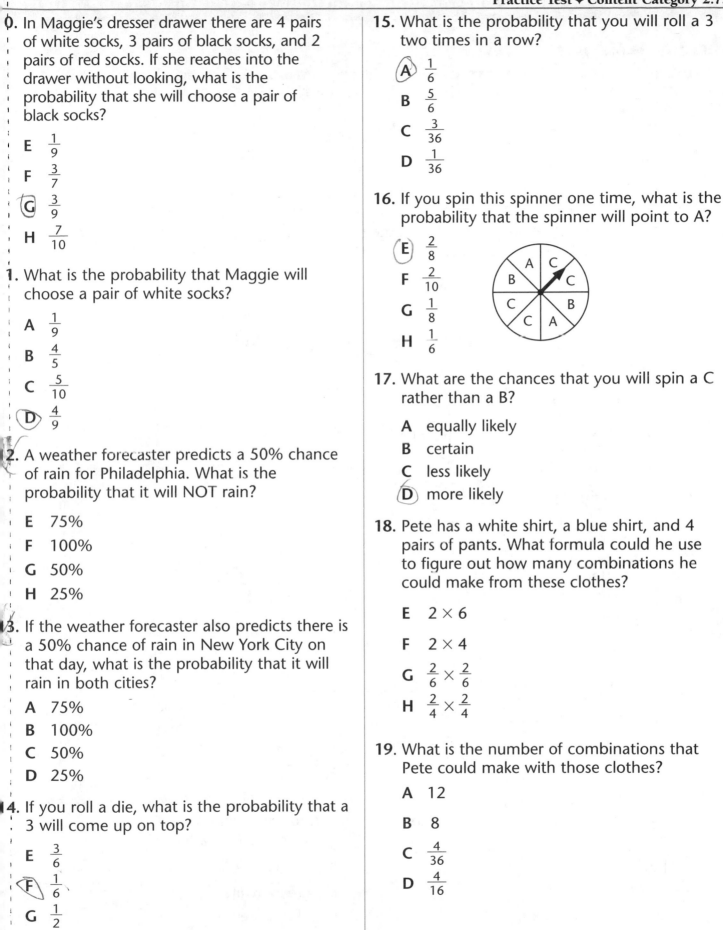

17. What are the chances that you will spin a C rather than a B?

A equally likely

B certain

C less likely

D more likely

18. Pete has a white shirt, a blue shirt, and 4 pairs of pants. What formula could he use to figure out how many combinations he could make from these clothes?

E 2×6

F 2×4

G $\frac{2}{6} \times \frac{2}{6}$

H $\frac{2}{4} \times \frac{2}{4}$

19. What is the number of combinations that Pete could make with those clothes?

A 12

B 8

C $\frac{4}{36}$

D $\frac{4}{16}$

Ready Reference

patterns regularities in situations such as those in nature, events, shapes, designs, and sets of numbers; *example:* spirals on pineapples, geometric designs in quilts, the number sequence 3, 6, 9, 12...

Think About It

You watch as your friend makes a bracelet. She places two round beads on a wire. Then she adds a square bead, a diamond bead, and two more round beads. Your friend is called to the telephone. As she leaves the room, she hands you the wire. "Add more beads in the same pattern," she says. What pattern is she using?

Here's How

Step 1 Recognize and describe the pattern.

1. There are _____ different-shaped beads on the wire.

2. First there are two_____round_____beads, then one _____ bead, then one _____ bead, then two _____ beads.

3. The first and second beads are the same shape as the _____ and _____ beads. So, the pattern is only _____ beads long.

4. The pattern is _____.

Step 2 Reproduce and extend the pattern.

5. The last two beads are both _____.

6. In the pattern, they are followed by a _____.

7. That bead is followed by a _____.

Practice

1. This is a color pattern: white–blue–blue–red–white–blue. What is the next color in this pattern?

   A   white

   B   blue

   C   red

   D   green

2. This is a color pattern: green–white–green–blue–green–white. What is the next color sequence in this pattern?

   E   green–blue

   F   green–white

   G   blue–green

   H   blue–white

Use this pattern to answer Problems 3–6.

3. How many kinds of marbles do you need to make this pattern?

A nine

B six

C three

D ten

4. What is a good description of this pattern?

E There are two striped marbles, then a black marble.

F Every third marble is a solid color.

G Every other marble is striped.

H Every other marble is a solid color.

5. What would the next marble be in this sequence?

A black

B striped

C white

D spotted

6. If you added a marble to the beginning of the row, what kind of marble would it be?

E black

F striped

G spotted

H white

7. An elevator was on the first floor. It went up 4 floors, and then it went down 2 floors. It went up 4 more floors and then down 2 floors. On what floor is the elevator?

A fourth

B fifth

C sixth

D seventh

8. On the first day of the month, a school cafeteria sold 85 cartons of milk. On the second day, 92 cartons were sold. On the third day, 99 cartons were sold. If this pattern continued, how many cartons were sold on the fifth day of the month?

E 100

F 106

G 113

H 120

Use the table below to answer Problems 9–10.

The owner of Al's Diner keeps a record of the number of lunch specials sold daily. The table shows the results for part of a week.

Specials	Monday	Tuesday	Wednesday	Thursday	Friday	Saturday
#1	28	32	36		44	
#2	13	16		22		28

9. What number should be added to Wednesday's total for Special #2?

A 20

B 18

C 21

D 19

10. What number should be added to the chart for Saturday for Special #1?

E 48

F 40

G 46

H 50

Think About It

Patterns are everywhere in the world. Special relationships between items make patterns. How often these relationships happen affect the pattern's order, or sequence. Look at the pattern. What is the next shape in this pattern?

Shape A   Shape B   Shape C

Here's How

Compare Shape A and Shape B.

1. What part of a circle is shown in Shape A? _____ $\frac{1}{4}$ or one quarter _____

2. What part of a circle is shown in Shape B? _____

3. What was added to Shape A to form Shape B? _____

Compare Shape B and Shape C.

4. What part of a circle is shown in Shape C? _____

5. What was added to Shape B to form Shape C? _____

6. What is being added each time to make the pattern? _____

7. What would Shape D look like? _____

Practice

1. Which is the next shape in this pattern?

   A   C

   B   D

2. Which is the next shape in this pattern?

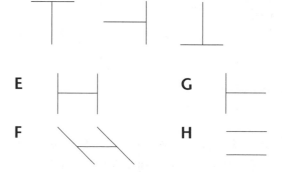

   E   G

   F   H

3. Which is the next shape in this pattern?

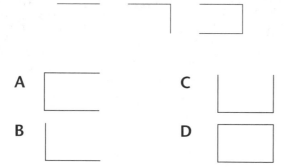

   A   C

   B   D

4. Which is next in this pattern?

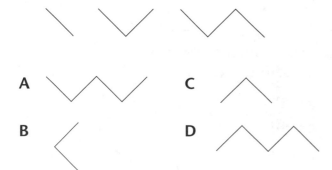

   E   G

   F   H

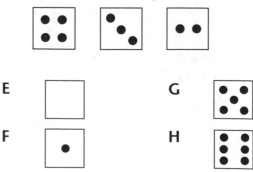

5. Which is the next shape in this pattern?

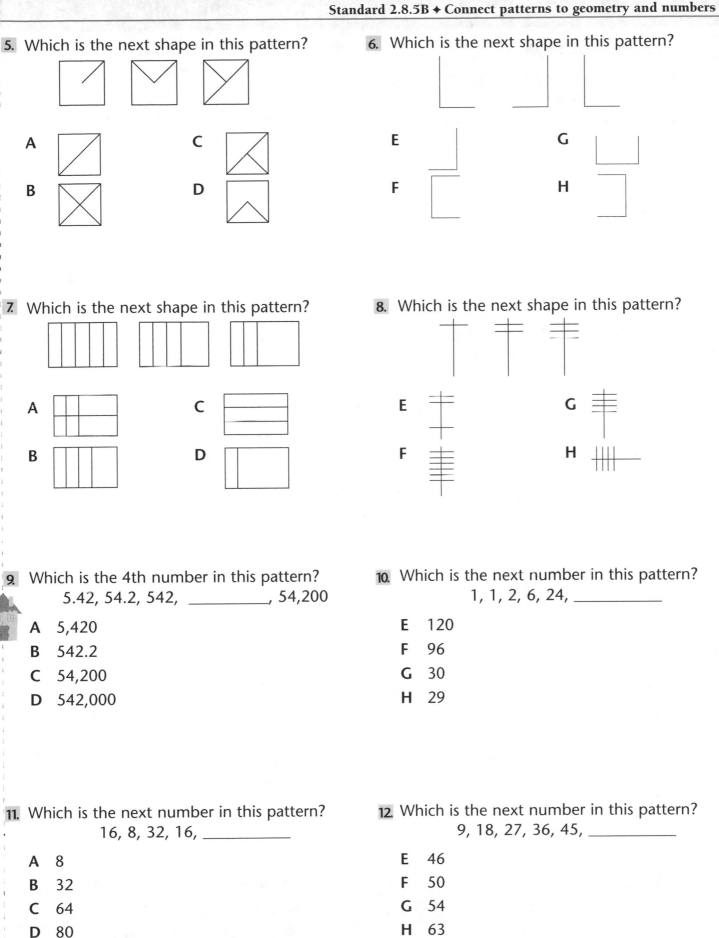

A

C

B

D

6. Which is the next shape in this pattern?

E

G

F

H

7. Which is the next shape in this pattern?

A

C

B

D

8. Which is the next shape in this pattern?

E

G

F

H

9. Which is the 4th number in this pattern?

5.42, 54.2, 542, _____, 54,200

A   5,420
B   542.2
C   54,200
D   542,000

10. Which is the next number in this pattern?

1, 1, 2, 6, 24, _____

E   120
F   96
G   30
H   29

11. Which is the next number in this pattern?

16, 8, 32, 16, _____

A   8
B   32
C   64
D   80

12. Which is the next number in this pattern?

9, 18, 27, 36, 45, _____

E   46
F   50
G   54
H   63

Think About It

Some animals can form new organisms by splitting. Certain worms stretch until they split in half. Each half becomes a new worm! Suppose a worm splits in half. Each of the two new worms then splits in half. If this continues five times, how many worms would there be?

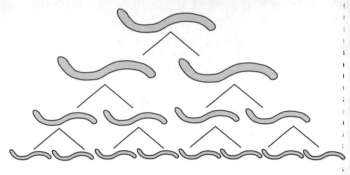

Here's How

Step 1 Make a diagram.

1. Count the number of worms in each row of the diagram. Row 1 has one worm. Row 2 has _____ worms. Row 3 has _____ worms. Row 4 has _____ worms.

2. Write the numbers in sequence: 1, _____, 4, _____

3. Recognize the pattern.
   Look at the first and second numbers. They are 1 and 2. Think about what you do to the first number to get the second number. You multiply 1 by _____ to get 2.

   Look at the second and third numbers. They are 2 and _____. Think about what you do to the second number to get the third number. You multiply 2 by _____ to get 4.

   Look at the third and fourth numbers. They are _____ and 8. What do you do to the third number to get the fourth number? You multiply 4 by _____ to get 8.

Step 2 Describe the pattern.

4. Explain the action done to each number: You multiply each number by _____ to get to the next number in the pattern.

Step 3 Extend the pattern.

5. Find the next two numbers in this pattern.
   Think 8 × 2 = 16, so the fifth number is 16.
   Think 16 × 2 = _____, so the sixth number is _____.

6. If the worm splits 5 times, there would be _____ worms in all.

Practice

1. Which shows the rule for this pattern?
   2, 4, 6, 8, 10

   A   Add 1 to each number.

   B   Multiply each number by 2.

   C   Add 2 to each number.

   D   Multiply each number by 1.

2. Which shows the rule for this pattern?
   5, 10, 15, 20, 25

   E   Add 5 to each number.

   F   Multiply each number by 5.

   G   Multiply each number by 2.

   H   Add 10 to each number.

3. Which shows the rule for this pattern?
4, 16, 64, 256

   A Add 12 to each number.
   B Multiply each number by 2.
   C Add 8 to each number.
   D Multiply each number by 4.

4. Which shows the rule for this pattern?
6, 7, 9, 12, 16, 21

   E Add 1 to each number.
   F Add 1, then 2, then 3, then 4, then 5.
   G Multiply each number by 3.
   H Multiply each number by 4.

5. Which shows the rule for this pattern?
66, 60, 54, 48, 42

   A Multiply each number by 2.
   B Subtract 2 from each number.
   C Subtract 6 from each number.
   D Subtract 6, then 5, then 4, then 3.

6. Which shows the rule for this pattern?
1, 1, 2, 6, 24

   E Multiply by 1, then 2, then 3, then 4.
   F Add 1, then 2, then 3, then 4.
   G Multiply each number by 4.
   H Multiply each number by 3.

7. Which shows the rule for this pattern?
54, 45, 37, 30, 24

   A Subtract 9 from each number.
   B Subtract 9, then 8, then 7, then 6.
   C Divide each number by 9.
   D Divide each number by 3.

8. Which shows the rule for this pattern?
500, 100, 20, 4

   E Subtract 400 from each number.
   F Divide each number by 3.
   G Subtract 400, then 300, then 200.
   H Divide each number by 5.

9. Which is the next number in the pattern
52, 48, 44, …?

   A 40
   B 42
   C 43
   D 38

10. Which is the next number in the pattern
13, 15, 19, 25, …?

   E 26
   F 30
   G 33
   H 35

11. Which is the next number in the pattern
100, 95, 85, 70, …?

   A 60
   B 65
   C 55
   D 50

12. Which is the next number in the pattern
63, 61, 66, 64, …?

   E 65
   F 69
   G 68
   H 70

13. Which is the next number in the pattern
23, 31, 28, 36, …?

   A 22
   B 29
   C 21
   D 33

14. Which is the next number in the pattern
16, 8, 32, 16, …?

   E 8
   F 32
   G 64
   H 80

Think About It

Dylan and Thomas went fishing yesterday. Together, they caught 26 fish. Dylan caught 13 fish. How many fish did Thomas catch? You can write a mathematical equation to solve this problem.

Here's How

Write an open sentence or expression.

1. What do you need to find out? _____

2. What do you know? _____

3. How many fish did Dylan catch?_____ How many fish did the boys catch in all? _____

4. Circle the open sentence that will help you solve this problem.

$$13 - \square = 26 \qquad 26 + \square = 13 \qquad 26 - \square = 13$$

5. Use a mathematical symbol, called a variable, to stand for the unknown number. $26 - x = 13$ (You can use any letter to stand for the unknown number.)

6. Solve the equation. $x =$ _____

Use counters to solve the problem.

1. How many fish did Dylan catch? _____ Put this number of counters in a pile.

2. How many fish did the boys catch in all? _____ Make a second pile of counters to represent Thomas' fish. Begin counting at 14 and stop at 26. Count the number of counters in Thomas' pile. How many fish did Thomas catch? _____

3. Write and solve the open sentence you circled in number 4. _____

Practice

Use counters to help solve Problems 1–9.

1. $17 + x = 26$

   A 17
   B 11
   C 8
   D 9

2. $y - 8 = 13$

   E 5
   F 21
   G 20
   H 6

3. $20 \times m = 220$

   A 11
   B 1
   C 9
   D 10

4. $x \div 12 = 51$

E   611

F   63

G   612

H   61

5. $y + 15 = 31$

A   16

B   15

C   46

D   17

6. $17 + m = 24$

E   6

F   13

G   9

H   7

7. $b - 11 = 14$

A   26

B   25

C   23

D   32

8. $39 - j = 13$

E   26

F   16

G   25

H   21

9. $40 - x = 15$

A   24

B   35

C   25

D   30

Use this pattern of paperclips to answer Problems 10–11.

Figure 1   Figure 2   Figure 3

10. Which number sequence could describe the pattern of paperclips?

E   1, 2, 3

F   1, 3, 5

G   2, 3, 4

H   2, 4, 6

11. Which equation describes the pattern of paper clips?

A $2 \times 2 \times 2 = x$

B $2 + 4 + 6 = x$

C $2 + 2 + 2 = x$

D $x + 2 = 4$

12. Will baked 48 cupcakes. He divided them into 8 containers. Which equation shows how to find how many cupcakes are in each container?

E $48 \div 8 = k$

F $8 \div 48 = k$

G $8 + k = 48$

H $48 - k = 8$

13. Carol Anne ran 27 laps today. She ran 12.2 laps in the morning. Which equation shows how many laps she ran in the afternoon?

A $12.2 + 27 = x$

B $27 + x = 12.2$

C $27 \div x = 12.2$

D $27 - x = 12.2$

14. Mike bought a package of 32 baseball cards. Of the 32 cards, 7 are doubles—cards he already owns. Which equation shows how to find the number of new cards that are not doubles?

E $7 \times m = 32$

F $32 - 7 = m$

G $m - 7 = 32$

H $32 \div 7 = m$

15. Every day, Jason spends 42 minutes reading. Which equation shows how much time he spends reading in a week?

A $42 \div 7 = y$

B $42 + 7 = y$

C $42 \times 7 = y$

D $42 - 7 = y$

Ready Reference

inequality a mathematical sentence that contains a symbol;
example: >, <, ≥, ≤, or ≠, in which the terms on either side
of the symbol are unequal; *example:* $x < y$, $7 > 3$, $n \geq 4$

Think About It

Katie saved $5 to buy stickers. At Sticker World, 4 packages of 8
stickers each cost $5. At Toy Depot, 5 packages of 6 stickers each
cost $5. How can Katie calculate where she will get the most
stickers for her money?

Here's How

Step 1 Write multiplication facts.

Sticker World	Toy Depot
Number of packages = 4	Number of packages = _____
Stickers in each package = 8	Stickers in each package = _____
Multiplication fact: $4 \times 8 = n$	Multiplication fact: _____

Step 2 Compare the amounts.

1. Write each multiplication fact: $4 \times$ _____ = _____   _____ $\times 6 =$ _____

2. Compare the products. Use <, >, or =.   _____

3. At Sticker World, Katie will get 32 stickers for $5. At Toy Depot, Katie will
get _____ for $5.

4. Where should Katie buy her stickers? _____

Practice

Use this information to answer Problems 1–4.

Alan wants to buy some juice. He can buy 2 packages of 4 juice boxes or 3 packages of
3 juice boxes for the same amount of money.

1. Which shows how much juice he will get in
2 packages containing 4 juice boxes each?

 A $2 \times 3 = 6$

 B $2 \times 6 = 12$

 C $2 \times 4 = 8$

 D $2 \times 5 = 10$

2. Which shows how much juice he will get in
3 packages containing 3 juice boxes each?

 E $3 \times 3 = 9$

 F $3 \times 2 = 6$

 G $3 \times 4 = 12$

 H $3 \times 6 = 18$

3. Which expression compares the products?

A $6 < 12$

B $8 < 12$

C $10 > 9$

D $8 < 9$

4. Which packages of juice should Alan buy to get the most juice for his money?

E 2 packages of 4 juice boxes

F 3 packages of 3 juice boxes

G They are both the same amount of juice.

H 4 packages of 2 juice boxes

Circle the symbol that will make each expression correct.

5. 8×5 _____ 4×10

A $<$

B $>$

C $=$

D $^\wedge$

6. 3×9 _____ 5×5

E $<$

F $=$

G $^\wedge$

H $>$

7. 7×2 _____ 3×5

A $>$

B $<$

C $^\wedge$

D $=$

8. 6×4 _____ 8×3

E $=$

F $>$

G $^\wedge$

H $<$

9. 8×8 _____ 10×7

A $^\wedge$

B $<$

C $=$

D $>$

10. 6×6 _____ 4×8

E $=$

F $^\wedge$

G $<$

H $>$

Use this information to answer Problems 11–14.

Mrs. Ling can buy 2 packages with 10 bagels in each package or, she can buy 3 packages that each have 6 bagels for the same amount of money.

11. Which shows the number of bagels in 2 packages containing 10 bagels each?

A $2 \times 6 = 12$

B $2 \times 3 = 6$

C $2 \times 10 = 20$

D $2 \times 20 = 40$

12. Which shows the number of bagels in 3 packages containing 6 bagels each?

E $3 \times 10 = 30$

F $3 \times 6 = 18$

G $3 \times 9 = 27$

H $3 \times 8 = 24$

13. Which expression compares the products?

A $40 > 30$

B $12 < 18$

C $20 < 24$

D $20 > 18$

14. Which packages of bagels should Mrs. Ling buy to get the most for her money?

E 2 packages of 10 bagels

F Both cost the same amount.

G 3 packages of 6 bagels

H 6 packages of 3 bagels

Ready Reference

equation a statement of equality between two mathematical expressions;
example: $x + 5 = y - 2$

expression a mathematical phrase that can include operations, numerals, and variables. In algebraic terms: $2l + 3x$; in numeric terms: $13.4 - 4.7$

Think About It

There are 63 boxes of shoes on three shelves in the storeroom of the Shoe Palace. The top shelf holds the least number of boxes. The bottom shelf holds the most. Each shelf holds 7 more boxes than the one above it. There are 14 boxes of shoes on the top shelf. How do you determine the number of boxes on the other two shelves?

Here's How

Solve by writing an equation.

1. How many boxes are on the top shelf? _____

2. What is the total number of boxes on all three shelves? _____

3. Write an open sentence using what you know.

Top Shelf		Middle Shelf		Bottom Shelf
14	+	(14 + 7)	+	$x = 63$
				$35 + x = 63$
				$x = $ _____

Solve by making a table.

Shelf	Number of Boxes
Top	14
Middle	
Bottom	

1. If each shelf holds 7 more boxes than the one above it, what do you add to find out how many boxes are on the middle shelf? _____

2. What do you add to find the number of boxes on the third row? _____

3. How can you check your answer? _____

Practice

Use this information to answer Problems 1–4.

Four boxes hold a total of 240 pencils. The boxes are placed in a line. The first box has the greatest number of pencils. The last box has the least number of pencils. Each box has twice as many pencils as the one behind it. The last box has 16 pencils. How many pencils are in all four boxes?

1. Which will help you calculate how many pencils are in the third box?

A $240 - 16 = x$

B $16 + 16 = x$

C $240 - 32 = x$

D $32 + 32 = 64$

2. Which will help you calculate how many pencils are in the second box?

E $240 - 32 = x$

F $32 + 16 = x$

G $16 \times 2 = x$

H $32 + 32 = x$

3. Which is a true statement about the pencils?

A the third box < 16

B the second box < 16

C the third box > 16

D the second box $= 16$

4. Which shows how to check your answer?

E $16 + 32 + 64 + 128 = 240$

F $240 - 128 = 112$

G $32 + 64 = 96$

H $16 + 32 + 64 = 112$

Use the graph to answer Problems 5–8.
Cameron watched the birds that came to his bird feeder in a one-hour period. He made a graph showing the number and types of birds he saw.

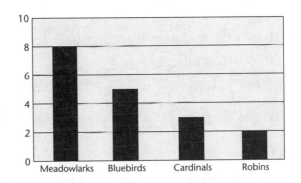

5. Which equation describes the number of birds Cameron saw in an hour?

A $x + 3 + 5 + 8 = 18$

B $x - 3 - 2 - 1 = 18$

C $x - 5 - 3 - 2 = 18$

D $x + 8 + 5 + 2 + 3 = 18$

6. How many birds in all did Cameron see in an hour?

E 20

F 10

G 15

H 18

7. Which is a true statement about the birds Cameron saw?

A meadowlarks $<$ robins

B cardinals $>$ bluebirds

C bluebirds $>$ cardinals

D robins $=$ meadowlarks

8. If $x =$ the total number of birds, which expression equals the number of meadowlarks?

E $x - (4 + 1) - (2 + 1) - (1 + 1)$

F $x \times 2 \times 3 \times 1$

G $x - 6 - 2 - 3$

H $x + (10 - 2) + (10 - 5) + (10 - 7)$

Think About It

There are many strategies you can use to solve problems and number sentences. Sometimes you will use mental math. You can use basic facts and patterns to find quotients for larger numbers.

Here's How

Use counters or other concrete materials.

Elaine baked 18 muffins. She wants to divide them evenly among 3 baskets. How can you use counters to find out how many muffins she should put in each basket?

Step 1 Use a model for the dividend.

1. How many muffins did Elaine bake? _____
   Place this number of counters on a flat surface.

Step 2 Name the divisor.

2. Into how many baskets can the muffins be placed? _____

3. What is the divisor? _____

Step Use the dividend and the divisor to solve the problem.

4. Separate the counters into 3 equal groups. How many counters are in each group? _____
   What is the quotient? _____
   How many muffins will be in each basket? _____

5. Write the division fact that you modeled with the counters. _____

Use basic facts.

Each class needs 20 yards of crepe paper to decorate their classroom for a party. If there is 180 yards of crepe paper, how many classes can decorate their classrooms?

Step 1 Write the number sentence. $180 \div 20 = n$

Step Use basic facts to find the quotient.

$$18 \div 2 = \underline{\hspace{1cm}}$$
$$180 \div 20 = \underline{\hspace{1cm}} \quad \text{Think: 18 tens} \div \text{2 tens} = 9$$

How many classes can decorate? _____

Use patterns of zeros.

$$18 \div 2 = \underline{\hspace{1cm}}$$
$$180 \div 20 = \underline{\hspace{1cm}}$$
$$1,800 \div 20 = \underline{\hspace{1cm}}$$
$$18,000 \div 20 = \underline{\hspace{1cm}}$$

Practice

Use this information to answer Problems 1–2.

Will baked 48 cupcakes. He wants to store the cupcakes in containers that each hold six cupcakes.

1. Use counters to help you. How many groups of six can you divide the counters into?

   A   12

   B   8

   C   3

   D   14

2. Which of these number sentences describes Will's problem?

   E $48 \div 4 = 12$

   F $6 \div 2 = 3$

   G $84 \div 6 = 14$

   H $48 \div 6 = 8$

Use this information to answer Problems 3–4.

Mae, Bud, and Lou earned $36 washing cars. They need to divide the money equally.

3. Which describes the problem that Mae, Bud, and Lou need to solve?

   A $36 \div 3 = x$

   B $36 \div 6 = x$

   C $3 \times 36 = x$

   D $3 \times 3 = x$

4. How much money did Lou earn from washing cars?

   E $3

   F $6

   G $9

   H $12

5. The factory made 20,000 widgets in 40 days. How many were made each day?

   A   5

   B   50

   C   500

   D   5,000

6. The stadium holds 72,000 people. There are 90 sections. How many people does each section hold?

   E   8

   F   800

   G   80

   H   8,000

7. The school band raised $600 for uniforms. If each uniform costs $20, how many uniforms can be ordered?

   A   3,000

   B   300

   C   30

   D   3

8. The tickets to Paris cost $900 each. How much would it cost for 90 people to fly to Paris?

   E $8,100,000

   F $810,000

   G $81,000

   H $8,100

9. The Booster Club raised $54,000 for a charity. If 600 people each donated the same amount of money, how much did each person give?

   A $90

   B $9

   C $900

   D $9,000

10. Each class raised $70 for a field trip. If the total amount of money raised was $560, how many classes raised money?

    E   6

    F   7

    G   8

    H   9

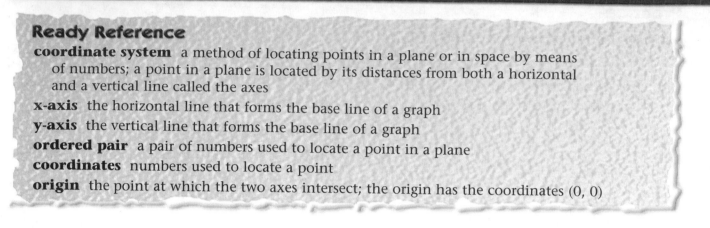

Ready Reference

coordinate system a method of locating points in a plane or in space by means of numbers; a point in a plane is located by its distances from both a horizontal and a vertical line called the axes

x-axis the horizontal line that forms the base line of a graph

y-axis the vertical line that forms the base line of a graph

ordered pair a pair of numbers used to locate a point in a plane

coordinates numbers used to locate a point

origin the point at which the two axes intersect; the origin has the coordinates (0, 0)

Think About It

A grid is a kind of map. You can find your way around the grid using pairs of numbers called ordered pairs. An ordered pair can be used to find the location of a point on a grid. How do you find the ordered pair of the point shown on the grid?

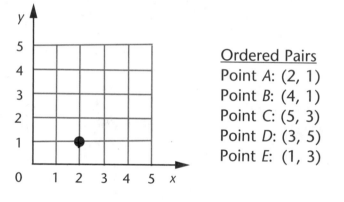

Ordered Pairs
Point A: (2, 1)
Point B: (4, 1)
Point C: (5, 3)
Point D: (3, 5)
Point E: (1, 3)

Here's How

Locate the ordered pairs.

1. The order of the numbers in an ordered pair is important. The first number tells you to move along the horizontal or x–axis. The second number tells you to move along the vertical or y–axis. The point at (2, 1) is different than the point at (1, 2).

2. The point shown on the grid above is Point A (2, 1). To locate the point, start at 0, go to the right 2 spaces, and then move up 1 space.

3. Locate Point B (4, 1). Move 4 spaces to the right. Move up 1 space.

4. Locate Point C (5, 3). Move 5 spaces to the right. Move up _____ spaces.

5. Locate Point D (3, 5). Move _____ spaces to the right. Move up 5 spaces.

6. Locate Point E (1, 3). Move _____ space to the right. Move up _____ spaces.

Practice

Use the grid to answer Problems 1–6.

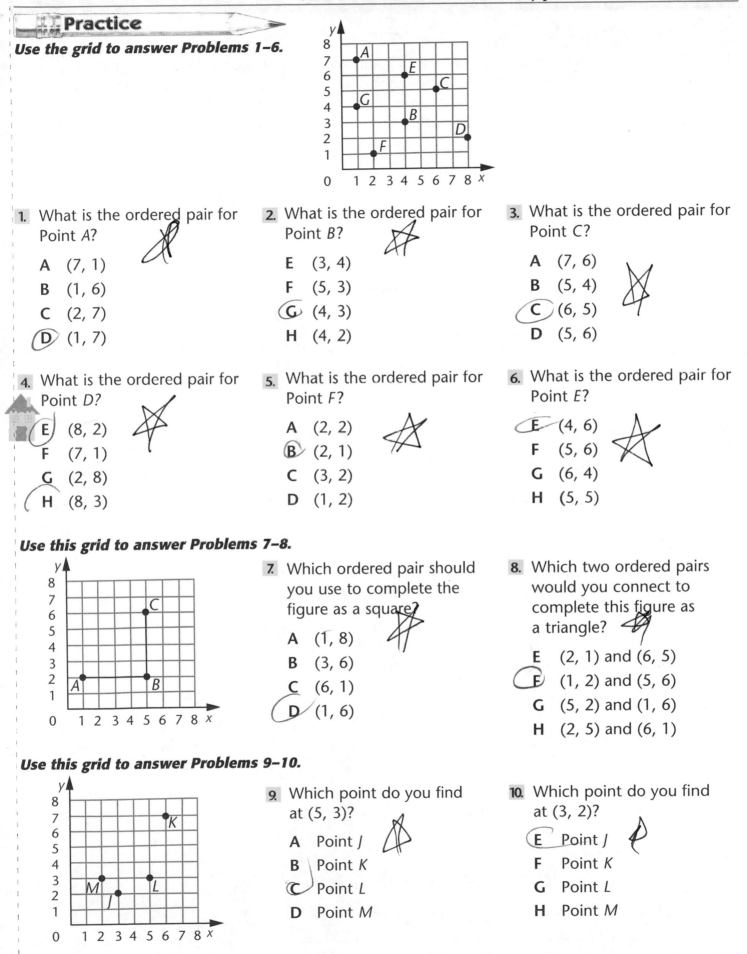

1. What is the ordered pair for Point *A*?

   A (7, 1)
   B (1, 6)
   C (2, 7)
   D (1, 7)

2. What is the ordered pair for Point *B*?

   E (3, 4)
   F (5, 3)
   G (4, 3)
   H (4, 2)

3. What is the ordered pair for Point *C*?

   A (7, 6)
   B (5, 4)
   C (6, 5)
   D (5, 6)

4. What is the ordered pair for Point *D?*

   E (8, 2)
   F (7, 1)
   G (2, 8)
   H (8, 3)

5. What is the ordered pair for Point *F?*

   A (2, 2)
   B (2, 1)
   C (3, 2)
   D (1, 2)

6. What is the ordered pair for Point *E?*

   E (4, 6)
   F (5, 6)
   G (6, 4)
   H (5, 5)

Use this grid to answer Problems 7–8.

7. Which ordered pair should you use to complete the figure as a square?

   A (1, 8)
   B (3, 6)
   C (6, 1)
   D (1, 6)

8. Which two ordered pairs would you connect to complete this figure as a triangle?

   E (2, 1) and (6, 5)
   F (1, 2) and (5, 6)
   G (5, 2) and (1, 6)
   H (2, 5) and (6, 1)

Use this grid to answer Problems 9–10.

9. Which point do you find at (5, 3)?

   A Point *J*
   B Point *K*
   C Point *L*
   D Point *M*

10. Which point do you find at (3, 2)?

    E Point *J*
    F Point *K*
    G Point *L*
    H Point *M*

Think About It

The snack bar at Town Cinema is very busy on Saturdays. The manager is considering hiring a new worker. She made a table to show the number of customers who visited the snack bar during a 10-hour period one Saturday. Can you use the data in the table to make a graph to show during what 3-hour shift an additional worker would be most needed?

Hours	12–1	1–2	2–3	3–4	4–5	5–6	6–7	7–8	8–9	9–10
# of Customers	14	18	20	14	10	16	22	29	24	13

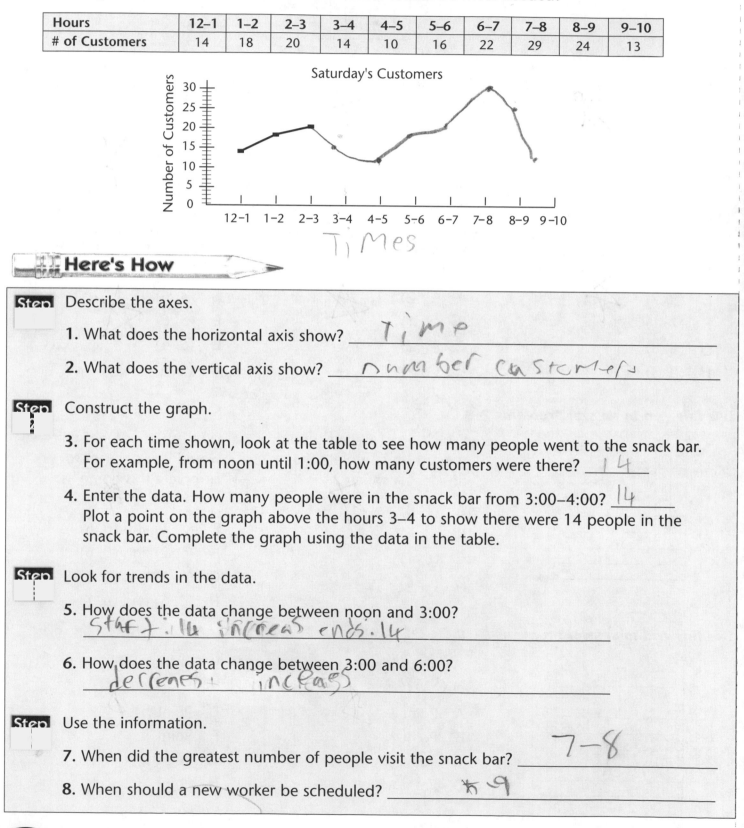

Saturday's Customers

Here's How

Step 1 Describe the axes.

1. What does the horizontal axis show? _Time_

2. What does the vertical axis show? _number customers_

Step 2 Construct the graph.

3. For each time shown, look at the table to see how many people went to the snack bar. For example, from noon until 1:00, how many customers were there? _14_

4. Enter the data. How many people were in the snack bar from 3:00–4:00? _14_
Plot a point on the graph above the hours 3–4 to show there were 14 people in the snack bar. Complete the graph using the data in the table.

Step 3 Look for trends in the data.

5. How does the data change between noon and 3:00? _Start: 14 increas ends: 14_

6. How does the data change between 3:00 and 6:00? _decreas + increas_

Step 4 Use the information.

7. When did the greatest number of people visit the snack bar? _7–8_

8. When should a new worker be scheduled? _7–9_

Practice

Use the bar graph to answer Problems 1–4.
The 4th, 5th, and 6th grades collected empty cans to recycle for an Earth Day project.

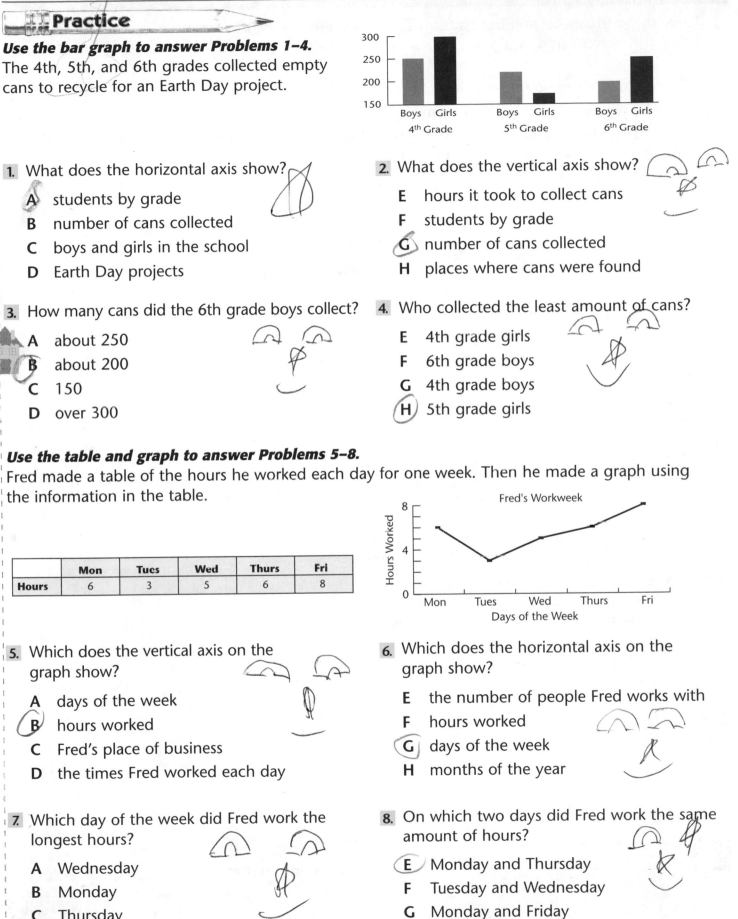

1. What does the horizontal axis show?
   - A students by grade
   - B number of cans collected
   - C boys and girls in the school
   - D Earth Day projects

2. What does the vertical axis show?
   - E hours it took to collect cans
   - F students by grade
   - G number of cans collected
   - H places where cans were found

3. How many cans did the 6th grade boys collect?
   - A about 250
   - B about 200
   - C 150
   - D over 300

4. Who collected the least amount of cans?
   - E 4th grade girls
   - F 6th grade boys
   - G 4th grade boys
   - H 5th grade girls

Use the table and graph to answer Problems 5–8.
Fred made a table of the hours he worked each day for one week. Then he made a graph using the information in the table.

	Mon	Tues	Wed	Thurs	Fri
Hours	6	3	5	6	8

5. Which does the vertical axis on the graph show?
   - A days of the week
   - B hours worked
   - C Fred's place of business
   - D the times Fred worked each day

6. Which does the horizontal axis on the graph show?
   - E the number of people Fred works with
   - F hours worked
   - G days of the week
   - H months of the year

7. Which day of the week did Fred work the longest hours?
   - A Wednesday
   - B Monday
   - C Thursday
   - D Friday

8. On which two days did Fred work the same amount of hours?
   - E Monday and Thursday
   - F Tuesday and Wednesday
   - G Monday and Friday
   - H Thursday and Friday

1. Look at the triangular number patterns shown. Determine the next number in the pattern. Show this pattern using numbers.

- **SHOW** each step of your math work.
- **EXPLAIN** why you solved the problem as you did.
- **WRITE** an explanation describing what you did and why you solved the problem as you did, **EVEN** if you used mental math or a calculator.
- **WRITE** your answer in the spaces provided.

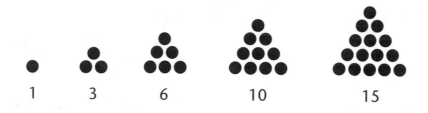

1	3	6	10	15

Explanation

Next number in pattern _____

Pattern in numbers _____

0–5 Points

Score _____

2. Use Grid 1 and Grid 2 to answer the questions in Parts A and B below.

- **READ** the problem and break it into parts to solve it.
- **SHOW** each step of your math work.
- **EXPLAIN** why you solved the problem as you did in the spaces below.
- **WRITE** your answer in the space provided.

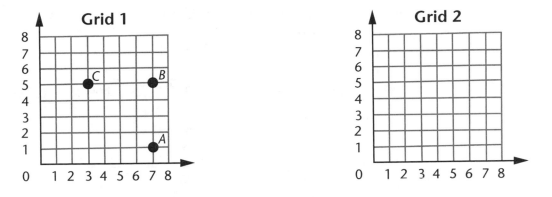

Part A Identify the ordered pair (point *D*) you should plot in Grid 1 to complete the figure as a square. _____

Explain why you chose this ordered pair.

Part B Plot point *A*, point *B*, and point *C* on Grid 2 to form a triangle. Which ordered pairs did you use?

point *A* _____   point *B* _____   point *C* _____

Explain your selection.

0–5 Points
Score _____

3. Sydney is keeping a record of the number of yards of gold and silver ribbon she has on each day for a project she is working on. The table below shows the results for last week. Use your understanding of patterns to complete the table. Explain how you solved the problem.

- **READ** the problem carefully and decide how to solve it.
- **EXPLAIN** why you solved the problem as you did.
- **WRITE** an explanation describing what you did and why you solved the problem as you did, **EVEN** if you used mental math or a calculator.
- **WRITE** your answers in the spaces provided.

Ribbon	Monday	Tuesday	Wednesday	Thursday	Friday	Saturday
Gold	7	$5\frac{2}{3}$		3		
Silver	9		$6\frac{1}{2}$	$5\frac{1}{4}$		

Explanation

Pattern for gold ribbon _____

Pattern for silver ribbon _____

0–5 Points
Score _____

4. Tim is 10 and Wendy is 9. Tim says that he can write two different number sentences that describe their age difference. Write the number sentences. Explain how you solved the problem.

- **READ** the problem carefully and decide how to solve it.
- **SHOW** each step of your math work.
- **EXPLAIN** why you solved the problem as you did.
- **WRITE** an explanation describing what you did and why you solved the problem as you did, **EVEN** if you used mental math or a calculator.
- **WRITE** your answers in the spaces provided.

Explanation

| Number sentences _____ |
| _____ |

| 0–5 Points |
| Score _____ |

1. Here is a color pattern:
red–orange–orange–blue–red–orange.
What is the next color in this pattern?

   A   blue

   B   red

   C   orange

   D   white

2. What is the next number in this pattern?
3, 6, 12, 24, 48, _____

   E   51

   F   96

   G   63

   H   54

3. What is the rule used in this pattern?
5, 6, 8, 11, 15

   A   Add 1, then 2, then 3, then 4.

   B   Divide by 1, then add 1.

   C   Multiply by 1, then add 1.

   D   Add 2, then subtract 1.

4. What is the rule used in this pattern?
10, 20, 40, 80, 160

   E   Add 10.

   F   Multiply by 3, then subtract 10.

   G   Divide by 5, then multiply by 10.

   H   Multiply by 5, then divide by 2.

5. The librarian had 39 books to put back on
the shelves. Students returned 17 more
books. How many books does the librarian
need to shelve now?

   A   22

   B   56

   C   60

   D   12

6. If each person receives 188 coins out of
3,948 coins, which expression shows how
many people will share the coins?

   E $3{,}948 + y = 188$

   F $3{,}948 \div y = 188$

   G $3{,}948 - y = 188$

   H $3{,}948 \times y = 188$

7. Max needs to buy some pencils. A store
sells 2 packages of 15 pencils and
4 packages of 8 pencils for the same
amount of money. Which equation shows
how many pencils are in 2 packages of
15 pencils?

   A $15 - 2 = 13$

   B $15 \div 5 = 3$

   C $2 + 15 = 17$

   D $2 \times 15 = 30$

8. Which shows how many pencils are in four
packages of 8 pencils?

   E $8 \div 4 = 2$

   F $4 + 8 = 12$

   G $8 \times 4 = 32$

   H $8 - 4 = 4$

9. Which expression compares the number
of pencils in both sets of packages?

   A $32 > 30$

   B $2 < 4$

   C $15 > 8$

   D $12 < 17$

10. Meg and Joy were collecting cans for a food drive. They need 150 cans. They have collected 112 cans. How many more cans do they need?

E 262

F 32

G 135

H 38

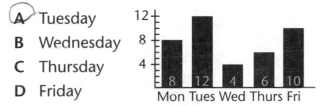

11. John received a homework pass after reading 25 pages of his book. On which day did he receive his pass?

A Tuesday

B Wednesday

C Thursday

D Friday

12. Madeline took 40 photographs during her vacation. Each day she took 4 more pictures than the day before. She took 4 pictures on the first day and 16 pictures on the last day. How many photographs did she take on the third day?

E 8

F 10

G 6

H 12

13. Which equation will help calculate how many photographs Madeline took on the third day?

A $12 + 16 = x$

B $4 + 4 + 4 = x$

C $8 + 8 = x$

D $4 + 16 = x$

14. The fifth grade voted on which animal they would prefer for a class pet. They posted the results of the voting in a table. How many more students voted for the rabbit than the lizard?

E 3

F 15

G 16

H 2

Pet	Votes
Gerbil	6
Rabbit	9
Lizard	7

15. (4, 7) is an ordered pair. What does the number 4 indicate?

A 4 on the horizontal axis

B 4 on the vertical axis

C 4 on the diagonal axis

D 4 on the circular axis

16. Lee asked five classmates to record how many hours they spent playing video games for one week. She put the results in a bar graph. What does the vertical axis show?

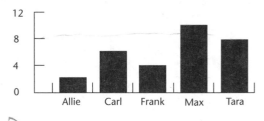

E classmates of Lee

F hours playing video games

G days of the week

H video games played

17. Who played video games for 8 hours during the week?

A Carl

B Frank

C Max

D Tara

Ready Reference

polygon a union of segments connected end to end, such that each segment intersects exactly two others at its endpoints

regular polygon a polygon in which all sides have the same measure and all angles have the same measure

quadrilateral a four-sided polygon

Think About It

Geometry is the study of different shapes. The pieces of a jigsaw puzzle have unique shapes. The small shapes fit together to make one larger shape. Almost everything you can see has some kind of shape. What are some terms that help describe those shapes?

Here's How

Plane figures

1. Plane figures are two-dimensional shapes. They are flat. A polygon is a closed plane figure that is made up of at least three line segments and each endpoint is connected to only two line segments. Which of these figures is a polygon? _____

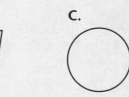

   A.   B.   C.

2. A quadrilateral is a polygon with four sides. Which of these figures is a quadrilateral? _____

   D.   E.   F.

Curved figures

1. Curved figures are geometric shapes that do not have straight sides. A circle is a simple closed curve that has every point along its outside edge at an equal distance from the center.

Practice

1. Which is the best definition of a triangle?

   A   an almost quadrilateral
   B   a polygon with three sides
   C   a geometric shape
   D   a plane figure

2. Which is the best definition of a square?

   E   a quadrilateral with equal sides
   F   a polygon
   G   a rectangle
   H   a four–sided shape

3. A special type of quadrilateral is a parallelogram. It has two pairs of parallel sides. Which shape is a parallelogram?

A

C

B

D

4. Another special type of quadrilateral is a trapezoid. A trapezoid has one pair of parallel sides. Which shape is a trapezoid?

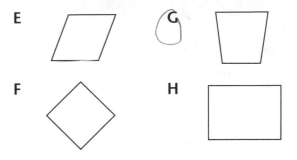

E

G

F

H

5. A special type of parallelogram is a rhombus. A rhombus has 4 congruent sides and no right angles. Which shape is a rhombus?

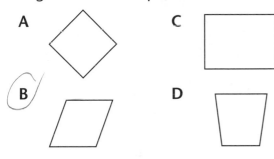

A

C

B

D

6. A rectangle is a parallelogram that has 4 right angles and only opposite sides that are congruent. Which shape is a rectangle?

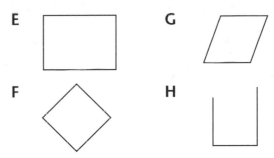

E

G

F

H

7. A pentagon is a polygon with 5 sides. Which shape is a pentagon?

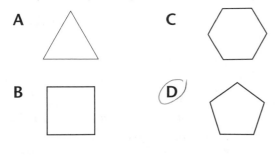

A

C

B

D

8. A hexagon is a polygon with 6 sides. Which shape is a hexagon?

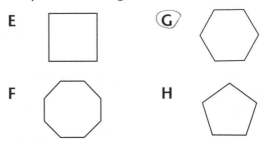

E

G

F

H

9. This shape is called a _____.

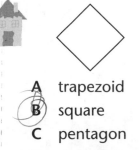

A trapezoid
B square
C pentagon
D rhombus

10. This shape is called a _____.

E triangle
F hexagon
G parallelogram
H square

Ready Reference

congruent having the same shape and the same size

Think About It

A triangle is a polygon with 3 sides. A quadrilateral is a polygon with 4 sides. Do all triangles look the same? Do all quadrilaterals look the same? There are many differences among them. How can you describe these differences?

Here's How

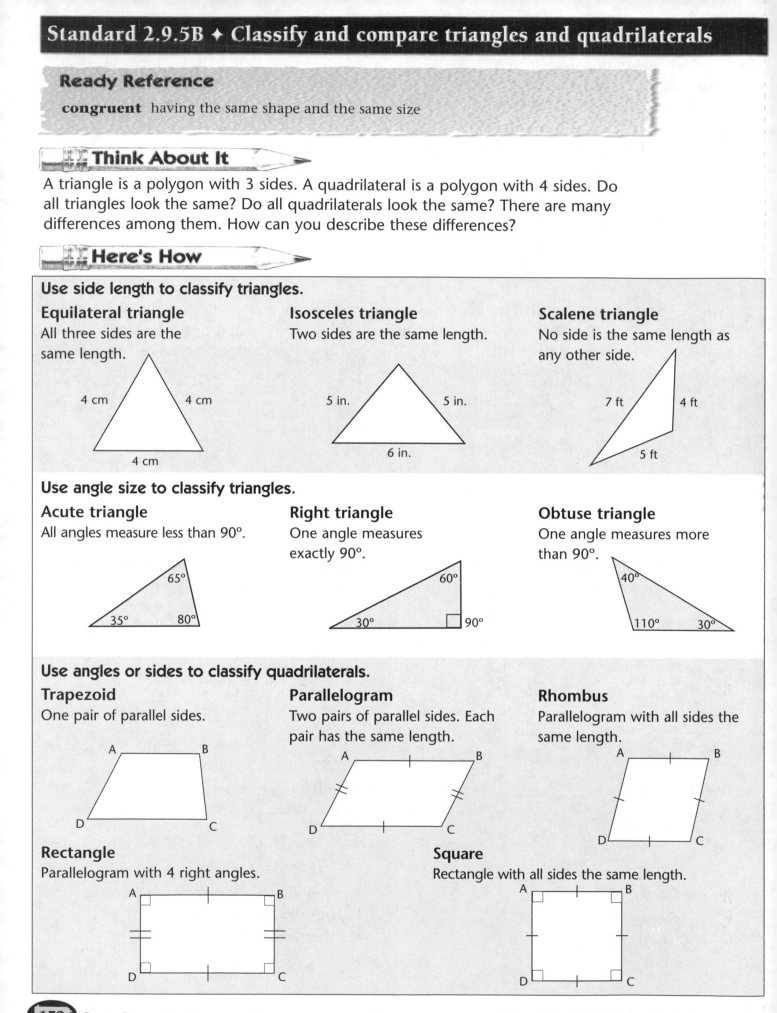

Use side length to classify triangles.

Equilateral triangle
All three sides are the same length.

4 cm   4 cm
4 cm

Isosceles triangle
Two sides are the same length.

5 in.   5 in.
6 in.

Scalene triangle
No side is the same length as any other side.

7 ft   4 ft
5 ft

Use angle size to classify triangles.

Acute triangle
All angles measure less than 90°.

65°
35°   80°

Right triangle
One angle measures exactly 90°.

60°
30°   90°

Obtuse triangle
One angle measures more than 90°.

40°
110°   30°

Use angles or sides to classify quadrilaterals.

Trapezoid
One pair of parallel sides.

A   B
D   C

Parallelogram
Two pairs of parallel sides. Each pair has the same length.

A   B
D   C

Rhombus
Parallelogram with all sides the same length.

A   B
D   C

Rectangle
Parallelogram with 4 right angles.

A   B
D   C

Square
Rectangle with all sides the same length.

A   B
D   C

Practice

1. What is this type of triangle called?

   A an equilateral triangle

   B an isosceles triangle

   C a congruent triangle

   D a scalene triangle

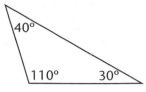

7 in.   7 in.

8 in.

2. What is this type of triangle called?

   E a right triangle

   F an acute triangle

   G a parallel triangle

   H an obtuse triangle

40° 110° 30°

3. What do all quadrilaterals have in common?

   A parallel sides

   B 4 congruent sides

   C right angles

   D four sides

4. How is a rhombus different from a square?

   E It does not have parallel sides.

   F It does not have right angles.

   G It does not have four sides.

   H It does not have congruent sides.

5. What is another way to classify a rectangle?

   A square

   B trapezoid

   C parallelogram

   D rhombus

6. How many sides are congruent in an isosceles trapezoid?

   E two

   F three

   G four

   H none

7. Which one of these shapes is NOT a parallelogram?

   A square

   B rhomboid

   C trapezoid

   D rhombus

8. Which of the following statements is NOT true about a rectangle?

   E It has four sides.

   F It has four right angles.

   G It has opposite sides that are congruent.

   H It has four congruent sides.

9. What is the best term to describe this shape?

   A rhombus

   B rectangle

   C trapezium

   D isosceles trapezoid

10. What is the best term to describe this shape?

    E a triangle

    F a square

    G a rhomboid

    H a trapezoid

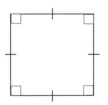

Ready Reference
circumference the distance around a circle
diameter a line segment that passes through the center of a circle and has both endpoints on the circle
radius a line segment with one endpoint on the center of a circle and an endpoint on the circle

Think About It

A circle has no beginning and no end. It is a simple closed curve. Look at the circle. How do you measure its circumference, diameter, and radius?

Here's How

Step 1 Place a piece of string the distance around the circle and cut the string.

Step 2 Measure the piece of string with a ruler. This is the circumference of the circle. The circumference of this circle is _____ in.

Step 3 Cut a piece of string equal to the length of the diameter of the circle.

Step 4 Compare the pieces of string. Are they the same length? _____ How many pieces of string the length of the diameter equal the length of string that measured the circumference? _____ What is the length of the diameter? _____ in.

Step 5 Divide the length of the diameter in half to find the radius. The radius of this circle is _____ in.

Practice

Use a piece of string and a ruler to measure the circumference of each circle in Problems 1–4.

1. What is the circumference of this circle?

   A $2\frac{3}{4}$ in.

   B 4 in.

   C 3 in.

   D $3\frac{1}{2}$ in.

2. What is the circumference of this circle?

   E $2\frac{1}{2}$ in.

   F 3 in.

   G $3\frac{1}{2}$ in.

   H 4 in.

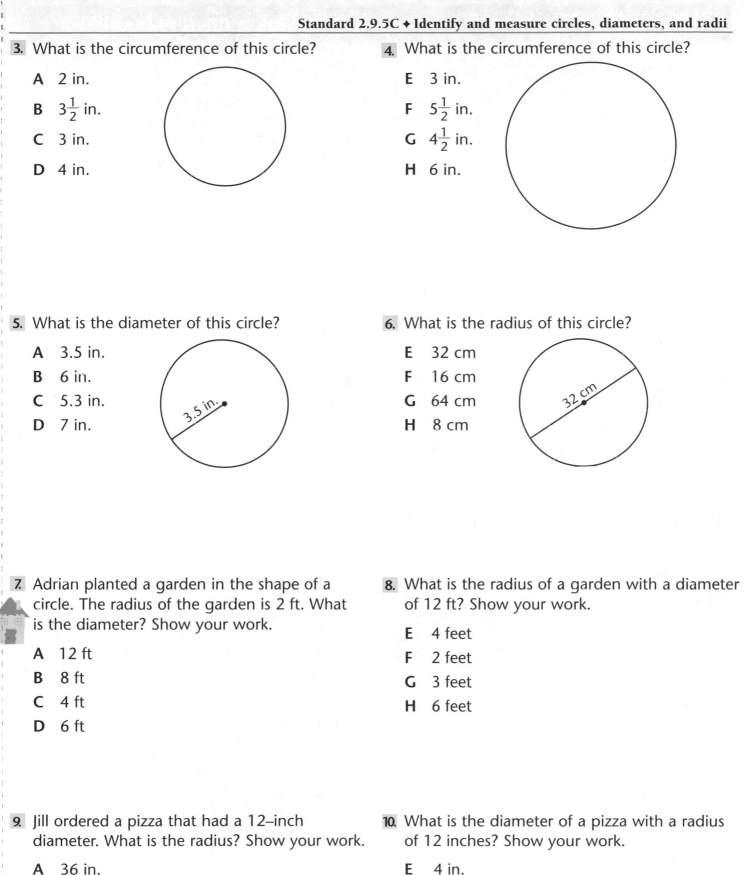

3. What is the circumference of this circle?

   A 2 in.

   B $3\frac{1}{2}$ in.

   C 3 in.

   D 4 in.

4. What is the circumference of this circle?

   E 3 in.

   F $5\frac{1}{2}$ in.

   G $4\frac{1}{2}$ in.

   H 6 in.

5. What is the diameter of this circle?

   A 3.5 in.

   B 6 in.

   C 5.3 in.

   D 7 in.

   3.5 in.

6. What is the radius of this circle?

   E 32 cm

   F 16 cm

   G 64 cm

   H 8 cm

   32 cm

7. Adrian planted a garden in the shape of a circle. The radius of the garden is 2 ft. What is the diameter? Show your work.

   A 12 ft

   B 8 ft

   C 4 ft

   D 6 ft

8. What is the radius of a garden with a diameter of 12 ft? Show your work.

   E 4 feet

   F 2 feet

   G 3 feet

   H 6 feet

9. Jill ordered a pizza that had a 12–inch diameter. What is the radius? Show your work.

   A 36 in.

   B 24 in.

   C 6 in.

   D 48 in.

10. What is the diameter of a pizza with a radius of 12 inches? Show your work.

    E 4 in.

    F 24 in.

    G 36 in.

    H 6 in.

Think About It

Circles, triangles, squares, and rectangles are two-dimensional, or flat, shapes. Sometimes you see a flat shape as part of a solid, or three-dimensional, figure. When you look at a can of soup, for example, you find a circle at the top and bottom of the can. When you look at a box, you might see a square or rectangle as one side of the box. How are the solid figures constructed?

Here's How

Look at these space figures. They are solid, three-dimensional objects. Notice that they may have *faces*, or flat sides. They may have *edges*, line segments where two faces meet. They may have a *vertex* or *vertices*, a point where three or more edges meet.

Cube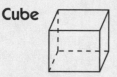

A cube has 8 vertices, _____ faces, and 12 edges. All the faces of a cube are squares.

Rectangular Prism

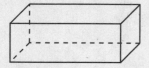

A rectangular prism has _____ vertices, 6 faces, and _____ edges.

Pyramid

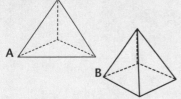

Pyramid A is a triangular pyramid. It has _____ faces, _____ vertices, and _____ edges. All the faces are triangles. The base is a _____.

Pyramid B is a square pyramid. It has 5 faces, _____ edges, and _____ vertices. The base is a _____.

Cylinder

A cylinder has 0 edges, 0 faces, and 0 vertices. It has _____ flat surfaces. The flat surfaces are _____.

Cone

A cone has _____ flat surface shaped like a circle.

Sphere

A sphere has _____ flat surfaces.

Practice

1. On which of these space figures would you find a triangle?

   A cube
   B rectangular prism
   C cylinder
   D square pyramid

2. On which of these space figures would you find a circle?

   E sphere
   F cone
   G rectangular prism
   H triangular prism

3. On which of these space figures would you find a square?

   A cylinder
   B cone
   C cube
   D sphere

Choose the correct name of each figure in Problems 4–9.

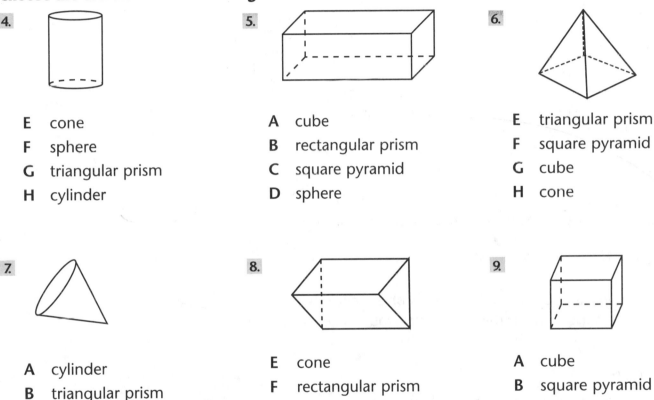

4.
   E cone
   F sphere
   G triangular prism
   H cylinder

5.
   A cube
   B rectangular prism
   C square pyramid
   D sphere

6.
   E triangular prism
   F square pyramid
   G cube
   H cone

7.
   A cylinder
   B triangular prism
   C cone
   D square pyramid

8.
   E cone
   F rectangular prism
   G triangular prism
   H square pyramid

9.
   A cube
   B square pyramid
   C rectangular prism
   D triangular prism

10. If you cut out 2 congruent circles and a rectangle, which space figure could you make?

    E rectangular prism
    F cylinder
    G cone
    H triangular prism

11. If you cut out 4 congruent triangles and a square, which space figure could you make?

    A cube
    B triangular prism
    C cone
    D square pyramid

Ready Reference

geoboard a board with pegs aligned in grid fashion that permits rubber bands to be wrapped around pegs to form geometric figures

Think About It

There are many ways to draw or create two-dimensional shapes. You can use objects such as straws, toothpicks, or string to make the outlines of flat shapes. You can use pattern blocks to create shapes. Then you can often use flat shapes to construct space shapes, or three-dimensional objects. Certain tools will help you draw flat shapes. What are some of these tools?

Here's How

Use a ruler.

1. How long is one side? _____

2. Use a ruler to make sure that each side of a square is the same length.

Use a compass.

A compass will help you measure radii and diameters.

3. What is the radius of this circle? _____

4. Open the compass as wide as the radius of the circle to draw a circle congruent to this one. Draw your circle to the right.

Use a protractor.

A protractor will help you measure and draw angles.

5. What is the measure of Angle *XYZ*? _____

Practice

1. If you wanted to copy a circle, which tool would you most likely use?

   A ruler

   B compass

   C string

   D protractor

2. If you wanted to copy a triangle, what tool could you use to measure and draw the angles?

   E protractor

   F compass

   G ruler

   H paper clip

Use this information to answer Problems 3–4.

Mae is using pattern blocks to make shapes. She is using blocks just like Shape A.

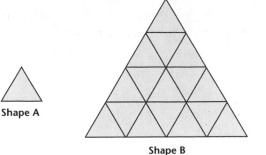

Shape A

Shape B

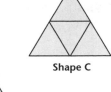

Shape C

3. How many pattern blocks shaped like Shape A do you find in Shape B?

A   10

B   12

C   13

D   16

4. How many groups of pattern blocks like Shape C do you find in Shape B?

E   3

F   5

G   4

H   6

Use the geoboard pictured here to answer Problems 5–6.

5. What shape has been made on this geoboard?

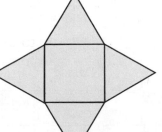

A   rectangle

B   square

C   triangle

D   circle

6. How many units long is the length of each side?

E   8 units

F   6 units

G   4 units

H   5 units

7. What space shape can be made by folding this flat shape?

A   triangular prism

B   cube

C   square pyramid

D   sphere

8. What space shape can be made by folding this flat shape?

E   cube

F   rectangular prism

G   cylinder

H   triangular prism

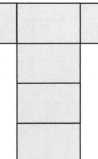

✏️ Think About It

Many everyday objects are examples of solid geometric shapes. Buildings, furniture, toys, and food containers are examples of solid geometric shapes. How many different space shapes do you see around you?

✏️ Here's How

Look at the picture. There is an alphabet letter on some of the geometric figures. Write the name of the figure beside the alphabet letter. The first one is done for you.

A   sphere _____

B _____

C _____

D _____

E _____

F _____

G _____

H _____

Practice

1. Which is shaped like a cereal box?

   A cube

   B rectangular prism

   C triangular prism

   D cone

2. Which is shaped like a soccer ball?

   E cylinder

   F cone

   G sphere

   H cube

3. Which is shaped like a can of soup?

   A triangular prism

   B sphere

   C cone

   D cylinder

4. Which is shaped like a die?

   E cube

   F square pyramid

   G rectangular prism

   H cylinder

5. Which is shaped like a party hat?

   A cylinder

   B sphere

   C cone

   D square pyramid

6. Which is shaped like a wedge of cheese?

   E cone

   F square pyramid

   G triangular prism

   H cube

7. Which of the following objects is probably NOT a sphere?

   A ice cream cone

   B globe

   C baseball

   D basketball

8. Which of the following objects is probably NOT a rectangular prism?

   E a bar of soap

   F a textbook

   G a shoe box

   H a drinking glass

9. A slice of pie is most like a

   A rectangular prism.

   B triangular prism.

   C cube.

   D cone.

10. A slice of a tree trunk is most like a

   E cylinder.

   F square pyramid.

   G sphere.

   H cone.

11. A camping tent is most like a

   A rectangular prism

   B cylinder

   C square pyramid

   D cube

Ready Reference

tessellation a repetitive pattern of polygons that covers an area with no holes and no overlaps; *example*: floor tiles

✏ Think About It

Hunter was asked to name a tessellation that is found in nature. He thought of a honeycomb. Is a honeycomb an example of a tessellation?

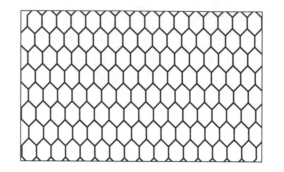

✏ Here's How

Step 1 Recognize the traits of tessellations.

1. How do you know when a pattern is a tessellation? It is a pattern that has no _____ and no _____.

Step 2 Carefully observe a honeycomb.

2. What shape makes up a honeycomb? _____

3. Are there holes between the shapes? _____ Are there any overlaps? _____

4. Is a honeycomb an example of a tessellation? _____

✏ Practice

Use this information to answer Problems 1–4.
Jed painted this pattern as a border around his room.

1. What shape makes up the pattern that Jed painted?

   A   circle

   B   square

   C   triangle

   D   rectangle

2. Which of the following is true about the pattern of shapes in this border?

   E   There are holes between the shapes.

   F   The shapes overlap.

   G   The shapes are not polygons.

   H   No two shapes are alike.

3. Which of the following statements is true about Jed's border?

   A   The pattern is a tessellation.

   B   The pattern is not a tessellation.

   C   The pattern does not repeat.

   D   The pattern does not overlap.

4. Which of the following statements is NOT true about tessellations?

   E   The pattern is repetitive.

   F   The pattern is made up of polygons.

   G   The pattern has no holes in it.

   H   The pattern may overlap.

Use this information to answer Problems 5–6.

Mrs. Wilkes covered her kitchen floor with this pattern of floor tiles.

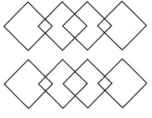

5. What shape makes up the floor tiles in Mrs. Wilkes' kitchen?

   A squares

   B rectangles

   C triangles

   D circles

6. Which of the following statements about the floor tiles is NOT true?

   E There are holes, or spaces, between the tiles.

   F The tiles overlap.

   G The floor pattern is a tessellation.

   H The tiles are a repeated pattern.

Use this information to answer Problems 7–8.

Mae made this shape with pattern blocks.

7. What polygon is used repeatedly to make this pattern?

   A squares

   B triangles

   C circles

   D rectangles

8. Which of the following statements is true about the pattern?

   E The triangles overlap.

   F There are holes in the pattern.

   G The triangles do not repeat.

   H The pattern is a tessellation.

9. Look at the pattern on the right. Why is this pattern NOT a tessellation?

   A The polygons do not repeat.

   B The polygons overlap.

   C There are holes between the polygons.

   D Rectangles are not polygons.

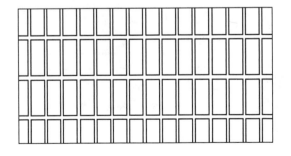

10. Which of the following would be the LEAST likely to have a tessellation pattern?

   E a necklace made of different beads

   F a woven rug

   G tiles on a floor

   H a sheet of graph paper

11. Which of the following would be the MOST likely to have a tessellation pattern?

   A a flower garden

   B books along a bookshelf

   C shingles on a roof

   D a checkerboard

Think About It

The perimeter of a plane figure is the distance around it, or the outside edge. The perimeter of a circle is called the circumference. The area is the number of square units that cover the surface of a plane figure. How can you determine the perimeter and area of triangles, quadrilaterals, and circles?

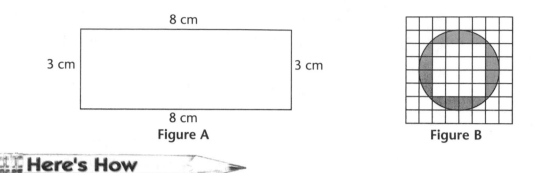

Figure A   Figure B

Here's How

Find the perimeter of a plane figure.

Look at Figure A. The perimeter of this rectangle is the distance around the outside. The formula for determining the perimeter of quadrilaterals is $P = length + length + width + width$. Another way to state the formula is $P = 2l + 2w$. $P = (2 \times 8) + (2 \times \underline{\hspace{1cm}}) = \underline{\hspace{1cm}}$ cm

Find the area of a plane figure.

Look at Figure A. The area of a plane figure is the number of sq units that cover the surface. The formula for determining the area of most quadrilaterals is $A = length \times width$ or $A = l \times w$. The area of Figure A is $A = 8 \times \underline{\hspace{1cm}} = \underline{\hspace{1cm}}$ square cm

Estimate the area of a circle.

1. Look at Figure B. Count the number of whole units that are inside the circle. There are _____ sq units inside the circle.

2. The shaded units inside the circle are not whole squares. There are _____ shaded units.

3. Add the number of units together. The estimated area of the circle is about _____ sq units.

Practice

Use these figures to answer Problems 1–4.

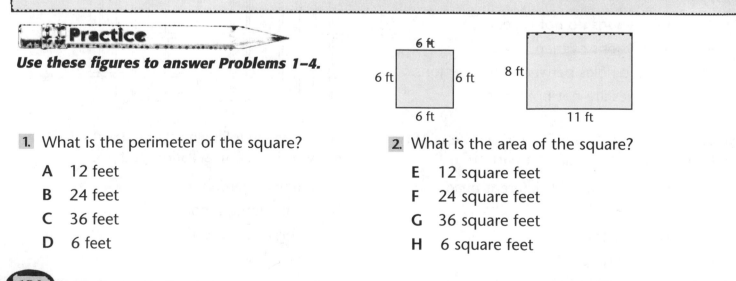

1. What is the perimeter of the square?

   A 12 feet

   B 24 feet

   C 36 feet

   D 6 feet

2. What is the area of the square?

   E 12 square feet

   F 24 square feet

   G 36 square feet

   H 6 square feet

3. What is the perimeter of the rectangle?

A 19 feet

B 16 feet

C 22 feet

D 38 feet

4. What is the area of the rectangle?

E 88 square feet

F 64 square feet

G 121 square feet

H 19 square feet

Use this information for Problems 5–8.

Sashi made a rectangular garden that is 4 feet long and 3 feet wide. She wants to put a fence around the edge of the garden and she wants to buy a plastic sheet to put over the garden.

5. What is a number sentence that Sashi can use to find the perimeter of her garden?

A $4 + 3 = P$

B $4 \times 3 = P$

C $4 + 4 + 3 + 3 = P$

D $4 - 3 = P$

6. What is the perimeter of Sashi's garden?

E 1 foot

F 14 feet

G 12 feet

H 7 feet

7. What is the number sentence that Sashi can use to find the area of her garden?

A $4 + 3 = A$

B $4 \times 3 = A$

C $4 + 4 + 3 + 3 = A$

D $4 - 3 = A$

8. What is the area of Sashi's garden?

E 7 square feet

F 14 square feet

G 1 square foot

H 12 square feet

9. What is the estimated area of Figure 1?

A 32 sq units

B 64 sq units

C 16 sq units

D 8 sq units

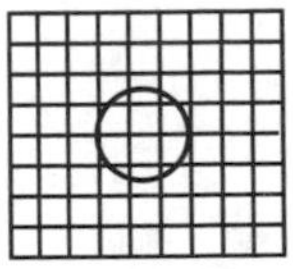

Figure 1

10. What is the estimated area of Figure 2?

E 25 sq units

F 24 sq units

G 52 sq units

H 42 sq units

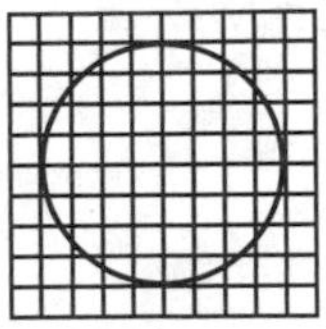

Figure 2

11. What is the estimated area of Figure 3?

A 6 sq units

B 12 sq units

C 20 sq units

D 24 sq units

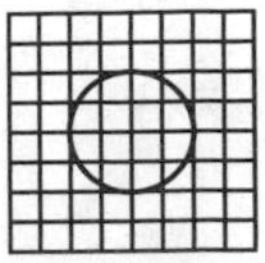

Figure 3

12. What is the estimated area of Figure 4?

E 16 sq units

F 14 sq units

G 12 sq units

H 32 sq units

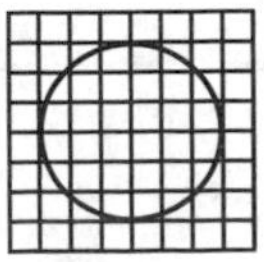

Figure 4

Think About It

Plane geometry is about shapes such as circles, squares, rectangles, and triangles. The basic building blocks of these shapes are points, lines, line segments, and angles. How do you define these geometric terms?

A plane is a flat surface that continues in all directions. A *point* is an exact location in space. A *line* is a straight set of points that goes on forever. A *line segment* is a part of a line with two endpoints. A *ray* is a part of a line with one endpoint that goes on forever in one direction. An *angle* is two rays with the same endpoint.

Here's How

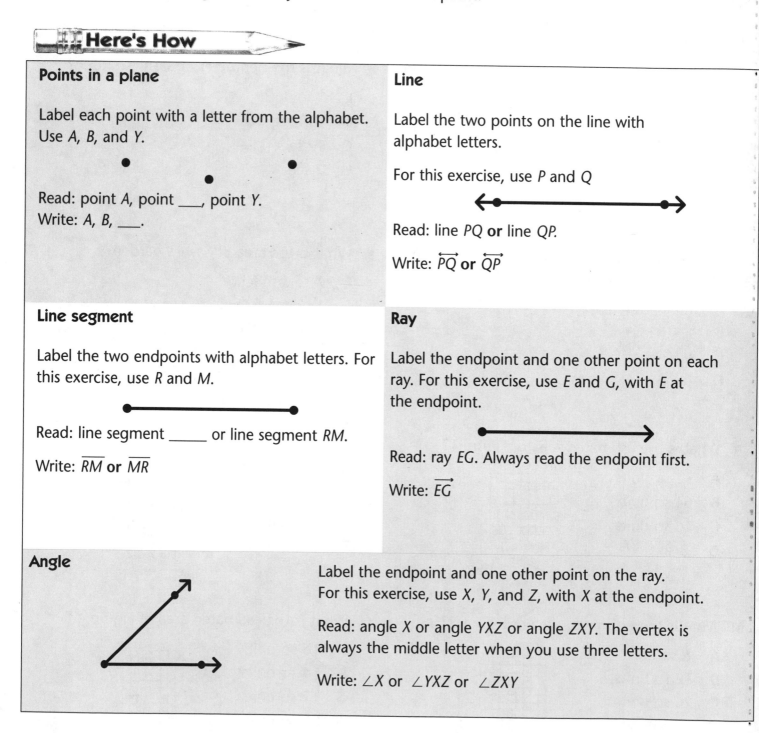

Points in a plane

Label each point with a letter from the alphabet. Use *A*, *B*, and *Y*.

Read: point *A*, point ___, point *Y*.
Write: *A*, *B*, ___.

Line

Label the two points on the line with alphabet letters.

For this exercise, use *P* and *Q*

Read: line *PQ* **or** line *QP*.

Write: $\overleftrightarrow{PQ}$ **or** $\overleftrightarrow{QP}$

Line segment

Label the two endpoints with alphabet letters. For this exercise, use *R* and *M*.

Read: line segment _____ or line segment *RM*.

Write: $\overline{RM}$ **or** $\overline{MR}$

Ray

Label the endpoint and one other point on each ray. For this exercise, use *E* and *G*, with *E* at the endpoint.

Read: ray *EG*. Always read the endpoint first.

Write: $\overrightarrow{EG}$

Angle

Label the endpoint and one other point on the ray. For this exercise, use *X*, *Y*, and *Z*, with *X* at the endpoint.

Read: angle *X* or angle *YXZ* or angle *ZXY*. The vertex is always the middle letter when you use three letters.

Write: ∠*X* or ∠*YXZ* or ∠*ZXY*

Practice

1. What is this figure called?

   A   a line

   B   a ray

   C   a line segment

   D   an angle

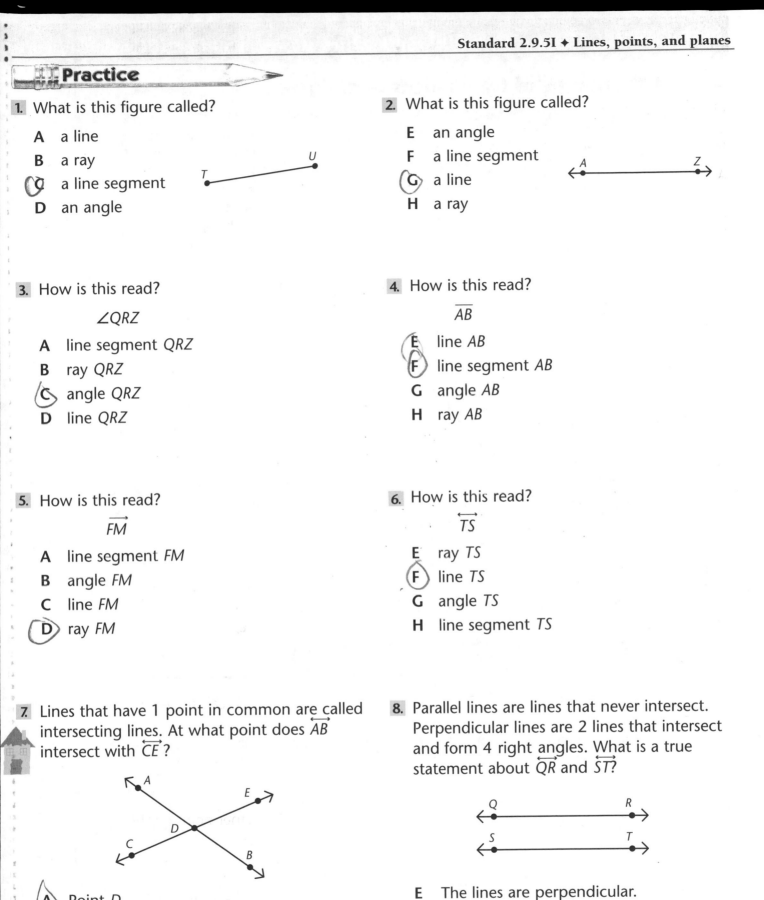

2. What is this figure called?

   E   an angle

   F   a line segment

   G   a line

   H   a ray

3. How is this read?

   ∠QRZ

   A   line segment QRZ

   B   ray QRZ

   C   angle QRZ

   D   line QRZ

4. How is this read?

   $\overline{AB}$

   E   line AB

   F   line segment AB

   G   angle AB

   H   ray AB

5. How is this read?

   $\overrightarrow{FM}$

   A   line segment FM

   B   angle FM

   C   line FM

   D   ray FM

6. How is this read?

   $\overleftrightarrow{TS}$

   E   ray TS

   F   line TS

   G   angle TS

   H   line segment TS

7. Lines that have 1 point in common are called intersecting lines. At what point does $\overleftrightarrow{AB}$ intersect with $\overleftrightarrow{CE}$?

   A   Point D

   B   Point C

   C   Point B

   D   Point E

8. Parallel lines are lines that never intersect. Perpendicular lines are 2 lines that intersect and form 4 right angles. What is a true statement about $\overleftrightarrow{QR}$ and $\overleftrightarrow{ST}$?

   E   The lines are perpendicular.

   F   The lines intersect.

   G   The lines are parallel.

   H   The lines form an angle.

Part 1 ✦ Properties of two-dimensional figures

Think About It

Plane figures are shapes that are two–dimensional, or flat. A circle is a plane figure. It is a closed curve in which the distances from the center point to the outside edge are all equal. Polygons are plane figures that are formed by joining three or more line segments. The line segments are joined only at the endpoints and each endpoint is connected to only two line segments. What are the many types of polygons and what is special about them?

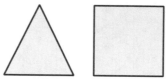

polygons

Here's How

1. A triangle is a polygon with three sides. It may be an equilateral triangle with three congruent sides, an isosceles triangle with two congruent sides, or a scalene triangle with no congruent sides. What type of triangle is shown above? _____

2. A quadrilateral is a polygon with four sides. There are three basic types of quadrilaterals. A trapezium has no parallel sides. A trapezoid has one pair of parallel sides. A parallelogram has two pairs of parallel sides. What kind of quadrilateral is shown above: a trapezium, a trapezoid, or a parallelogram? _____

3. There are four types of parallelograms. A rhomboid has no right angles and only opposite sides are congruent. A rhombus has no right angles and four congruent sides. A rectangle has four right angles and only opposite sides are congruent. A square has four right angles and four congruent sides. What kind of parallelogram is shown above? _____

Practice

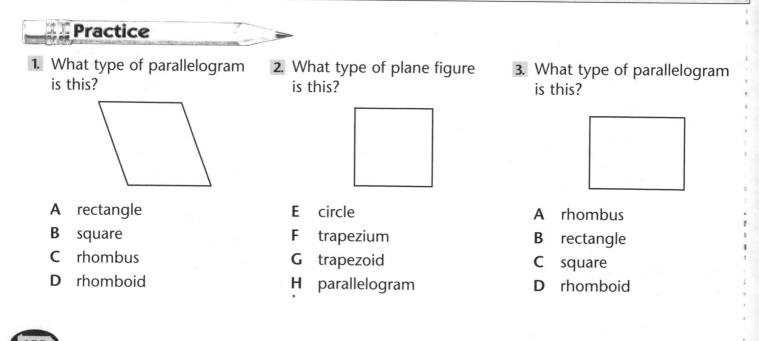

1. What type of parallelogram is this?

A   rectangle
B   square
C   rhombus
D   rhomboid

2. What type of plane figure is this?

E   circle
F   trapezium
G   trapezoid
H   parallelogram

3. What type of parallelogram is this?

A   rhombus
B   rectangle
C   square
D   rhomboid

4. What type of quadrilateral is this?

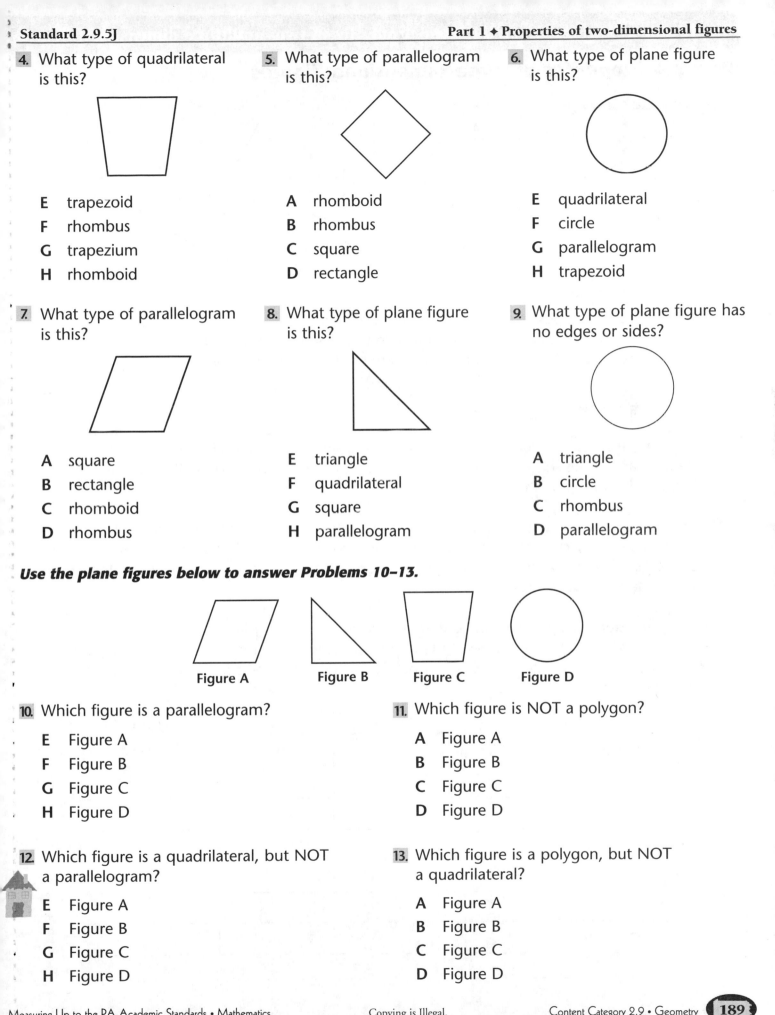

E   trapezoid

F   rhombus

G   trapezium

H   rhomboid

5. What type of parallelogram is this?

A   rhomboid

B   rhombus

C   square

D   rectangle

6. What type of plane figure is this?

E   quadrilateral

F   circle

G   parallelogram

H   trapezoid

7. What type of parallelogram is this?

A   square

B   rectangle

C   rhomboid

D   rhombus

8. What type of plane figure is this?

E   triangle

F   quadrilateral

G   square

H   parallelogram

9. What type of plane figure has no edges or sides?

A   triangle

B   circle

C   rhombus

D   parallelogram

Use the plane figures below to answer Problems 10–13.

Figure A   Figure B   Figure C   Figure D

10. Which figure is a parallelogram?

E   Figure A

F   Figure B

G   Figure C

H   Figure D

11. Which figure is NOT a polygon?

A   Figure A

B   Figure B

C   Figure C

D   Figure D

12. Which figure is a quadrilateral, but NOT a parallelogram?

E   Figure A

F   Figure B

G   Figure C

H   Figure D

13. Which figure is a polygon, but NOT a quadrilateral?

A   Figure A

B   Figure B

C   Figure C

D   Figure D

Part 2 ✦ Properties of three-dimensional figures

Ready Reference

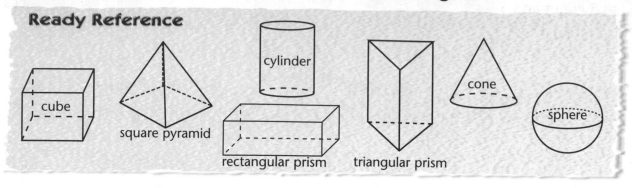

cube

square pyramid

cylinder

rectangular prism

triangular prism

cone

sphere

Think About It

Plane figures are flat shapes. If a shape is not flat, takes up space, and is three-dimensional, it is called a solid or space figure. The five most common solids are the sphere, the cone, the cylinder, the pyramid, and the prism. What are the special features of these shapes?

Here's How

1. The sphere, the cone, and the cylinder have curved sides. A sphere is like a ball. A cone has a circle base and is the shape of an ice cream cone. A cylinder has congruent circles for bases at its top and bottom. It is shaped like a can.

2. Prisms and pyramids are made up of polygon faces. In a prism, 2 congruent polygons are the bases and parallelograms are the sides. A cube is a prism. Other prisms are rectangular prisms and triangular prisms. A pyramid has one polygon for a base and triangles make up the sides. A square pyramid has a square for the base.

3. Three-dimensional shapes have faces that are flat sides made of plane figures. They have edges where two faces meet. They have a vertex (or vertices) which is the point where three or more edges meet, or a point like the tip of a cone. Look carefully at the space figures above. Then fill in the chart.

Name	Edges	Vertices	Faces	Shapes of Faces
Rectangular prism	12	8	6	rectangles
Sphere				
Square pyramid				
Cube				
Cylinder				
Cone				
Triangular prism				

Practice

1. This figure has 8 edges and 5 faces. Some of the faces are triangles. What is this figure called?

A cone
B triangular prism
C square pyramid
D cube

2. This figure has 12 edges and 6 faces. Its faces are squares. What is this figure called?

E square pyramid
F cube
G rectangular prism
H triangular prism

3. This figure has 0 edges, 0 vertices, and 0 faces. It is shaped like a ball. What is this figure called?

A cylinder
B circle
C cone
D sphere

4. This figure has 9 edges and 5 faces. Some of its faces are triangles. What is this figure called?

E rectangular prism
F triangular prism
G square pyramid
H cone

5. What is the name of this solid?

A cylinder
B cone
C square pyramid
D triangular prism

6. What is the name of this solid?

E cube
F square pyramid
G cone
H cylinder

Use these figures to answer Problems 7–10.

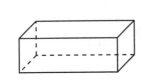 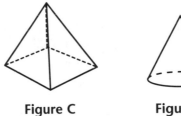

Figure A   **Figure B**   **Figure C**   **Figure D**

7. Which figure has faces that are rectangles?

A Figure A
B Figure B
C Figure C
D Figure D

8. Which figure has 2 congruent circles as bases?

E Figure A
F Figure B
G Figure C
H Figure D

9. Which figure has only 1 vertex?

A Figure A
B Figure B
C Figure C
D Figure D

10. Which figure has only 1 face that is a square?

E Figure A
F Figure B
G Figure C
H Figure D

Ready Reference

transformation an operation on a geometric figure by which each point gives rise to a unique image

rotation a transformation that maps every point in the plane to its image by rotating the plane around a fixed point or line

Think About It

Lay a book on your desk. Now "flip" the book as shown in the diagram. Is the book still the same size and shape? What is different about the book?

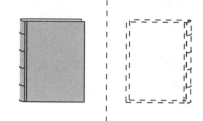

Here's How

Transformations

A transformation is a change of position of a figure. The book is still the same size and shape. If you traced around the book before and after you flipped it over, the shapes would be congruent. By flipping the book, you have made a transformation.

Flips and slides

Besides rotations, other kinds of transformations are making a figure bigger or smaller, flipping a figure to produce a mirror image, or sliding a figure to move it somewhere else along a line.

Turns

Take the book again and hold it by one corner. Keep the book flat on the desk but turn it in a circle with the corner staying in the same place. Now you have given the book a turn.

1. Are the figures similar? _____

2. Are all of the figures the same size? _____

3. What kind of transformation is this? _____

Practice

1. Which type of transformation do you see in this pattern?

   A flip
   B shapes made larger
   C slide
   D turn

2. Which type of transformation do you see in this pattern?

   E slide
   F flip
   G turn
   H shapes made smaller

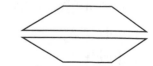

3. Which type of transformation do you see in this pattern?

A   turn

B   shapes made smaller

C   slide

(D) flip

4. Which type of transformation do you see in this problem?

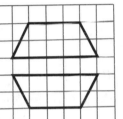

(E) slide

F   shapes made larger

G   flip

H   turn

5. What kind of transformation is shown in the grid below?

A   made bigger

B   made smaller

C   turn

(D) slide

6. What kind of transformation is shown in the grid below?

E   slide

(F) flip

G   made larger

H   turn

7. Picture a smaller triangle to the right of a larger triangle. What kind of transformation is this?

A   triangle made smaller

B   flip

(C) triangle made larger

(D) slide

8. Four congruent right triangles are side by side. The right angles are on the bottom left of each triangle. What kind of transformation is this?

E   triangle made larger

F   slide

(G) flip

H   triangle made smaller

9. A triangle is congruent but facing a different direction. What kind of transformation is this?

A   made smaller

(B) flip

C   turn

D   slide

10. A congruent triangle is upside down next to the original triangle. What kind of transformation is this?

E   slide

(F) turn

G   made larger

H   flip

Part 1 ✦ Parallel and perpendicular lines

Ready Reference

perpendicular lines two lines that intersect to form right angles; *example:* ⊥, ⌐, Γ

Think About It

When two streets cross each other, the place where the two streets meet is called the intersection. In geometry, when two lines cross each other at only one point, they are called intersecting lines. Two lines that intersect and form right angles are called perpendicular lines. Two lines that will never intersect are called parallel lines. What mathematical symbol looks like two perpendicular lines? What mathematical symbol looks like two parallel lines?

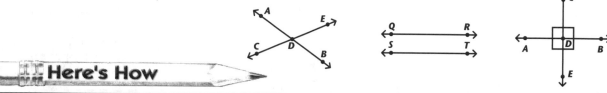

Here's How

Perpendicular lines

1. Look at the perpendicular lines. To indicate that lines are perpendicular, a square might be drawn at the point where the lines intersect. Perpendicular lines meet to form right angles. What mathematical symbol looks like two perpendicular lines? _____

2. Draw perpendicular lines.

Parallel lines

1. Look at the parallel lines. Parallel lines do not intersect. They are always the same distance apart from each other. What mathematical symbol looks like two parallel lines? _____

2. Draw parallel lines.

Practice

Use the pairs of lines to answer Problems 1–4.

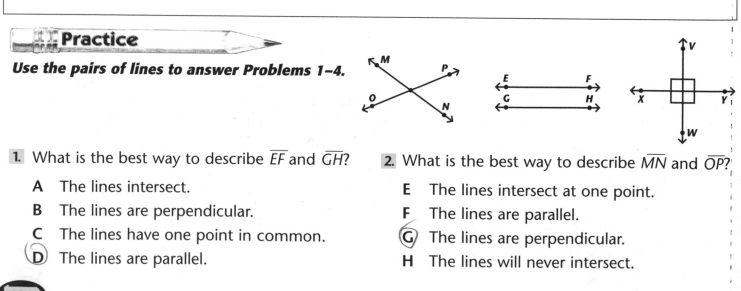

1. What is the best way to describe $\overline{EF}$ and $\overline{GH}$?

   A   The lines intersect.

   B   The lines are perpendicular.

   C   The lines have one point in common.

   D   The lines are parallel.

2. What is the best way to describe $\overline{MN}$ and $\overline{OP}$?

   E   The lines intersect at one point.

   F   The lines are parallel.

   G   The lines are perpendicular.

   H   The lines will never intersect.

3. What is the best way to describe $\overline{VW}$ and $\overline{XY}$?

   A The lines are parallel.

   B The lines will never intersect.

   C The lines are perpendicular.

   D The lines do not intersect.

4. What is another way to describe $\overline{EF}$ and $\overline{GH}$?

   E The lines are perpendicular.

   F The lines will never intersect.

   G The lines will intersect at one point.

   H The lines are intersecting lines.

Use the polygons below to answer Problems 5–10.

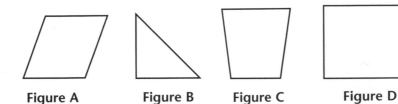

    Figure A   **Figure B**   **Figure C**   **Figure D**

5. Which two figures are parallelograms?

   A Figure A and Figure B

   B Figure A and Figure C

   C Figure B and Figure D

   D Figure A and Figure D

6. Which figure is a trapezoid?

   E Figure D

   F Figure C

   G Figure B

   H Figure A

7. Perpendicular lines meet to form right angles. Which two figures have right angles?

   A Figure A and Figure C

   B Figure B and Figure D

   C Figure A and Figure D

   D Figure A and Figure B

8. A rhombus is a parallelogram that has no right angles. Which figure is a rhombus?

   E Figure B

   F Figure D

   G Figure A

   H Figure C

9. Which figure is a parallelogram with right angles?

   A Figure D

   B Figure C

   C Figure B

   D Figure A

10. Which figure has a right angle but no parallel sides?

   E Figure C

   F Figure A

   G Figure D

   H Figure B

11. Which is an example of parallel lines?

   A the sides of a door

   B lines that form an X

   C the top and side of a window

   D two diameters of a circle

12. Which is an example of perpendicular lines?

   E lines that form an X

   F the edges of a cylinder

   G the corner of a room

   H the top and bottom edges of a book

Standard 2.9.5L ✦ Identify properties of geometric figures

Part 2 ✦ Similar, congruent, and symmetrical figures

Ready Reference

congruent having the same shape and the same size

similarity having the same shape but not necessarily the same size

symmetry a line of symmetry separates a figure into two congruent halves, each of which is a reflection of the other; *example:* ∅, the line through the center of the circle divides it into congruent halves

✏️ Think About It

Carl wants to know if the dotted line in the figure is a line of symmetry. He copied the figure onto a sheet of paper. Do you know how Carl can use the paper to determine if the line is a line of symmetry?

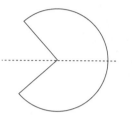

✏️ Here's How

Step 1 Make a model.

1. Place a sheet of paper over the figure. Trace the figure and the dotted line.

2. Carefully fold the paper along the dotted line. Do the outlines of the two halves of the figure match exactly? _____

Step 2 Determine symmetry.

3. Open the paper. Carefully observe the two parts on either side of the dotted line. Are they congruent? _____

4. Is the dotted line a line of symmetry? _____

✏️ Practice

Use the plane figures below to answer Problems 1–2.

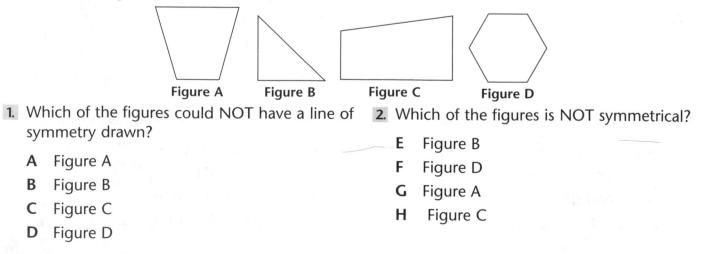

Figure A   Figure B   Figure C   Figure D

1. Which of the figures could NOT have a line of symmetry drawn?

  A   Figure A
  B   Figure B
  C   Figure C
  D   Figure D

2. Which of the figures is NOT symmetrical?

  E   Figure B
  F   Figure D
  G   Figure A
  H   Figure C

Use the figures below to answer Problems 3–4.

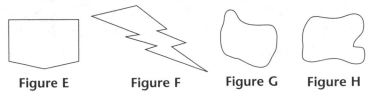

Figure E   **Figure F**   **Figure G**   **Figure H**

3. Which figure above could have a line of symmetry?

   A Figure E

   B Figure F

   C Figure G

   D Figure H

4. Which figure is symmetrical?

   E Figure H

   F Figure E

   G Figure F

   H Figure G

Use the figures below to answer Problems 5–6.

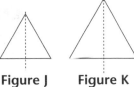

Figure J   **Figure K**

5. Do each of the triangles have lines of symmetry?

   A yes

   B no

   C only Triangle J

   D only Triangle K

6. How can the triangles be described?

   E They are congruent.

   F They are the same size, but not the same shape.

   G They are similar.

   H They are not symmetrical.

Use the figures below to answer Problems 7–8.

Figure 1   **Figure 2**   **Figure 3**   **Figure 4**

7. Which of these figures is not symmetrical?

   A Figure 1

   B Figure 2

   C Figure 3

   D Figure 4

8. Which two figures are congruent?

   E Figure 1 and Figure 2

   F Figure 2 and Figure 3

   G Figure 1 and Figure 3

   H Figure 2 and Figure 4

1. Study the figures labeled A and B below. Beside Figure A, draw three more shapes to make a slide pattern using the figure shown. For Figure B, draw one additional shape to create a flip pattern of the figure shown. After you complete the drawings, decide if the figures shown are similar. Are they congruent? Explain.

- **READ** the problem and break it into parts to solve it.
- **SHOW** each step of your math work.
- **EXPLAIN** why you solved the problem as you did.
- **WRITE** an explanation describing what you did and why you solved the problem as you did, **EVEN** if you used mental math or a calculator.
- **WRITE** your answer in the space provided.

Figure A

Figure B

Are the figures similar? _____

Are the figures congruent? _____

Are the figures similar? _____

Are the figures congruent? _____

Explanation

0–5 Points

Score _____

2. Examine the figures identified as 1, 2, and 3. For each, identify the type of figure and the number of faces, edges, and vertices. How are a cube and a rectangular prism alike? How are they different?

- **EXPLAIN** your response to the question.
- **WRITE** your answers in the space provided.

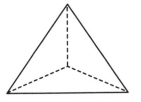

Figure 1

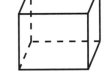

Figure 2

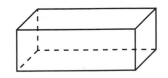

Figure 3

Type _____

Faces _____

Edges _____

Vertices _____

Type _____

Faces _____

Edges _____

Vertices _____

Type _____

Faces _____

Edges _____

Vertices _____

Explanation

0–5 Points
Score _____

3. Study the figures below. Circle the letters of the figures that are NOT polygons. Explain your choices. On the lines provided, identify the name for each shape shown.

- **READ** the problem and break it into parts to solve it.
- **EXPLAIN** why you solved the problem as you did.
- **WRITE** your answers in the space provided.

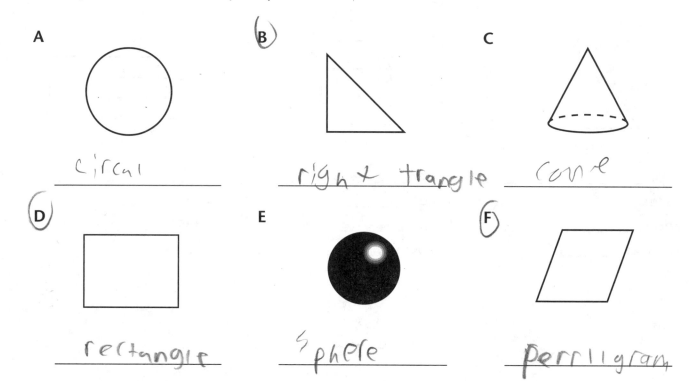

A

circal

B

right trangle

C

cone

D

rectangle

E

sphere

F

perrllgram

Explanation

a ficur is not made by lines
a cone is dose not have a line.
a sphere has no base
a circil

line

0–5 Points
Score _____

4. The items shown in the drawings represent everyday items you might find in your home or at school. Study the drawings carefully. Classify each object according to its three–dimensional shape. Then answer the question.

- **LOOK** carefully at each drawing to identify its shape.
- **ANSWER** the question and **EXPLAIN** your answer.
- **WRITE** your answers in the space provided.

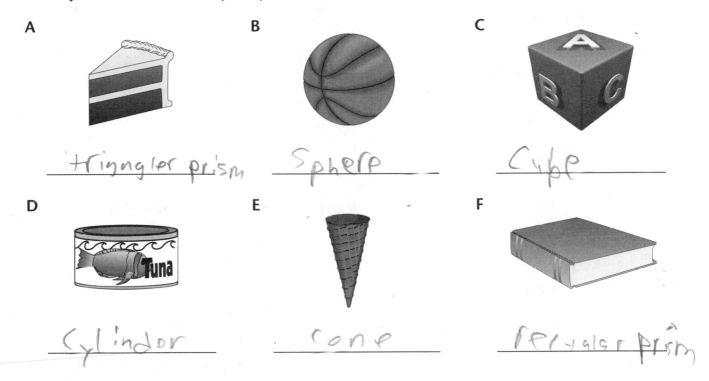

A

triangler prism

B

Sphere

C

Cube

D

Cylindor

E

cone

F

regular prism

How are a square and a cube related? Explain.

a cube has a face of a saqe

0–5 Points
Score _____

1. Which of the following is NOT a characteristic of all polygons?

   A   It has at least 3 line segments.

   B   Each endpoint is connected to only two line segments.

   C   The line segments are congruent.

   D   It is a closed plane figure.

2. Which line segments are perpendicular?

   E

   F

   G

   H

3. What is a triangle with two congruent sides called?

   A   equilateral triangle

   B   acute triangle

   C   scalene triangle

   D   isosceles triangle

4. Which shows an estimate of the area of this circle?

   E   10 square units

   F   6 square units

   G   16 square units

   H   8 square units

5. How many lines of symmetry does this figure have?

   A   2

   B   3

   C   4

   D   5

6. Which two of these figures are parallelograms?

   E   Figures A and B

   F   Figures A and C

   G   Figures B and C

   H   Figures B and D

7. Which figure is a rhombus?

   A   Figure C

   B   Figure D

   C   Figure A

   D   Figure B

8. Which figure is a trapezoid?

   E   Figure D

   F   Figure B

   G   Figure A

   H   Figure C

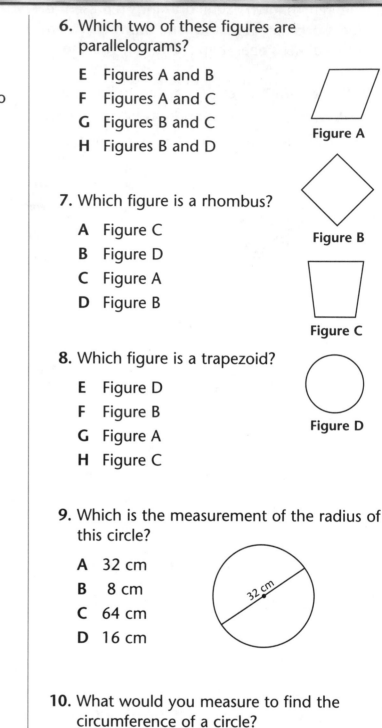

Figure A

Figure B

Figure C

Figure D

9. Which is the measurement of the radius of this circle?

   A   32 cm

   B   8 cm

   C   64 cm

   D   16 cm

10. What would you measure to find the circumference of a circle?

   E   The area inside the circle.

   F   A line segment that goes through the center point and has endpoints on the circle.

   G   The distance around a circle.

   H   A line segment with one endpoint in the center of the circle and the other on the circle.

11. How many faces, edges, and vertices does this figure have?

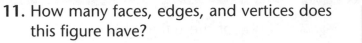

- **A** 4 faces, 6 edges, 4 vertices
- **B** 6 faces, 8 edges, 6 vertices
- **C** 6 faces, 12 edges, 8 vertices
- **D** 8 faces, 8 edges, 8 vertices

12. What is the figure in Problem 11 called?

- **E** cone
- **F** cube
- **G** triangular prism
- **H** square pyramid

Use these figures to answer Problems 13–15.

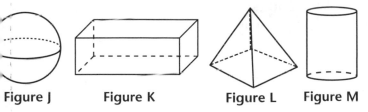

Figure J   Figure K   Figure L   Figure M

13. Which of these solids has triangles for faces?

- **A** Figure M
- **B** Figure L
- **C** Figure K
- **D** Figure J

14. Which two space figures have no square faces?

- **E** Figure J and Figure K
- **F** Figure L and Figure M
- **G** Figure K and Figure L
- **H** Figure J and Figure M

15. Which solid is a kind of prism?

- **A** Figure J
- **B** Figure K
- **C** Figure L
- **D** Figure M

16. What kind of space shape is a tennis ball?

- **E** cone
- **F** cylinder
- **G** sphere
- **H** triangular prism

17. What is a tessellation?

- **A** A pattern of shapes that covers an area without holes or overlaps.
- **B** A solid figure.
- **C** Lines that never intersect.
- **D** Figures that are the same shape but not the same size.

18. Which shows the perimeter of this figure?

- **E** 9 inches
- **F** 12 inches
- **G** 15 inches
- **H** 18 inches

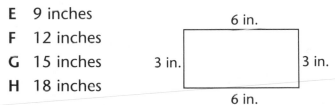

19. Bud made a butterfly garden in this shape. Which is the perimeter of his garden?

- **A** 12 ft
- **B** 24 ft
- **C** 16 ft
- **D** 32 ft

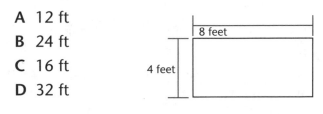

20. What is the measure of the area of Bud's garden?

- **E** 12 sq ft
- **F** 24 sq ft
- **G** 16 sq ft
- **H** 32 sq ft

Ready Reference

polygon a union of segments connected end to end, such that each segment intersects exactly two others at its endpoints

Think About It

Mr. Ridge drew a triangle on the chalkboard. He asked the class to determine whether the triangle he drew was a right triangle or some other type of triangle. He also asked the class to identify the legs and the hypotenuse of the triangle.

Here's How

Right angles and right triangles

Step 1 First, decide if the figure is a triangle. A triangle is a three-sided polygon. Count the number of sides on the polygon.

Step 2 Identify whether or not the triangle drawn is a right triangle. A right triangle is a triangle in which one of the angles measures exactly 90°. To determine if the triangle shown is a right triangle, use a protractor to measure each angle. Indicate the measure of each angle on the lines provided on the drawing.

1. Is the triangle shown a right triangle? How do you know? _____

   Note: The right angle of a right triangle may be identified by using the symbol in the angle shown.

2. In any triangle, the sum of all the angles must equal 180°. Write a number sentence that proves that the sum of the angles in the right triangle above equals 180°. _____

Step 3 Identify the legs and hypotenuse of the triangle.

3. The legs of a right triangle are the sides that form the right angle. Thus, a right triangle has two legs. Find and label the legs on the right triangle shown.

4. The hypotenuse of a right triangle is its longest side. Locate the longest side of the triangle shown. If necessary, use a ruler to confirm your choice. Label this side of the triangle as the hypotenuse.

Acute angles

1. An acute angle is an angle that has a measure less than 90°. Study the pictures below.

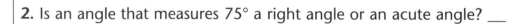

2. Is an angle that measures 75° a right angle or an acute angle? _____

Practice

1. Which of the following angle measurements would indicate that a triangle is a right triangle?

A   90°

B   45°

C   30°

D   60°

2. Which of the following make up the legs of a right triangle?

E   the longest side

F   the shortest side

G   the sides that form a right angle

H   the sides that do NOT form a right angle

3. Look at the figures shown below. Use a protractor to identify the one that is a right triangle.

A

B

C

D

4. Use a protractor to identify the right triangle below.

E

F

G

H

5. If one angle of a right triangle equals 90° and another angle equals 45°, what must the measure of the remaining angle be?

A   90°

B   45°

C   30°

D   60°

6. Look at the triangle below. Which line segment(s) form the hypotenuse of this triangle?

E $\overline{XY}$

F $\overline{XZ}$

G $\overline{YZ}$

H $\overline{ZX}$

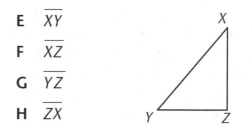

7. Which of the following is the hypotenuse of a right triangle?

A   the longest side

B   the shortest side

C   the sides that form a right angle

D   the mid-length side

8. Which of the symbols below are used to identify an angle as a right angle?

E   °

F   △

G

H   ∠

Ready Reference

geoboard a board with pegs aligned in grid fashion that permits rubber bands to be wrapped around the pegs to form geometric figures

✏️ Think About It

Groups of students in Mrs. Thornburg's class were provided with geoboards. Mrs. Thornburg asked each group to use rubber bands to form a right triangle on their geoboard.

✏️ Here's How

Make a right triangle like the one shown in the figure.

The pegs of a geoboard form a grid. The pegs in the grid are arranged in columns and rows.

1. Choose any column of pegs. Loop the rubber band around a peg near the top of the column. Count six or seven pegs down from the peg around which the rubber band is looped.

   Loop the other end of the rubber band around the second peg. This rubber band represents a leg of your right triangle.

2. Loop a second rubber band around the peg you just used at the bottom of the leg you formed. Count six or seven pegs over in the same row.

   Loop the other end of your rubber band around the second peg. This rubber band represents the second leg of your right triangle.

3. Use a third rubber band to complete your triangle. Loop this rubber band from the top of the first leg you made to the right side of the second leg you made. When in place, this rubber band forms the hypotenuse of your right triangle.

   Compare your triangle to the one shown. Use a protractor to measure the angle formed by the legs. The angle should measure 90°.

4. What other geometric shapes can you make with a geoboard?

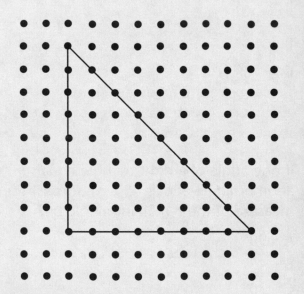

_____

_____

Practice

1. The students in Tommy's group used rubber bands to make triangles on geoboards. Which of the triangles made by the students is a right triangle?

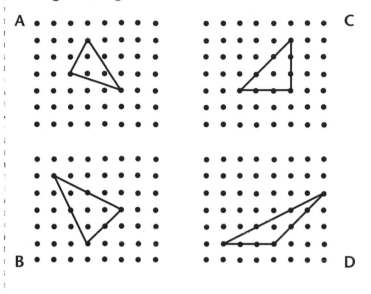

A B C D

2. Jorge's team made the triangle shown on a geoboard. Which rubber band forms the hypotenuse of this right triangle?

E $\overline{AB}$

F $\overline{AC}$

G $\overline{CB}$

H $\overline{BA}$

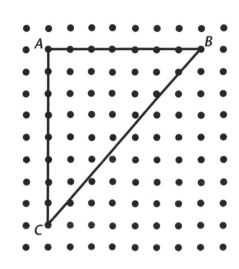

3. Sheila made the following shapes on her geoboard. Which of the shapes made by Sheila is a right triangle?

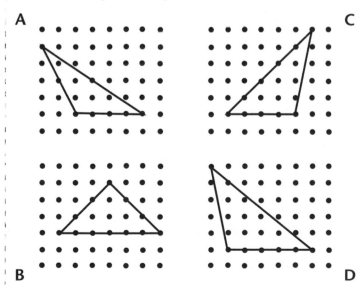

A B C D

4. Look at the right triangle shown. Which rubber band(s) form the leg(s) of this triangle?

E only $\overline{XY}$

F $\overline{XZ}$ and $\overline{XY}$

G only $\overline{XZ}$

H $\overline{XY}$ and $\overline{YZ}$

1. Look at the figures in the drawings below. Circle the letter beside any figure that shows a right triangle. Explain how you identified the right triangles.

- **REREAD** the problem and decide how to solve it.
- **CIRCLE** the letters of the correct responses.
- **WRITE** an explanation describing what you did and why you solved the problem as you did, **EVEN** if you used mental math or a calculator.

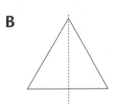 A

D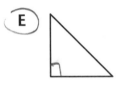

B

E

C

F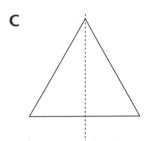

Explanation

a D e f are right because it has a right angel

2. Look at the drawings of the triangles shown below. For each drawing, identify the following by labeling the drawing with these terms: right angle, hypotenuse, leg, and acute angle. Then answer the question.

- **REREAD** the problem and break it into parts to solve it.
- **LABEL** the different parts of the triangle. **DRAW** lines to connect each label with its part.
- **USE** the appropriate symbol to identify the right angle of each triangle.
- **WRITE** an explanation describing what you did and why you solved the problem as you did, **EVEN** if you used mental math or a calculator.
- **WRITE** your answers in the space provided.

Figure 1

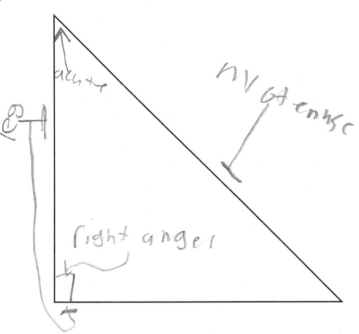

Figure 2

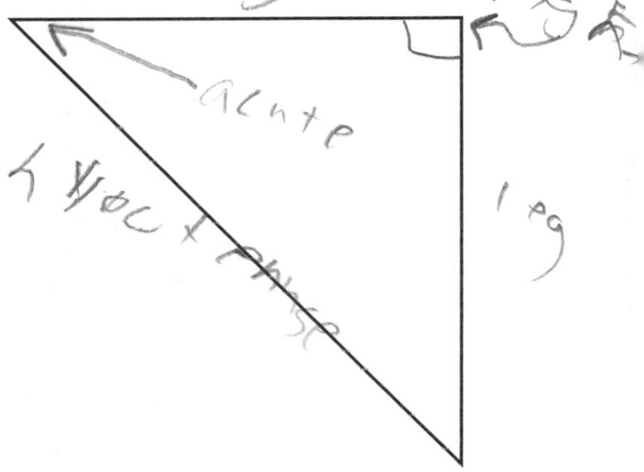

Explanation

How do you know the triangles above are right triangles?

they have a right angel

3. Use the grid below and a ruler to draw two right triangles. Label the first triangle A and include legs that measure 2 inches long each. Label the second triangle B and include one 2-inch leg and one 3-inch leg. Use the appropriate symbol to identify the right angle in each triangle.

- **REREAD** the problem and break it into parts to solve it.
- **LABEL** each triangle as instructed in the directions. **USE** the appropriate symbol to identify the right angle of each triangle. **DRAW** your triangles on the grids provided.
- **WRITE** an explanation describing what you did and why you solved the problem as you did, **EVEN** if you used mental math or a calculator.

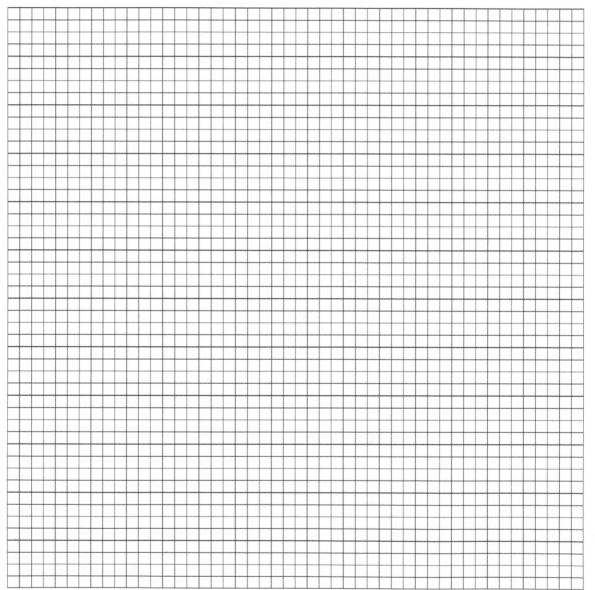

Explanation

0–5 Points

Score _____

4. For each triangle shown below, use a protractor to identify the measure of each angle. Write the measurement beside the angle it goes with. Show right angles using the appropriate symbol. If the triangle is a right triangle, circle the letter of the triangle.

- **REREAD** the problem and break it into parts to solve it.
- **LABEL** each triangle as instructed in the directions. **USE** the appropriate symbol to identify the right angle of each triangle.
- **WRITE** an explanation describing what you did and why you solved the problem as you did, **EVEN** if you used mental math or a calculator.

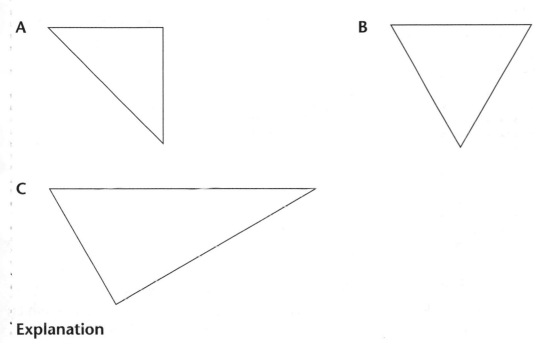

Explanation

0–5 Points
Score _____

1. Which of the following must a triangle have in order to be a right triangle?

   A one angle that measures 90°

   B one leg longer than the other

   C a hypotenuse that is shorter than either leg

   D one 45° angle

2. Each triangle below was formed on a geoboard. Which triangle is an example of a right triangle?

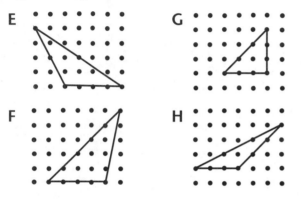

3. The sum of two of the angles in a right triangle equals 110°. What is the measure of the third angle?

   A 45°

   B 90°

   C 60°

   D 70°

4. Which of the symbols below might be used to identify the right angle in a right triangle?

   E

   F

   G

   H

5. Juan made a triangle on a geoboard. Which line segment(s) indicate the hypotenuse(s) of his triangle?

   A $\overline{DF}$

   B $\overline{DE}$

   C $\overline{DF}$ and $\overline{EF}$

   D $\overline{EF}$

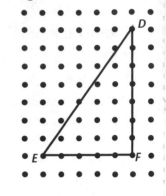

6. Look at the triangle for Problem 5 again. Which of the following identifies the right angle for this triangle?

   E ∠FED

   F ∠DFE

   G ∠DEF

   H ∠EDF

7. Use a protractor and your knowledge of the features of right triangles to determine which of the following is a right triangle.

   A

   B

   C

   D

8. One angle of a triangle measures 90°. A second angle measures 30°. What is the measure of the third angle?

   E 45°

   F 60°

   G 30°

   H 90°

9. What are the legs of a right triangle?

  A any three-sided polygon

  B the angle that measures exactly 90°

  C the sides that form the right angle

  D the longest side of the triangle

10. Look at the triangle shown below. Which line segments make up the leg(s) of this triangle?

  E only $\overline{AB}$

  F only $\overline{AC}$

  G $\overline{AC}$ and $\overline{AB}$

  H $\overline{AB}$ and $\overline{BC}$

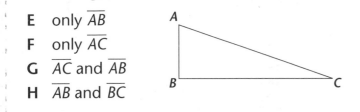

11. The pictures below show four triangles that were made on geoboards. Which triangle is a right triangle?

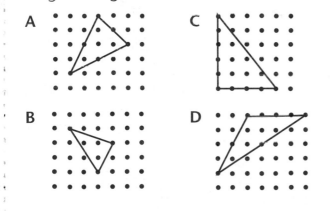

  A   **C**

  B   **D**

12. If one angle in a right triangle is equal to 90°, which of the following pairs of angles could be part of the same triangle?

  E 45°, 110°

  F 60°, 75°

  G 20°, 75°

  H 45°, 45°

13. The students studied the following drawing.

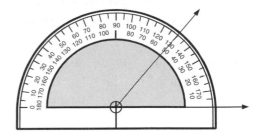

Ray said the angle measures 130°. Cassandra believes the angle measures 50°. Leon writes down 40° and Merry says it's 90°. Who is correct?

  A Ray

  B Cassandra

  C Leon

  D Merry

14. Which shows an acute angle?

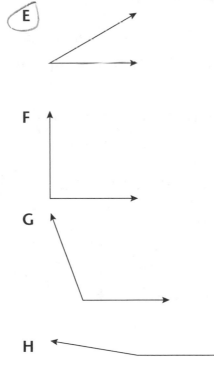

  E

  F

  G

  H

Think About It

Luke, Alma, Rico, and Jill collect baseball cards. Luke has 378 cards. Alma has 389 cards. Rico has 218 cards. Jill has 216 cards. Who has the greatest number of cards? Who has the least number of cards?

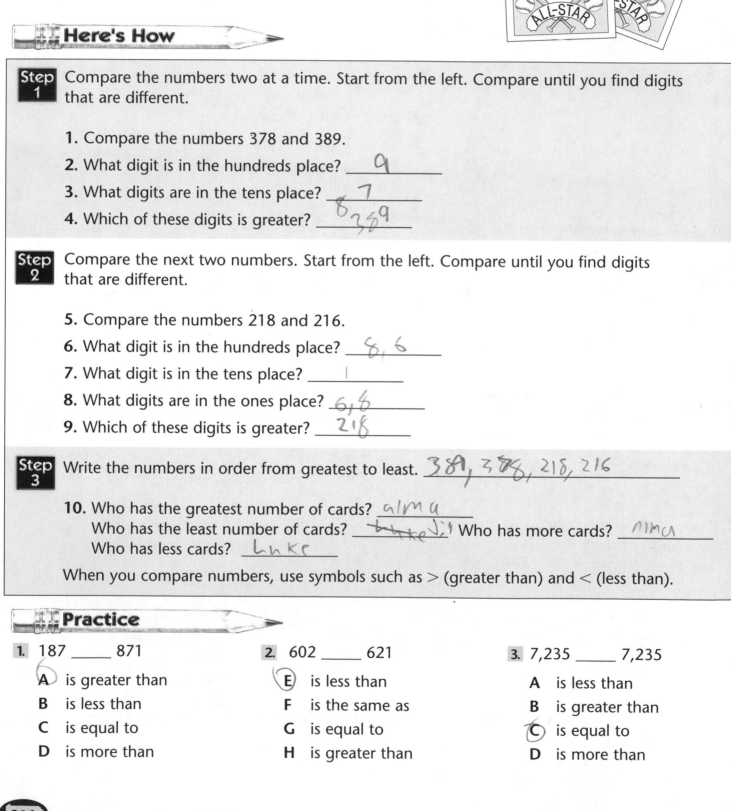

Here's How

Step 1 Compare the numbers two at a time. Start from the left. Compare until you find digits that are different.

1. Compare the numbers 378 and 389.

2. What digit is in the hundreds place? ___9___

3. What digits are in the tens place? ___7___

4. Which of these digits is greater? ___8 2 5 9___

Step 2 Compare the next two numbers. Start from the left. Compare until you find digits that are different.

5. Compare the numbers 218 and 216.

6. What digit is in the hundreds place? ___8, 6___

7. What digit is in the tens place? ___1___

8. What digits are in the ones place? ___6, 8___

9. Which of these digits is greater? ___218___

Step 3 Write the numbers in order from greatest to least. ___389, 378, 218, 216___

10. Who has the greatest number of cards? ___alma___
    Who has the least number of cards? ___~~Luke~~ Jill___ Who has more cards? ___alma___
    Who has less cards? ___Luke___

When you compare numbers, use symbols such as > (greater than) and < (less than).

Practice

1. 187 _____ 871

A is greater than
B is less than
C is equal to
D is more than

2. 602 _____ 621

E is less than
F is the same as
G is equal to
H is greater than

3. 7,235 _____ 7,235

A is less than
B is greater than
C is equal to
D is more than

4. 381 _____ 3,800

E is the same as
F is less than
G is greater than
H is equal to

5. 4,714 _____ 4,741

A ∧
B <
C >
D =

6. 9,114 _____ 9,111

E <
F =
G ∧
H >

7. 167 + 393 _____ 650

A is less than
B is equal to
C is more than
D is greater than

8. 42 _____ 14 × 3

E is greater than
F is less than
G is equal to
H is more than

9. 745 + 980 _____ 1,752

A is equal to
B is less than
C is the same as
D is greater than

10. 3,328 _____ 6,923 − 3,596

E <
F ∧
G =
H >

11. 38 × 7 _____ 155

A =
B >
C <
D ∧

12. 120 ÷ 6 _____ 25

E ∧
F >
G <
H =

13. Marty has 336 cards. Don has 8 fewer cards than Marty. Rhea has 12 more cards than Don. How many cards does Rhea have?

A 340
B 336
C 328
D 316

14. Among Marty, Don, and Rhea, who has the most cards?

E Marty
F Don
G Rhea
H They all have the same number.

15. Andy has 117 album pages filled with cards. Maggie's card collection fills 12 fewer pages. Annie's collection fills 8 more pages than Maggie's. All the pages hold the same number of cards. Who has the most cards?

A Annie
B Maggie
C Andy
D Andy and Annie have the same number.

16. Among Andy, Maggie, and Annie, who has the least amount of cards?

E Annie
F Maggie
G Andy
H Andy and Annie have the same amount.

Think About It

One way to organize information so that it will be easy to read is to make a graph. A bar graph uses bars of different heights to display the information. A circle graph uses fractional parts of the circle to show information. Look at the bar graph below. The title is "Races Won in October." Who won the most races? Who won the least number?

Here's How

Races Won in October

Number of Races (y-axis: 0–8)

Julie: 5, Ken: 1, Jose: 3, Maria: 7, Pam: 2

1. Who are the race participants?
   Julie Ken Jose Maria
   Pam

2. How many races did Julie win? ___5___

3. How many races did Ken win? ___1___

4. How many races did Jose win? ___3___

5. How many races did Maria win? ___7___

6. How many races did Pam win? ___2___

7. Who won the most races? ___Maria___

8. Who won the least number of races? ___Ken___

9. How is it easy to tell who won the most races on the bar graph?
   the bar is taller

10. How is it easy to tell who won the least number of races?
    it is shorter

Practice

Use the information in the bar graph for Problems 1–6.

FAVORITE KINDS OF MOVIES

MYSTERY
ADVENTURE
ANIMAL

0   20   40   60   80
NUMBER OF STUDENTS

1. Which kind of movie was NOT voted on by the students?

   (A) love stories

   B   mysteries

   C   adventure

   D   animal

2. How many students voted for mysteries as their favorite kind of movie?

   E   20

   F   30

   G   40

   H   60

3. How many students voted for adventure as their favorite kind of movie?

   A 20

   B 40

   C 60

   (D) 80

4. How many students voted for animal as their favorite kind of movie?

   E 10

   (F) 20

   G 40

   H 60

5. Which kind of movie received the most votes?

   A mystery

   (B) adventure

   C animal

   D love story

6. Which kind of movie received the fewest votes?

   E mystery

   F adventure

   (G) animal

   H love story

Study the circle graph to answer Problems 7–12.

HOW MIRANDA SPENDS HER GIFT MONEY

BOOKS $3 · MOVIES $2 · $15 CLOTHES

7. What is one thing that Miranda did NOT spend her money on?

   A movies

   (B) food

   C clothes

   D books

8. How much money did Miranda spend on movies?

   E $4

   F $3

   G $15

   (H) $2

9. How much money did Miranda spend on clothes?

   A $4

   B $3

   (C) $15

   D $2

10. How much money did Miranda spend on books?

   E $4

   (F) $3

   G $15

   H $2

11. What did Miranda spend most of her money on?

   A movies

   B food

   (C) clothes

   D books

12. What did Miranda spend the least amount of her money on?

   (E) movies

   F food

   G clothes

   H books

Ready Reference
maximum the greatest number in a set of data
minimum the least number in a set of data

Think About It

The manager of a grocery store wonders when the grocery store is the busiest so he can have more cashiers work during the busy periods. He counted the customers who came to the store one Saturday and made a bar graph showing the results. When did the greatest, or maximum number of customers visit the store? When did the least, or minimum number of customers visit the store?

Here's How

Step 1 Find out what each axis of the graph shows.

1. What does the vertical axis show? _____

2. What does the horizontal axis show? _____

Step 2 Interpret the bars on the graph.

3. Write the number of customers for each time on the graph:

9:00 _____   10:00 _____   11:00 _____   12:00 _____   1:00 _____

2:00 _____   3:00 _____   4:00 _____   5:00 _____

Step 3 Analyze the bar graph to answer the questions.

4. When did the maximum number of customers come to the store? _____

5. When did the minimum number of customers come to the store? _____

Practice

Use this information to answer Problems 1–4.
Mrs. Clymer asked 30 students to record how many hours of television they watched for one week. She made a frequency table showing the results.

Hours Watched	Number of Students
0–5 hours	ЖЖ I
6–10 hours	IIII
11–15 hours	ЖЖ ЖЖ
16–20 hours	ЖЖ III
21–25 hours	II

1. What is the maximum number of students in any time period?

A 8
B 6
C 10
D 30

2. How many hours of television did the maximum number of students watch?

E 21–25 hours
F 0–5 hours
G 16–20 hours
H 11–15 hours

3. What is the minimum number of students in any time period?

A 2

B 4

C 6

D 10

4. How many hours of television did the minimum number of students watch?

E 0–5 hours

F 21–25 hours

G 11–15 hours

H 6–10 hours

5. Mr. Chung's class read 65 books in 1999, 70 books in 1996, 60 books in 1997, and 50 books in 1998. What was the minimum number of books read from 1996 through 1999?

A 65

B 70

C 60

D 50

6. What was the maximum number of books read from 1996 through 1999?

E 65

F 70

G 60

H 50

Day	Low Temperature	High Temperature
Monday	28°	37°
Tuesday	36°	43°
Wednesday	35°	41°
Thursday	26°	30°
Friday	30°	34°

7. In the table above, what was the minimum temperature recorded for the five days?

A 30°

B 28°

C 26°

D 43°

8. In the table above, what was the maximum temperature recorded for the five days?

E 43°

F 37°

G 30°

H 26°

MONEY EARNED AT HOME EACH WEEK

Amount earned	Number of students
$2.00	4
$5.00	12
$10.00	3

9. What was the maximum amount of money earned by students in the table above?

A $2.00

B $5.00

C $10.00

D 12

10. What was the minimum amount of money earned by students in the table above?

E $2.00

F $5.00

G $10.00

H 3

Ready Reference

ratio a comparison of two numbers by division

▪ Think About It

Things change over time. We can measure how much things change to help predict what will happen in the future. Suppose that Anytown, U.S.A., has grown in population over the last ten years. How fast has the population grown? At what rate has the population grown?

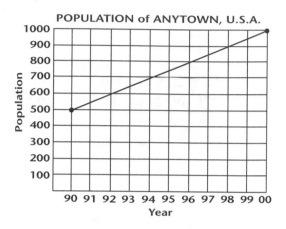

POPULATION of ANYTOWN, U.S.A.

▪ Here's How

1. Look at the graph showing the population of Anytown, U.S.A. from 1990–2000. The Census Bureau reported the population for the years 1990 and 2000. What was the population in 1990? _____ What was the population in 2000? _____ How much did the population grow each year?

2. To find the rate of change, use this ratio: Rate of change $= \dfrac{\text{Change in population}}{\text{Change in years}}$

3. For Anytown, U.S.A., the rate of change $= \dfrac{1{,}000 - 500}{2{,}000 - 1{,}990} = \dfrac{500}{10} =$ _____

4. The population of Anytown, U.S.A. grew at a rate of about _____ people per year.

▪ Practice

1. Jeff is on a vacation with his family. The first day his family drove 300 miles in 6 hours. Jeff wants to find the rate of speed his family travels. What is the ratio he should use?

   A $\dfrac{6 \text{ hours}}{300 \text{ miles}}$

   B $\dfrac{300 \text{ miles}}{6 \text{ hours}}$

   C $\dfrac{300 \text{ miles}}{60 \text{ minutes}}$

   D $\dfrac{6 \text{ hours}}{60 \text{ minutes}}$

2. How many miles did Jeff's family travel in one hour? Show your work.

   E 150 miles

   F 5 miles

   G 60 miles

   H 50 miles

3. A bakery can make 48 cakes in 8 hours. Which ratio shows the rate at which cakes are baked?

A $\dfrac{48 \text{ cakes}}{8 \text{ hours}}$

B $\dfrac{8 \text{ hours}}{48 \text{ cakes}}$

C $\dfrac{48 \text{ cakes}}{60 \text{ minutes}}$

D $\dfrac{24 \text{ cakes}}{2 \text{ hours}}$

4. How many cakes can be baked in 2 hours? Show your work.

E 24

F 8

G 12

H 6

5. Carol makes friendship bracelets for her friends. She can make 6 bracelets in 2 hours. What is the rate at which she can make bracelets?

A $\dfrac{2}{6}$

B $\dfrac{4}{12}$

C $\dfrac{6}{2}$

D $\dfrac{6}{4}$

6. How many bracelets can Carol make in 6 hours? Show your work.

E 12

F 18

G 36

H 24

7. Ted can read 90 pages in 3 hours. Which ratio shows the rate at which Ted reads?

A $\dfrac{90}{1}$

B $\dfrac{3}{1}$

C $\dfrac{30}{3}$

D $\dfrac{90}{3}$

8. At Ted's reading rate, how many pages is Ted reading in one hour? Show your work.

E 30

F 60

G 45

H 15

9. Dana earns $10 a month doing jobs around her house. Which ratio shows the money she earns in one month?

A $\dfrac{10}{30}$

B $\dfrac{10}{1}$

C $\dfrac{1}{10}$

D $\dfrac{4}{10}$

10. At Dana's rate of earning, how much money can Dana expect to earn in one year? Show your work.

E $100

F $52

G $120

H $520

Ready Reference

area the number of square units needed to cover a region
volume the amount of space enclosed in a space (3-dimensional) figure, measured in cubic units

Think About It

Suppose your mother wants to buy a tablecloth for the kitchen table. She needs to know the area of the kitchen table so that she will buy a tablecloth big enough to cover it. The area is the number of square units needed to cover a flat surface. How can she find the area of the kitchen table? Your mother also needs to measure a storage box to find out how much space is in it. The volume is how much space is inside a solid figure. How can she find the volume of the box?

Here's How

Find the area by counting the square units.

1. How many tiles long is the tabletop? _____

2. How many tiles wide is the tabletop? _____

3. Find the area by counting the tiles, or by multiplying *length* × *width*. What is the area of this table? _____ square units

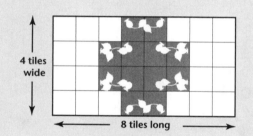

Find the area of irregular shapes.

1. Look at the dark tiles that form an irregular shape in the middle of this tabletop.

2. Count the square units to find the area of the irregular shape. Add the whole units and the half units together. The area of the irregular shape is _____ square units.

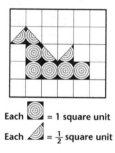

Each ◎ = 1 square unit

Each ◸ = $\frac{1}{2}$ square unit

Find the volume by counting unit cubes.

1. How many unit cubes are in each row? _____ This is the length.

2. How many rows are there? _____ This is the width.

3. There are _____ layers of cubic units. This is the height.

4. Find the volume by adding up the cubes or by multiplying *length* × *width* × *height*.

What is the volume of the box? _____

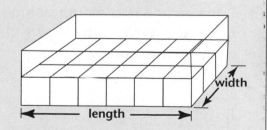

Practice

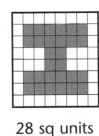

Figure 1

1. What multiplication sentence would help you find the area of Figure 1?

   A 8 × 4

   B 12 × 2

   C 4 × 4

   D 4 × 12

2. What is the area of Figure 1? Show your work.

   E 12 sq units

   F 16 sq units

   G 8 sq units

   H 24 sq units

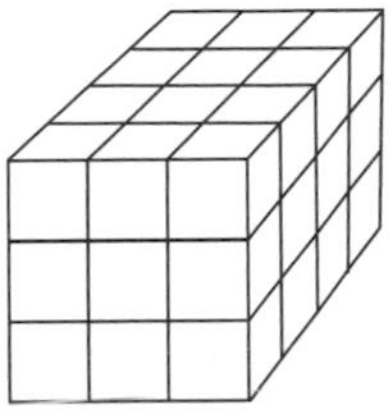

Figure 2

3. What is the height of Figure 2?

   A 3 units

   B 4 units

   C 9 units

   D 7 units

4. What is the volume of Figure 2?

   E 24 cubic units

   F 12 cubic units

   G 21 cubic units

   H 36 cubic units

Find the area of the dark tiles in Problems 5–7.

5.

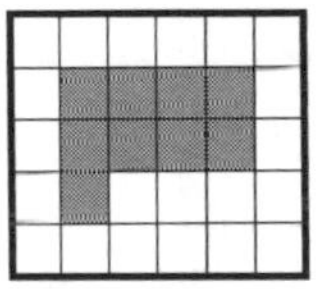

   A 30 sq units

   B 9 sq units

   C 8 sq units

   D 11 sq units

6.

   E 28 sq units

   F 64 sq units

   G 16 sq units

   H 36 sq units

7.

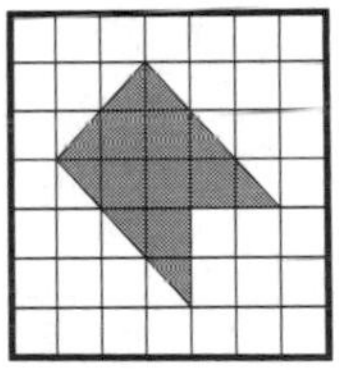

   A 49 sq units

   B 9 sq units

   C 25 sq units

   D 10 sq units

Find the volume of the space figures in Problems 8–10.

8.

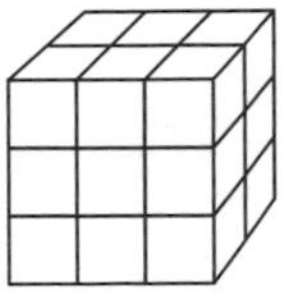

   E 9 cubic units

   F 6 cubic units

   G 18 cubic units

   H 36 cubic units

9.

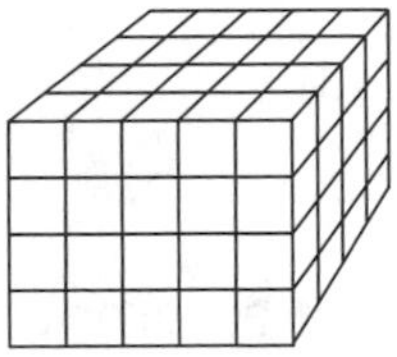

   A 40 cubic units

   B 20 cubic units

   C 24 cubic units

   D 80 cubic units

10.

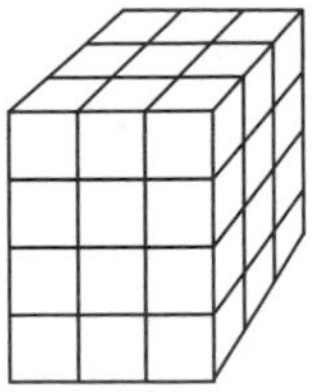

   E 36 cubic units

   F 12 cubic units

   G 24 cubic units

   H 18 cubic units

Think About It

Centimeters, inches, feet, yards, and meters are all units of measurement. They measure length. To measure volume you use cubic centimeters, cubic inches, cubic feet, cubic yards, and cubic meters. How do you decide which unit of measurement to use?

Here's How

1. Look at the pencil and the ruler. The point of the pencil is closest to 6 inches. The pencil is about _____ long.

2. If you wanted to measure the pencil using a different unit of measurement, would it be a good idea to use centimeters or meters? _____ Why? _____
   _____

3. Becky wants to carpet her room. She needs to measure the area of her room to find out how much carpet to buy. Should she measure her room in square inches, square centimeters, or square feet? _____ Why? _____
   _____

4. Area can be expressed as square units, sq units, or units^2. Volume can be expressed as cubic units or units^3.

Practice

Choose the BEST unit of measurement in Problems 1–6.

1. The area of a football field
   A cm^2
   B $in.^2$
   C yd^2
   D ft^2

2. The volume of a cereal box
   E $in.^3$
   F yd^3
   G m^3
   H ft^3

3. The area of this page in your book
   A ft^2
   B cm^2
   C yd^2
   D m^2

4. The volume of a refrigerator
   E m^3
   F $in.^3$
   G cm^3
   H ft^3

5. The area of a computer mouse pad
   A $in.^2$
   B yd^2
   C ft^2
   D m^2

6. The volume of a desk drawer
   E yd^3
   F m^3
   G $in.^3$
   H ft^3

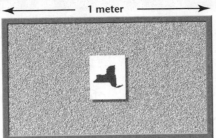

1 meter

7. What unit of measurement would you use to measure the area of the picture on the bulletin board above?

A ft²

B m²

C yd²

D cm²

8. What do you estimate is the area of the picture?

E 60 cm²

F 1 m²

G 10 ft²

H 2 yd²

2 ft

1 ft

5 ft

9. This bathtub is about 5 ft long. What unit of measurement would you use to measure its volume?

A in.³

B ft³

C cm³

D m³

10. What do you estimate is the volume of the bathtub?

E 1,000 in.³

F 2,000 cm³

G 10 ft³

H 5 m³

Choose the BEST estimate in Problems 11–16.

11. The area of a soccer field

A 5,000 in.²

B 5,000 ft²

C 5,000 cm²

D 5,000 m²

12. The volume of a backpack

E 1,200 in.³

F 1,200 ft³

G 1,200 m³

H 1,200 yd³

13. The area of a bedroom

A 90 m²

B 90 ft²

C 90 in.²

D 90 yd²

14. The volume of a CD box

E 168 in.³

F 168 m³

G 168 cm³

H 168 ft³

15. The area of a poster

A 6 ft²

B 6 in.²

C 6 yd²

D 6 cm²

16. The volume of a grocery sack

E 1,368 yd³

F 1,368 m³

G 1,368 ft³

H 1,368 in.³

1. Zeke read that a square room is 12 ft wide. How can Zeke find the perimeter and area of this room using only this one measurement? Find the perimeter and area of the room.

- **REREAD** the problem carefully. **IDENTIFY** any information that is needed to solve the problem.
- **SHOW** each step of your math work.
- **ANSWER** the question.
- **WRITE** an explanation describing what you did and why you solved the problem as you did, **EVEN** if you used mental math or a calculator.
- **WRITE** your answers in the spaces provided.

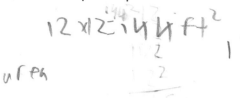

$$12 \times 12 = 144 \, ft^2$$

area

How can you find perimeter and area from only one measurement?

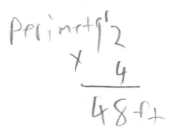

$$Perimeter$$
$$\times \, 4$$
$$48 \, ft$$

Explanation

I got perimeter I took what Zeke knew wich is 12 and all 4 sides to get area I x LxW wich is
12 X 12 = 144

| Perimeter | 48 |
| Area | 144 |

0–5 Points

Score _____

2. Barry made a table to show the number of bags of leaves he filled for one week. The table he made is shown below. Study the data in the table. Then identify the greatest and least values shown.

- **REREAD** the problem carefully. **IDENTIFY** any information that is needed to solve the problem.
- **SHOW** each step of your math work.
- **WRITE** an explanation describing what you did and why you solved the problem as you did, **EVEN** if you used mental math or a calculator.
- **WRITE** your answers in the spaces provided.

Explanation

I found the smallest bar wich is wed and lined up to the number line. I found the biges by locking at the biges bar and lined up with the number line

Greatest value 4 wed

Least value 12 tues

0–5 Points

Score _____

3. Study the shape shown. Find the area and volume for the figure. Then explain how you found the area and the volume of this shape.

- **REREAD** the problem carefully. **IDENTIFY** any information that is needed to solve the problem.
- **SHOW** each step of your math work.
- **WRITE** an explanation describing what you did and why you solved the problem as you did, **EVEN** if you used mental math or a calculator.
- **WRITE** your answers in the spaces provided.

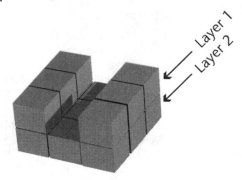

Explanation

Area of Layer 1 _____

Area of Layer 2 _____

Volume of shape _____

0–5 Points

Score _____

4. Assume that you are 58 in. tall. If you were to grow $\frac{1}{4}$ inch every month, how tall would you be in six months? Make a chart to show your predicted growth.

- **REREAD** the problem carefully. **IDENTIFY** any information that is needed to solve the problem.
- **DEVELOP** a chart to record your predicted growth.
- **SHOW** each step of your math work.
- **WRITE** an explanation describing what you did and why you solved the problem as you did, **EVEN** if you used mental math or a calculator.
- **WRITE** your answers in the spaces provided.

Make your chart here.

Explanation

| Total growth _____ |
| New height _____ |

| 0–5 Points |
| Score _____ |

1. Compare 1,476 and 1,467.

   (A) 1,476 is greater than 1,467.

   B 1,476 is equal to 1,467.

   C 1,476 is less than 1,467.

   D 1,476 is the same as 1,467.

2. Compare 699 and 969.

   E 699 = 969

   F 699 % 969

   (G) 699 < 969

   H 699 > 969

3. Last summer, Will read a book that had 245 pages. Liz read a book that had 12 fewer pages than Will's. Emily read a book that had 30 more pages than Liz's. Who read the most pages?

   A Will

   B Liz

   (C) Emily

   D Emily and Will read the same amount.

4. Which of these compares the number of pages read by Will and Liz?

   (E) 245 > 233

   F 245 < 233

   G 245 = 245

   H 245 + 233

5. This graph shows how many students were absent during one week. What day were the most students absent?

   A Wednesday

   B Friday

   (C) Tuesday

   D Monday

6. Which shows numbers in order from greatest to least?

   E 718, 493, 384, 871

   F 871, 384, 493, 718

   G 384, 493, 718, 871

   (H) 871, 718, 493, 384

7. According to the graph below, in which year did the fifth grade have the most race winners?

   A 1995

   (B) 1997

   C 1998

   D 2000

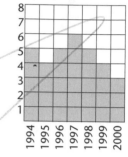

8. Look at the graph below. Which two students did the most homework?

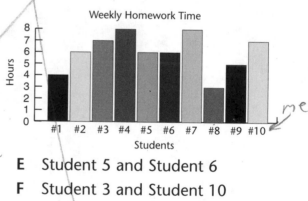

   Weekly Homework Time

   E Student 5 and Student 6

   F Student 3 and Student 10

   G Student 2 and Student 5

   (H) Student 4 and Student 7

9. In the graph above, which student spent the least amount of time on homework?

   A Student 1

   B Student 9

   (C) Student 8

   D Student 7

10. Study the graph. Who played the most games?

E Philip

F Sam

G Mario

H Nora

BASKETBALL GAMES PLAYED

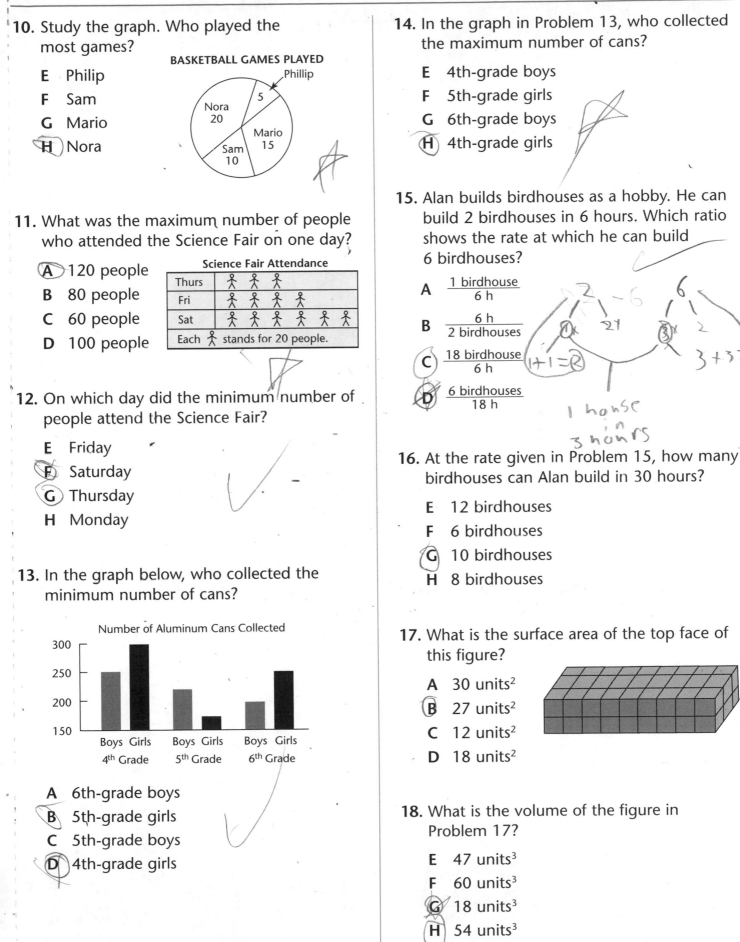

Phillip 5
Nora 20
Mario 15
Sam 10

11. What was the maximum number of people who attended the Science Fair on one day?

A 120 people

B 80 people

C 60 people

D 100 people

Science Fair Attendance

Thurs	🚶 🚶 🚶			
Fri	🚶 🚶 🚶 🚶			
Sat	🚶 🚶 🚶 🚶 🚶 🚶			

Each 🚶 stands for 20 people.

12. On which day did the minimum number of people attend the Science Fair?

E Friday

F Saturday

G Thursday

H Monday

13. In the graph below, who collected the minimum number of cans?

Number of Aluminum Cans Collected

A 6th-grade boys

B 5th-grade girls

C 5th-grade boys

D 4th-grade girls

14. In the graph in Problem 13, who collected the maximum number of cans?

E 4th-grade boys

F 5th-grade girls

G 6th-grade boys

H 4th-grade girls

15. Alan builds birdhouses as a hobby. He can build 2 birdhouses in 6 hours. Which ratio shows the rate at which he can build 6 birdhouses?

A $\frac{1 \text{ birdhouse}}{6 \text{ h}}$

B $\frac{6 \text{ h}}{2 \text{ birdhouses}}$

C $\frac{18 \text{ birdhouse}}{6 \text{ h}}$

D $\frac{6 \text{ birdhouses}}{18 \text{ h}}$

16. At the rate given in Problem 15, how many birdhouses can Alan build in 30 hours?

E 12 birdhouses

F 6 birdhouses

G 10 birdhouses

H 8 birdhouses

17. What is the surface area of the top face of this figure?

A 30 units²

B 27 units²

C 12 units²

D 18 units²

18. What is the volume of the figure in Problem 17?

E 47 units³

F 60 units³

G 18 units³

H 54 units³

Math Journal

Your Math Journal will help you track where you've been, where you are now, and where you're going. Keeping a Math Journal can be fun and can help you improve your math skills. Your Math Journal is divided into two sections.

Math At Home and *How I Use Math Every Day*

Math I Do Well and *What I Can Improve*

You should add to your Math Journal throughout the year. Start by reading *Math At Home*. Think about all the times you use math outside of school. Use *How I Use Math Every Day* to note what you are doing when you use math.

As you learn and practice math in your classroom and for homework, make notes on the *Math I Do Well* and *What I Can Improve* pages. List skills you need to work on using *What I Can Improve*. After you have improved in that area, don't forget to cross it out or put a ✓ next to the skill. Then write that math skill on your *Math I Do Well* page. Keeping track of where you need to improve and what you do well will help you improve your test scores.

How I Use Math Everyday

I built a doghouse for my dog, Barney. I made a plan and measured the boards.

Math I Do Well

Rounding decimals
Making bar graphs
Adding decimals
Subtracting decimals
Multiplication by 1 and 2 digits
Stem-and-leaf plots

What I Can Improve

✓ *Subtracting decimals*
✓ *Finding the mean*
Stem-and-leaf plots
Double bar graphs
Order of operations

Think About It

You use math at home every day. Do you save money from a job or allowance? How do you use math in the kitchen? How do you use math in your room?

Here's How

Start Saving Now!

Have you ever earned any money for doing jobs at home or for your neighbors? Do you have a business or know anyone who does? Have you ever received money for your birthday or for another holiday? Do you receive an allowance? Do you save money? Being smart about money is a smart thing to do, no matter what age you are!

When you save money in a bank, the bank pays you interest on your money. In other words, they pay you for saving your money. The longer you leave the money in the bank, the more money the bank will give you. Suppose you saved $20 a month for 20 years and the bank paid you 5% interest. You would have put $4,800 into the bank. But at the end of 20 years, you would have $8,220.67! The bank would have paid you $3,420.67 for saving your money. It's worth it to start saving now, no matter how much or how little you can save.

Kitchen Math!

You use math in many different ways in the kitchen. Here are just a few examples.

1. When you use a recipe, you use math to measure ingredients. If you want to double a recipe, you use math to decide how much you need of each ingredient.
2. When you shop for groceries, you use math.
3. You use math when you cook to decide how much time it will take to prepare a meal.
4. When you cook or bake, you use math to tell you what time your food will be done.
5. You use math to set the temperature in your oven.
6. You use math to decide what size containers to put lunches or leftovers in.
7. You use math to find out what size tablecloth to buy.

There's Math in Your Room!

Look around your room at home. Here are a few ways you probably use math in your room.
1. When you set your alarm clock you use math.
2. To find out how much paint you need to buy to paint your room, you measure the walls.
3. What furniture will fit in your room? You need to measure to make sure it will fit.
4. What pictures and posters will fit on your walls? What size picture frame do you need for your pictures?
5. What temperature should you set the thermostat?
6. How much fabric do you need for curtains?

Math Journal • How I Use Math Every Day

Keep track of how you use math in your everyday life. Use this Math Journal page to jot down how you use math at home, with your friends, and with your family. Compare your notes with your classmates and share your ideas with your teacher and your family.

Math Journal ◆ What I Do Well

We all have things we do well. Some people can sing beautifully or paint or play chess. What kinds of math are you good at? Keep track of all the things you do well in math on this page. Share your ideas with your family and your teacher. Keep adding to your list. You'll be surprised at all the things you can do in math. Watch your list grow!

Math Journal ◆ What I Can Improve

We all have ways we can improve. What kinds of math do you need to improve? Keep track of the math subjects you need to improve on this page. Share your ideas with your family and your teacher. As you improve in a certain math subject, draw a line through it or put a ✓ next to it. Then write it on your *What I Do Well* page. You'll be surprised at how you can improve your math. Watch your list shrink!

Glossary

A

acute angle an angle with a measure less than 90°

angle two rays with the same endpoint

area the number of square units needed to cover a region; $A = l \times w$

C

circumference the distance around a circle

common factor a number that is a factor of two or more numbers; *example:* 1,2,3, and 6 are common factors of 6 and 12

common multiple a multiple of 2 or more numbers; *example:* 8 is a common multiple of 2 and 4

composite number any positive integer exactly divisible by one or more positive integers other than itself and 1

congruent having the same shape and the same size

coordinate system a method of locating points in the plane or in space by means of numbers; a point in the plane is located by its distances from both a horizontal and a vertical line called the axes

coordinates numbers used to locate a point

D

decimal a number expressed using a decimal point; part of a whole

deductive reasoning the process of reasoning from statements accepted as true to reach a conclusion

diameter a line segment that passes through the center of a circle and has both endpoints on the circle

E

equilateral a geometric figure having all sides the same length

equation a statement of equality between two mathematical expressions; *example:* $x + 5 = y - 2$

element a member of a set

estimate an approximate answer that is close to exact

expanded notation writing the number in expanded form to show the value of each digit; *example:* $15,629 = 10,000 + 5,000 + 600 + 20 + 9$

expression a mathematical phrase that can include operations, numerals, and variables; in algebraic terms: $2l + 3x$; in numeric terms: $13.4 - 4.7$

F

factor the number or variable multiplied in a multiplication expression

fraction a number that names part of a whole

G

geoboard a board with pegs aligned in grid fashion that permits rubber bands to be wrapped around pegs to form geometric figures

greatest common factor (GCF) the greatest number that is a factor of each of two or more numbers; *example:* the GCF of 24 and 48 is 12

H

hypotenuse the longest side of a right triangle and opposite the right angle

I

inductive reasoning generalizations made from particular observations in a common occurrence

inequality a mathematical sentence that contains a symbol; *example:* $>, <, \geq, \leq$, or $\neq$, in which the terms on either side of the symbol are unequal; *example:* $x < y$, $7 > 3$, $n \geq 4$

isosceles triangle a triangle with at least two congruent sides

L

least common denominator (LCD) the least common multiple of the denominators of two or more fractions; *example:* the LCD of 4 and 3 is 12

least smallest in magnitude or degree

least common multiple (LCM) the least number, other than 0, that is the common multiple of two or more numbers; *example:* 6 is the least common multiple of 2 and 3

leg in a right triangle, one of the two sides that form the right angle

line a straight set of points that goes on forever

line segment a part of a line with two endpoints

M

maximum the greatest number in a set of data

mean the sum of the set of numbers divided by *n*, the number of numbers in the set

median the number that lies in the middle when a set of numbers is arranged in order. If there are two middle values, the median is the mean of these values

minimum the least number in a set of data

mode the number(s) that occurs most often in a set of numbers; *example:* in the set 1, 2, 3, 3, 5, 8; the mode is 3

multiple a number that is the product of a given integer and another integer; *example:* 0, 3, 6, 9… are multiples of 3

N

negative number a whole number that is less than zero

O

obtuse angle an angle with a measure greater than 90° and less than 180°

ordered pair a pair of numbers used to locate a point in a plane

origin the point at which the two axes intersect; the origin has the coordinates (0,0)

P

parallel always the same distance apart

parallel lines lines in the same plane that never intersect

parallelogram a quadrilateral with two pairs of parallel sides

patterns regularities in situations such as those in nature, events, shapes, designs, and sets of numbers; *example:* spirals on pineapples, geometric designs in quilts, the number sequence 3, 6, 9, 12…

perimeter the distance around a closed figure; $P = l + l + w + w$, or $P = 2l + 2w$

perpendicular lines two lines that intersect to form right angles; *example:* ⊥ ⌐ ⌐

place value the value of a digit based on its position in a number

plane a flat surface that continues in all directions

point an exact location in space

polygon a union of segments connected end to end, such that each segment intersects exactly two others at its endpoints

prime number an integer greater than one whose only positive factors are 1 and itself; *example:* 2, 3, 5, 7, 11, 13, 17, and 19

probability a number from 0 to 1 that indicates how likely something is to happen

Q

quadrilateral a four-sided polygon

R

radius a line segment with one endpoint on the center of a circle and an endpoint on the circle

range the difference between the greatest number and the least number in a set of data

ratio a comparison of two numbers by division

ray a part of a line with one endpoint that goes on forever

rectangle a parallelogram with four right angles

regroup use 1 ten to form 10 ones, 1 hundred to form 10 tens, and so on

regular polygon a polygon in which all sides have the same measure and all angles have the same measure

rhombus a parallelogram with all four sides equal in length

right angle an angle that measures exactly 90°

right triangle a triangle containing a right angles

rotation a transformation that maps every point in the plane to its image by rotating the plane around a fixed point or line

round write a number as the nearest ten, hundred, thousand, and so on.

S

scalene triangle a triangle with no congruent sides

similarity having the same shape but not necessarily the same size

simple event an event whose probability can be obtained from consideration of a single occurrence; *example:* the tossing of a coin is a simple event

square a rectangle with all sides the same length

symmetry a line of symmetry separates a figure into two congruent halves, each of which is a reflection of the other; *example:* ⊘, the line through the center of the circle divides it into congruent halves

T

tessellation a repetitive pattern of polygons that covers an area with no holes and no overlaps; *example:* floor tiles

transformation an operation on a geometric figure by which each point gives rise to a unique image

tree diagram a diagram used to show the total number of possible outcomes in a probability experiment

trapezoid a quadrilateral with exactly two parallel sides

triangle a three-sided polygon

V

Venn diagram a display that pictures unions and intersections of sets

volume the amount of space enclosed in a space (3-dimensional) figure, measured in cubic units

X

x-axis the horizontal line that forms the base line of a graph

Y

y-axis the vertical line that forms the base line of a graph